LONGMAN HISTORY STUDIES IN DEPTH

A History of South Africa

Martin Roberts

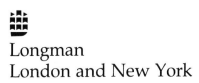

Longman
London and New York

Longman Group UK Ltd,
Longman House, Burnt Mill, Harlow,
Essex CM20 2JE, England
amd Associated Companies throughout the world.

Published in the United States of America
by Longman Inc., New York

First published 1990
Second impression 1993

Set in 10/11 point Palatino Linotron
Produced by Longman Singapore Publishers Pte Ltd
Printed in Singapore

ISBN 0582 00268 0

British Library Cataloguing in Publication Data
Roberts, Martin, *1941–*
    South Africa.
    1. South Africa, history
    I. Title
    968

    ISBN 0–582–00268–0

Library of Congress Cataloging-in-Publication Data
Roberts, Martin.
    South Africa/Martin Roberts.
       p. cm.
    Includes bibliographical references.
    ISBN 0–582–00268–0:
    1. South Africa – History. I. Title.
DT1787.R62   1990
968–dc20   90–5616
               CIP

The publisher's policy is to use paper manufactured from sustainable forests.

Contents

List of maps

Introduction

South Africa in the modern world

Here are three reports about South Africa, which all appeared in British newspapers within the same few days.

Report 1 (from the *Guardian*) told how three women and a man, members of the African National Congress, were killed in Gaborone, Botswana, in a night raid by members of the South African Defence Force. The raiders crossed the border from South Africa in a minibus and escaped by helicopter.

Report 2 (from the *Independent*) described how Chris Heunis, the government minister responsible for black townships, had apparently changed his mind about Oukasie. This township had been part of the town of Brits for more than fifty years. Now Brits' population was growing and the whites wanted the people of Oukasie to be moved 24 km away. Earlier Heunis appeared to have promised that no one from Oukasie would be forced to move. Now he was saying that the township would be closed and that its inhabitants would be 'persuaded' to leave.

Report 3 (again from the *Guardian*) was about the film *Cry Freedom* which described the friendship of the black leader Steve Biko with the white newspaper editor Donald Woods. Biko 'died in police custody' and Woods, banned by the South African government, had to flee from South Africa to get his book about Biko published. United International Pictures, the international distributors of the film, postponed its showing in South Africa because they feared that the government would punish those cinema owners who screened it.

The week of these reports happened to be the last week of March 1988, but South Africa has held the attention of the world's media, week in week out, for the last forty years. The reason for this attention lies in the extraordinary and tragic situation which developed there and which caused increasing dismay and anger in the rest of the world.

Political and civil rights in the Western world

If you live in Britain or the USA, there are some things you can take for granted. Once you reach the age of eighteen, for example, you are free to vote in national elections for the politicians whom you wish to govern your country. All adult Britons and Americans can vote in national elections and the politicians who win the majority form the government. If you do not like a government, you can criticise it and look forward to the next election which will never be more than a few years away. You can choose where you live, as long as you have enough money, and, if you have some ability and some qualifications, you can expect a choice of jobs. There is hardly any censorship of films and plays, while the press, radio and television are as free to say what they like as anywhere in the world.

There is still much racism in Britain and the USA and black people suffer serious inequality when trying to get a job or find somewhere to live, yet such discrimination is against the law. This means that they have legal and political ways of challenging their disadvantages and they are recognised in law as full and equal citizens.

The contrasting situation in South Africa

In South Africa in 1988, blacks outnumbered whites by six to one yet this huge black majority could not take for granted any of your political and legal rights. A white parliament and president had political power. Blacks could not vote in national elections. Their most popular political party, the African National Congress (see Report 1 above), was banned. Its leaders were either in prison or in exile. Blacks could not live, work or travel as they wished. The government interfered continually in their affairs (see Report 2 above) and prevented them from watching any film, play or television programme or from reading any newspaper report which it disliked (see Report 3 above). At the same time, the whites had the best land, the best jobs and their average standard of living was amongst the highest in the world. The average black wage was a small fraction of the white average and thousands of blacks lived close to starvation.

For the first sixty years of the twentieth century the blacks protested peacefully against this unfairness. Their peaceful protests got them nowhere. On the contrary, their leaders were fined, beaten and sometimes imprisoned. When from 1961 they turned to violence, the white government replied with greater violence. Three times in less than thirty years, in 1960, 1976–77 and 1984–86, South Africa appeared to be on the edge of revolution but each time white rule survived.

This book has two main aims: the first is to outline the history of South Africa to show how the roots of

Black protest: the students' march in Soweto to protest about having to learn Afrikaans, June 1976

An armed personnel carrier of the South African Defence Force patrols a black township during the troubles of 1985–86

the present situation lie deep in the past; the second is to present some of the evidence which historians are using to work out what happened and why.

It is divided into three sections. The first, which takes the story from the earliest times to the middle of the nineteenth century, describes how the whites took some of the best farmland from the blacks.

The second, which explains how the discovery of diamonds and gold brought great changes to modern South Africa, shows how the whites took control of industry as well as increasing their hold on the land.

The third, which begins with the victory of the National Party in the election of 1948, describes the apartheid schemes which the white, mainly Afrikaner government used to keep the white minority under political and economic control and the appalling suffering which these policies caused to the blacks.

It ends in 1990 with the whites still in power (and the Nationalists yet again victorious at white election time), but more uncertain than ever before about the future of their multi-racial country in which they were an increasingly small minority and apparently more ready to talk with black leaders about major reforms. For example, F. W. de Klerk, the white State President, cancelled the ban on the African National Congress and released from prison its most famous leader, Nelson Mandela.

A note on the evidence

Imagine a history of modern Ireland based almost entirely on English evidence, or a history of Israel written only from an Arab point of view. Such histories would be unbalanced and give only a one-sided view of the subject.

One of the problems of the history of South Africa is that most of the evidence, visual as well as written, is provided by whites. This is particularly true for the years before 1870. Modern historians use oral history (see page 10) and anthropology (see page 7) to gain a better understanding of black societies in the past but these methods can only get so far. The sources most frequently used by historians to describe and explain South Africa's history were written by whites and their tendency to one-sidedness needs to be remembered.

Glossary

Many different terms are used in books and newspaper articles to describe the various racial groups in South Africa. Here are some of the most common.

Afrikaans   the language of the white population of Dutch origin, based on Dutch but influenced by English, French and Malay.

Afrikaner   the Afrikaans word meaning African; used of whites mainly of Dutch descent; see also *Boer* below.

Bantu   general name given to the languages spoken by the black majority, for example, Sotho-Tswana, Nguni; often used by the South African government to distinguish such peoples from the whites, Indians and coloureds.

Black   widely used to describe all the peoples of South Africa not of European descent including Bantu speakers native to Africa (also sometimes called Africans), Indians (thousands of whom came to work in the sugar plantations of Natal during the nineteenth century) and coloureds (see below).

Boer   Afrikaans for farmer and generally used during the nineteenth century to describe the Afrikaner; passed out of use in the early twentieth century.

Bushman   see *San* below.

Coloured   people of mixed racial descent, from Khoikhoi, slaves brought to the Cape, and from whites; frequently called Cape Coloured since they have mostly lived in the Cape Town area.

Hottentot   see *Khoikhoi* below.

Kafir (meaning unbeliever) and *native*   terms frequently used in the past by whites to describe blacks. Both terms are disliked by blacks since they include a sense of contempt.

Khoikhoi   meaning 'men of men', yellow-skinned herdsmen who were the first native inhabitants of Southern Africa; whites often called them *Hottentots*, a name which also included a sense of contempt.

Khoisan   the name modern historians use to include all the yellow-skinned peoples of Southern Africa, herdsmen as well as hunters.

San   the Khoikhoi name for another people: hunters, whom settlers from Europe usually called Bushmen; nowadays *San* is preferred to *Bushman* for the same reasons that *Khoikhoi* is preferred to **Hottentot**.

This book simply uses 'black' and 'white' in the main text except when it is necessary to be more precise. However, many of the above terms are used in the sources.

PART ONE THE LAND AND ITS PEOPLES FROM THE EARLIEST TIMES TO THE MIDDLE OF THE NINETEENTH CENTURY

Chapter 1 The earliest inhabitants

The geography of Southern Africa

South Africa lies at the southernmost tip of the African continent. The Atlantic and the Indian oceans surround it to the west, south and east and its northern borders are the Kalahari desert, the Orange and Limpopo rivers. It is more than a million square km, nearly six times the size of Britain and twice the size of Texas. The distance from Pretoria to Cape Town is about 1300 km, similar to the distance from London to Rome or from New York to St Louis.

Most of the country is plateau between 600 and 2000 m high. The plateau tilts upwards from west to east so that its eastern edge is divided from the nearby coast by the spectacular Drakensberg mountains which rise in a number of places to 3300 m or more.

Climate and rainfall

The line of latitude 30' South runs across the middle of South Africa, so it is roughly the same distance from the Equator as North Africa, Florida and southern California. The climate is sub-tropical, warm with long periods of sunshine, though with winter frosts on the plateau.

The main rain-bearing winds blow in from the east over the Indian ocean against the mountains so the east coast gets the heaviest and most regular rainfall. This reduces greatly from east to west. Indeed, the only region in the west to get good regular rainfall is round Cape Town (the Cape), where, during the winter, westerly winds blow in from the Atlantic.

In comparison with Britain and Western Europe, South Africa is a dry country. The amount of rainfall can vary greatly from year to year and drought is a constant worry. None of the rivers is navigable for any distance (in some dry years the Orange river stops flowing altogether). The long smooth coastline has few good natural harbours. In contrast to these natural disadvantages, South Africa is extremely rich in minerals such as iron, coal, diamonds and gold.

Human settlement

The climate and soil have made it possible for human beings to live in most parts of South Africa for thousands of years. Up to the end of the seventeenth century the east coast, thanks to its heavy rainfall and its fertile pastures, was the most populated region. Farmers bred cattle in large numbers and grew a variety of crops. Such mixed farming was also possible on the eastern plateau. In the much drier west settled farming was not possible. People moved, with their sheep and cattle, from pasture to pasture or gathered roots and berries and hunted wild game. The countryside teemed with game, especially antelope, which was hunted for food, particularly in times of cattle disease and drought.

The first peoples

Fossil remains

In the often mysterious story about how the human species first came into existence, Southern African discoveries are important. Our knowledge of early people comes mostly from fossil remains, often hidden deep in the earth. At various sites, notably in the caves of Sterkfontein near Johannesburg and Makapansgat in the Transvaal (see map on page 2), South African archaeologists have found the remains of creatures which walked upright and had human-like teeth but whose brains were still ape-like in size. They had lived between 1,000,000 and 3,000,000 years ago. These 'hominids' as they are called, not yet humans but no longer apes, mark an important stage in our evolution.

Hunter-gatherers who used stone tools

More archaeological evidence proves that 10,000 years ago people who were skilled makers of stone tools lived all over South Africa. They hunted game and gathered roots as well as nuts and berries. These hunters were probably the ancestors of the hunters whom the first Europeans saw when they began to settle in the Cape in the seventeenth century.

SOURCE WORK: Geographical features

Source A: Southern Africa: main climatic regions

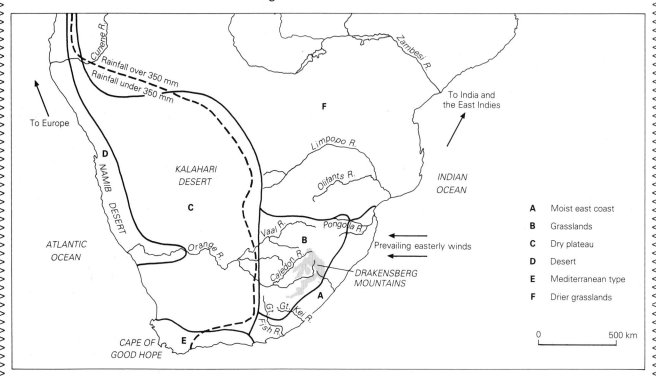

A	Moist east coast
B	Grasslands
C	Dry plateau
D	Desert
E	Mediterranean type
F	Drier grasslands

Source B: Southern Africa: the main peoples, about 1700

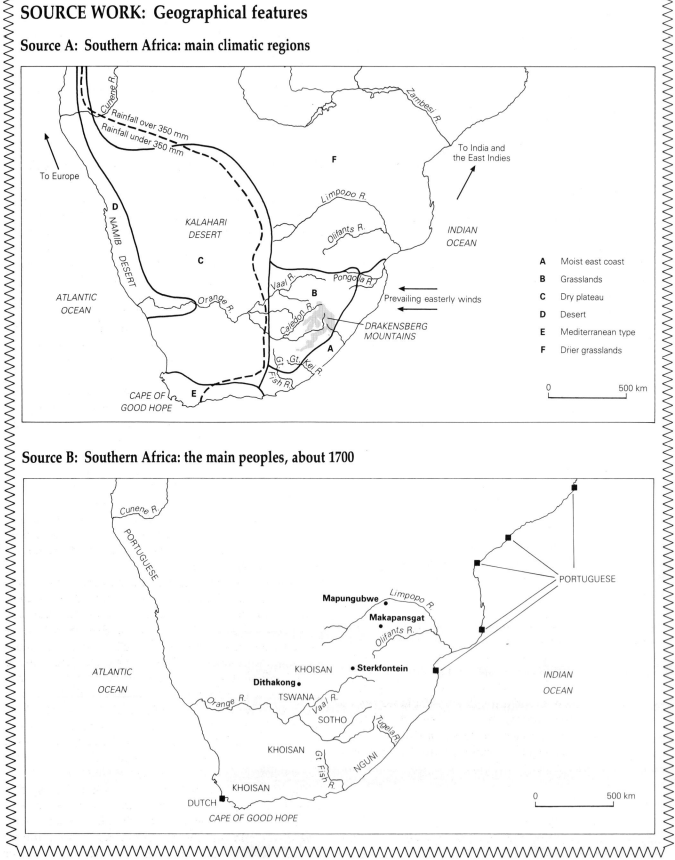

1 (a) Look at Source A. Which two regions of South Africa can count on a good regular rainfall?

    (b) Which region of South Africa was most heavily populated in AD 1700? Give two reasons for this.

2 Why do you think that the line indicating the eastern limit of 350 mm annual rainfall is included on Source A?

3 For each of the following peoples (see Source B) (i) the Nguni, (ii) the Sotho-Tswana and (iii) the Khoisan, explain:

    (a) what kind of farmers they are likely to have been;

    (b) how important hunting would have been to them.

The first herdsmen

In the Namib desert (on the western coast to the north of the Orange river, see Source A) and in the south-west near Cape Town, archaeologists have found remains of people who used stone tools but also herded sheep and cattle and could make pottery. At some time more than 2000 years ago, hunter-gatherers who lived to the north of South Africa learned how to herd sheep and cattle. They probably made their way southwards from what is now Botswana into the Orange valley. Some moved westwards along the Orange river to the coast and then southwards towards the Cape, while others continued southwards across the Orange river until they reached the south coast and then turned westwards towards the Cape.

The term 'Khoisan'

The herdsmen called themselves 'Khoikhoi' (men of men) to show they were different from the hunter-gatherers whom they called San. The first Europeans also used separate names for them, calling the Khoikhoi 'Hottentots' and the San 'Bushmen'. Modern historians have invented the term 'Khoisan' to cover both groups since their languages and way of life had much in common.

If you put your tongue against your teeth or against the roof of your mouth and pull it back sharply, you can make a number of sounds, as when you tut to show you do not like something or when you imitate the noise of horses' hooves. All Khoikhoi and San speech included various click sounds. Both peoples were yellow-skinned and though the Khoikhoi prided themselves on their herds, they also hunted and gathered like the San, especially in times of drought. Both peoples often lived closely together, with the San ready to act as herdsmen for the Khoikhoi in return for milk.

The San

The San were skilful hunters. They could discover the tracks of animals from the tiniest clues and then, with the dogs they had tamed, pursue them across miles of difficult country. They made their kills by accurate shooting with poisoned arrows from simple bows or by traps. Their arrows were cleverly designed. The main shaft was joined to the point by a torpedo-shaped link. When the arrow point hit the animal, the link and shaft usually fell away, so that the point with its poison (made from the larvae of a beetle) would be more likely to stay embedded in the animal until the poison took effect. As well as meat, the San ate roots, berries, caterpillars and locusts and were particularly fond of wild honey. They stored water in the shells of ostrich eggs.

While the hunting of large animals was done by the men, the women hunted smaller animals and gathered the roots and berries. Their main tool was a digging stick weighted by a stone.

The San were seldom more than 1.5 m high with yellowy-brown skin. They lived in small groups usually between twenty-five and seventy in number. When there were no caves nearby, they put up shelters of grass and wood and hollowed out shallow trenches in the ground in which to sleep. The few clothes they needed were made from animal skins and their tools from stone, wood or bone.

The leader of each small group was the senior male. He also guarded the fire, which was considered sacred, and would decide when and in what direction the group should move. Otherwise the San seem to have treated each other, women as well as men, as equals and to have co-operated closely together. They shared their food carefully and acted quickly to stop quarrels since the death or injury of even one adult member of the group would affect their ability to get the food which they needed for survival. For similar reasons of survival the size of the group could not get too large. Children had to be spaced so those babies who arrived too soon would be left to die in the wild.

The San believed that the world was full of spirits, some friendly, some dangerous and some a mixture of the two. Sickness was due to evil spirits which medicine men could cure by the correct ritual dance and by touch. Particular animals or insects, like the eland or

San hunters armed for an expedition: a painting by Samuel Daniell, about 1830

San hunters (centre) fight Bantu-speaking farmers for cattle: a San rock painting

praying mantis, hid powerful gods. The San's music and dance and their magnificent rock paintings linked them, they believed, to the spirit world.

The Khoikhoi

Like the San, the Khoikhoi hunted, fished and gathered roots and berries. However, their herds gave them sour milk to add to their diet. This improvement may have been the main reason why they were taller on average than the San. Cattle were seldom killed for food, only for special celebrations or in times of famine.

The Khoikhoi lived a more settled life than the San since they could stay in one place for as long as their herds had enough pasture. Usually they moved according to the seasons, for example to the coastal pastures in the summer and inland in the winter.

Their herds also made it possible for them to live in larger groups than the San. A typical camp numbered thirty to fifty huts with about 150 to 250 inhabitants. The huts were made of a framework of thin poles bent into semi-circles, covered with mats of woven reeds and, in winter, with skins. The huts themselves formed a large circle, often surrounded by a brushwood fence inside which the herds would sleep at night.

The Khoikhoi wore loin cloths, leather cloaks and sandals and fur hats. They could make pottery and copper blades for tools and weapons, and they trained their oxen to carry both them and their goods.

The inhabitants of a camp usually consisted of one extended family group or clan. At the heart of this group were the male relatives, each with their wives and children. The men controlled the cattle, which were the wealth of the clan. Women were treated as inferior and had little say in clan affairs. Neither the clan leaders nor the clans themselves were strong. They formed and re-formed as they moved from pasture to pasture and frequently raided each other's herds. In times of drought, good pasture would be in short supply and the clans would battle to control it. Those who lost would have to move off, either to find new pastures or to turn entirely to hunting and gathering.

The Khoikhoi believed that the spirits of their ancestors lived on after death and that their graves were holy places. Their supreme god was the god of rain who spoke through the thunderstorms. By prayers and by sacrifices, they hoped to bring rain when it was needed.

The Khoisan: the earliest inhabitants of South Africa

By AD 1500 there were probably about 20,000 San scattered across the area between the Orange river and the south and west coasts. Rather more Khoikhoi, about 100,000 by recent calculations, herded their flocks along the Orange valley and the southern coastal belt. These, not the black Bantu-speaking farmers nor the white settlers of the Cape, were the first inhabitants of South Africa.

A Khoikhoi settlement: a drawing by James Chapman, about 1868

The Drakensberg mountains in Natal divide the well-watered coastlands from the drier central plateau.

The Mediterranean climate of the Western coast of Cape Province is ideal for the cultivation of vines and citrus fruit. This vineyard near Stellenbosch, to the east of Cape Town, was photographed in 1986.

SOURCE WORK: Different views of the San

The first written evidence about the San and indeed South African history generally was written by Europeans. While this written evidence appears to tell us much more than paintings or archaeological remains, it has its problems. Most of it is written from a white viewpoint and most of the first white travellers in South Africa took it for granted that they were superior to the yellow and black-skinned peoples already living there. In their eyes, Europe was Christian and civilised, while Africa was pagan and savage (see Source A).

Nowadays far fewer Europeans think of themselves as superior to other peoples. There are many reasons for this change. One is the fact that between 1914 and 1945 Europeans fought the two most cruel wars in human history. Another is that they know much more about other peoples and realise that different though they may be, they have strengths as well as weaknesses.

Source A: A white traveller in the eighteenth century

O. F. Mentzel was a German who joined the Dutch East India Company (see Chapter 2) and worked in Cape Town from 1732 to 1740. He was the tutor of the children of a rich Cape Town merchant and travelled quite extensively in the countryside to the north and east of Cape Town.

'Having no cattle and often lacking edible roots ... they [the San whom Mentzel, like most whites, called Bushmen] are forced to steal ... and to risk their lives to fill their stomachs. They therefore do not easily let slip an opportunity to stalk and overwhelm the tame Hottentots, to drive off and steal some of their cattle ... They have become accustomed to lazy days that even when they drive small herds of cattle to their hiding places, they are far too indolent [lazy] to tend and graze them ... Instead they kill them off to the last one ... rather than take the slightest trouble in looking after them ...

By nature they are apparently not savage or cruel, but the persecution of Europeans who shoot them like dogs and the bitter hunger when they have nothing to eat, make them audacious [bold] and desperate so they risk their lives and become bloodthirsty. They can however be tamed ... and, if they are gently persuaded, become servants. Especially those taken young can easily be trained and used ...'

O. F. Mentzel, *Geographical and Topographical Description of the Cape of Good Hope*, 1785

Source B: The San peoples still living today

Laurens van der Post (1906–) has been a farmer, a soldier, and explorer in some of Africa's least known regions. In 1956 he led an expedition into the Kalahari desert and lived among the San for a number of weeks filming as well as writing about their way of life. This extract describes one group beside whom he camped.

'They were always going about work of some kind. The younger men ... were always out hunting for game ... Daily too the younger women and children went out with their grubbing sticks to look for food in the sands of the desert. Whenever I accompanied them the intelligence ... and speed with which they harvested the earth never ceased to astonish me ...

While the hunters were out, the older people did the maintenance work of the community: repaired the bows and arrows ... and prepared the poisons used in hunting ... They also cured and tanned the skins of the buck brought back by the hunters. When I looked back at the laborious methods used on our own farms I was amazed by the speed and skill with which they worked.

They loved also to play ... they had a game of chequers that the men played on squares in the sand ... Once, when we had helped them to hunt for food, they played another game which we called 'Bushman badminton' ... Sometimes, too, they had a mimic war. The pantomime was based on some half-forgotten historical fact ...

Also these Bushmen made music. Nxou was constantly at it and the instrument which he played was like a bow and most popular ...'

Laurens van der Post, *The Lost World of the Kalahari*, Hogarth Press, 1958

1 Who were the Hottentots described by Mentzel?

2 Why should the San seen by Mentzel have been so hungry?

3 What are the main differences between Mentzel's and Van der Post's accounts?

4 Why do you think Van der Post values the San more highly than Mentzel?

5 What are the strengths and weaknesses of each of Mentzel's and Van der Post's accounts for building a picture of the San before 1750?

The Bantu-speaking black farmers

The Early Iron Age

The evidence of archaeologists suggests that by AD 400 iron-working farmers had settled widely across the north and east of South Africa. They lived in small villages in the most fertile valleys of the eastern coast or on the best grasslands of the north-eastern plateau. Their main grain crops were millet and sorghum but they grew other plants, such as melon, and herded goats as well as sheep and cattle. The balance between herding and crop cultivation depended on the climate and soil of their region, and they added wild game, nuts and berries to their diet.

The Late Iron Age

From around AD 1000 some of these communities began to change. They grew in size and produced better pottery and ironwork. There is evidence to show they also mined gold and traded with more distant peoples beyond Africa.

Just south of the Limpopo river is Mapungubwe, the Hill of Jackals (see map, page 2). A rich town stood there from about AD 1100 to 1300. On the flat, easily defended hilltop were the chiefly residences and below, along stone-walled terraces, the smaller but solid homes of the less wealthy people. In the hilltop graves archaeologists found gold and ivory carvings, glass beads and pottery from China. Mapungubwe probably grew rich by trading its local gold and ivory for goods from East Africa and Asia.

The iron-working farmers were larger than the Khoisan. They had darker skins and spoke a Bantu language. They were the ancestors of the present black majority of South Africa who still speak Bantu languages.

Older history books about South Africa describe the Bantu-speaking farmers coming across the Limpopo between 1500 and 1600 and spreading across the land in 'migrations', waves of people moving rapidly southwards. Often these migrations were shown as thick black arrows on a map. White South Africans used to argue that blacks and whites arrived in South Africa at much the same time and that therefore the whites had as much right to the land as the blacks. In fact, the archaeological evidence proves that black farmers had settled widely in South Africa hundreds of years before

A Nguni settlement. Note the thatched semi-circular homes and the cattle pen

the arrival of the whites. It also indicates that their settlement of the land was probably a slower, more gradual movement than the word 'migration' suggests. As the farmers cleared land for their crops and found new pastures, they built more homesteads. Once their children became adults, some at least would want new land of their own. So the area of settlement expanded, generation by generation.

The black farmers' way of life

The importance of cattle

With the passing of time, cattle became even more important. A man's wealth and importance was measured by the number of his cattle. He could normally only take a wife when he had paid *lobola* (the bride-price) in cattle to his future wife's family. Since men were allowed a number of wives, those richest in cattle had the most wives and, consequently, the most children. The larger a man's family, the more help he would have with his crops and with his cattle. Thus his wealth would increase. Men rich in cattle would lend them out to their followers. By the *mafisa* system, their followers had use of the milk and sometimes the offspring of the cattle. In this way, chiefs may have first built up their power.

The women not only looked after the children, the home and the meals, but they also worked in the fields, ground the corn and made the pottery. Their men treated them as inferiors and gave them no say in public affairs.

Chiefs and their power

As well as owning many cattle, a chief also had to be the most senior male amongst his relatives and related through his male ancestors to the most famous ancestors of his people. A chief's main tasks included judging disputes, usually about cattle or land, protecting his people, flocks and lands, and holding ceremonies to ensure rain. Since his power was believed to come from the ancestor spirits, he would be obeyed without question. Nonetheless he usually asked the advice of the senior male family heads before making important decisions.

As young men and women reached adulthood, they took part in initiation ceremonies. A group who went through the ceremony together became an 'age-regiment'. The male age-regiments were the units which a chief would use to form an army, either to raid his neighbours or to defend his people from the raids of others.

The Sotho-Tswana and the Nguni

By AD 1600, the black farmers had developed into two main Bantu language-speaking groups, the Sotho-Tswana and the Nguni. The most obvious difference between the two language groups was the click sounds which the Nguni used. These came from the Khoisan with whom they mingled.

Most of the Sotho-Tswana peoples had settled on the eastern plateau. They lived in large towns; Dithakong, for example, had between 15 and 20,000 inhabitants. These towns were usually divided into wards, in each of which lived groups of related families. Their houses had foundations and walls of stone. Immediately outside the town lay the cultivated fields and beyond them the grazing lands. A *pitso*, or assembly of household heads, met to discuss major problems.

The Nguni of the eastern coastlands, whose settlements reached as far south as the Great Fish river, built their homes out of reeds, grass and wood rather than stone. They seem to have lived in villages rather than towns and their chiefs, at least until 1600, ruled over smaller numbers than did the Sotho-Tswana chiefs. However, after 1600 some chiefs not only raided their neighbours but they also conquered their lands to form larger political units. By 1750, the Xhosa was the most powerful of the southern Nguni peoples and seventy years later, among the northern Nguni, the Zulu had overcome their main rivals.

The chief's homestead, with his many wives and their children, could be a quarrelsome place. Rival wives and sons often argued bitterly about who should succeed to the chiefdom and such arguments could lead to a group splitting off, or to murder or war. Towards the end of the eighteenth century violent disputes between the chiefs and within the chiefs' families appear to have become more common both among the Sotho-Tswana and the Nguni.

The black farmers and the Khoisan

How much fighting there was between the black farmers and the lighter-skinned Khoisan is hard to say. The blacks had the more advanced technology. Their more powerful chiefs and better-armed and better-organised warriors meant that they would eventually win any war, even if they lost the odd battle or two. Certainly they succeeded in taking possession of the best land for their type of farming. In these regions, the Khoi became herdsmen-servants, or were absorbed through marriage, or moved away westwards with their herds. The San were driven off what had been their hunting grounds into the mountains. Their cave paintings show that they did not go without a fight.

SOURCE WORK: The black oral tradition

Oral history is spoken history, often taking the form of tales told round the fireside generation after generation. The black farming peoples of South Africa had a rich oral history, some of which is now written down. Obviously such oral evidence is important for our understanding of South Africa's past but, like all evidence, it needs to be handled carefully. Over the years the tales may have changed but by how much is difficult to judge. An event which started a tale may well have got exaggerated in the telling to make it more entertaining. Sometimes the most famous chiefs become the heroes of far more events than could ever have been possible in reality.

Source A: The Tsonga people and mines of Musina

For centuries Musina (Messina) in the north-east of South Africa has been an important mining centre. The Tsonga people of that area handed down from generation to generation this story of how the first mining began there. The story was put into writing in the 1930s.

> The Musina people brought with them hammers and crowbars and bellows. The crowbar was for digging, and was made from a piece of iron inserted into the end of a heavy stick. The bellows were made out of cowhide or the skin of an antelope. They also plaited very long cords of leather which would not break. Then they made a big basket, tied the cords to it, and, getting into it, the sons of Musina went down the shaft. There they mined the copper by the light of candles made from the leaves of the mokxote tree... At that time there was neither girl nor youth nor man nor woman that stayed at home. The girls gathered the leaves of the mephane trees to make the fires with when drawing wires.
>
> When they were mining the copper they brought the ore to the surface in the skins of impala, buffalo or gnu. They brought the copper out in the form of stones or dust. The stones they then broke with hammers and put into winnowing baskets. They winnowed this and eliminated the dust, so that only the copper remained, which they put into crucibles and heated up...

Told to N. J. Warmelo by M. F. Mamedi in the 1930s

Source B: The Xhosa people: Rharhabe and the 'Hottentots'

In 1857 the first black Christian priest in South Africa, Tiyo Soga, married a Scotswoman while training for the ministry in Glasgow. One of his sons, J. Henderson Soga, wrote a history of the Xhosa. Henderson Soga realised that in his lifetime black society was changing so fast that the oral tales were in danger of being forgotten so he included in his written history all those which he thought to be true. One of these tales was about the famous eighteenth-century chief, Rharhabe.

> [Rharhabe was one of the sons of Chief Phalo. He was a brave warrior and a wise counsellor but he and Phalo's heir became such bitter rivals that Rharhabe decided that he must leave.]
>
> 'He therefore turned his eyes to the West... across the Great Kei River and prepared his section of the tribe to remove to a new country... He burnt his huts and... made for the Buffalo Drifts in the Kei. Arriving there he was at once intercepted by the Hottentots who occupied the country on the further bank...
>
> The opposing forces met at the drift and Rharhabe's people found it difficult to contend with two enemies in the shape of the current of water and the assegais [spears] of those who defended the opposite shore. The Kei was dyed red with the blood of heroes but in spite of this Rharhabe urged on his men to valiant deeds... The whole army having crossed, the Hottentots were driven back and their chief killed...
>
> He then opened communications with the Hottentot Queen Hoho whose husband was slain at the Kei. An amicable [friendly] agreement was reached by which all the rights to that part of the country lying between the Keiskamma and Buffalo Rivers was granted to Rharhabe by purchase.'

J. H. Soga, *The South-Eastern Bantu*, Witwatersrand University Press, 1930, p. 128

Using Source A:
1   How did the miners (a) dig the shafts? (b) light the shafts? (c) extract the pure copper from the copper ore?

2   How did cattle and wild game help the work of the miners?

3   The account gives no date for the beginning of mining at Musina. How would historians set about establishing that date?

Using Source B:
4   Which sections, if any, seem to be the most likely to be exaggerated?

5   What does it tell you (a) about Xhosa chiefs? (b) about the Xhosa and Khoikhoi ('Hottentots')?

6   How useful are these oral history sources to historians? What are their main weaknesses as reliable guides to the past?

Chapter 2 The Dutch settle in the Cape region, 1652–1795

White newcomers

The Portuguese and the sea-route to India

In the fifteenth and sixteenth centuries white seamen began to voyage further from their home ports in Europe. Some, like Christopher Columbus who worked for the rulers of Spain, sailed westwards across the Atlantic. Others, like the Portuguese Bartholomew Diaz, explored southwards down the west coast of Africa. They were all searching for a safe sea-route to the Indies (India, the East Indies and the Far East). They were looking for ways of bringing spices, silks and other luxuries back to Europe in bulk. In his search Columbus found America in 1492. Four years earlier, in 1488, Diaz had rounded the southern-most tip of Africa.

Diaz made a number of landings on the southern coast east of the Cape before his exhausted sailors forced him to turn homewards. In 1497 Vasco da Gama also landed on South African shores (and was wounded by some Khoikhoi). Unlike Diaz, he continued up the eastern coast before he struck out into open sea again and became the first European to sail to India.

The Portuguese, however, never showed much interest in South Africa. Compared to the Indies, the chances for profitable trade there seemed poor and the coast was dangerous. They only landed when forced to do so by bad weather.

The Dutch set up the Cape base in 1652

By 1600 the Dutch had overtaken the Portuguese to become the main European traders in the Indies. Their trade was controlled by a powerful commercial company, the Dutch East India Company (Vereenigde Oost-Indische Compagnie or VOC). Its ships were the first to use Table Bay as a regular stopping place for fresh water. In 1651, the merchants at the head of the company, known as the Lords Seventeen, decided to set up a permanent refreshment base there. They appointed Jan van Riebeeck to carry out this task, and he arrived at Table Bay with five ships in April 1652. When he left ten years later, he had successfully established the base.

The Lords Seventeen ordered the Cape base to be run as cheaply as possible. They instructed Van Riebeeck to build a fort and grow fresh corn and vegetables on the land close by to supply the passing ships. He

should get fresh meat from the Khoikhoi by peaceful barter. The VOC did not wish the base to be the centre of a European colony. They had no intention of getting involved in wars against the Khoikhoi, which would cost them men, money and equipment.

The Dutch settlement expands

Things turned out differently. Since land around the base did not produce enough fresh vegetables, Van Riebeeck gave land nearby to nine white farmers. The Khoikhoi regarded the land as theirs and fighting followed. The number of whites increased. In 1652 ninety had come. By 1662 there were 230, by 1717 about 2000, and by 1780 about 10,500. Some stayed in Cape Town to make a living out of the fleets which called in for rest, fresh food, water and repairs on the long voyages from Europe to the East Indies. Others became farmers. The first were arable farmers who grew corn, vegetables and vines in the well-watered valleys of the south-west Cape. Amongst them were more than 200 French Protestants (Huguenots), who had fled to the Protestant Netherlands after the French king began persecuting them in 1688.

The trekboers

In the eighteenth century, as the whites explored north and east across the mountain ranges of the Cape, they found land suitable for grazing. Many took to pastoral farming, which meant herding cattle and sheep like the Khoikhoi. These pastoral farmers were called *trekboers* or travelling farmers. Their normal way of marking out a farm was to walk a horse for half an hour from a central point in the direction of each of the main compass points. The circumference of the circle so made became the boundary of the farm. Such farms, 2500 hectares in size, were huge by European standards. The VOC tried to govern this huge area through officials known as *landrosts*. However, the trekboers got used to running their lives, and the lives of their black servants, more or less as they pleased.

By 1770, they had begun to graze their cattle in the land between the Sundays and Great Fish rivers (see map, page 12). There they met not just the now familiar Khoisan but a quite different people, the Xhosa. This meeting marked the start of a new stage in South Africa's history.

SOURCE WORK: The Dutch establish their base at Cape Town

Source A: The Cape and white expansion, 1652–1770

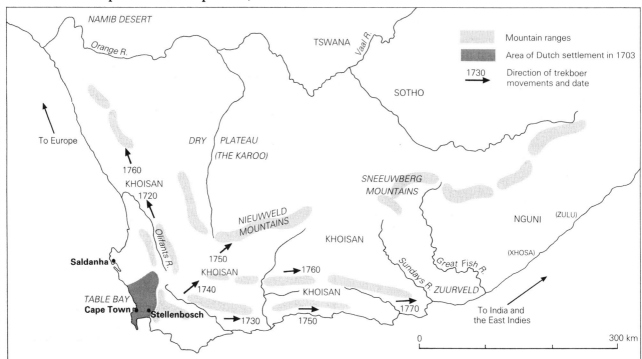

Source B: Cape Town in 1706

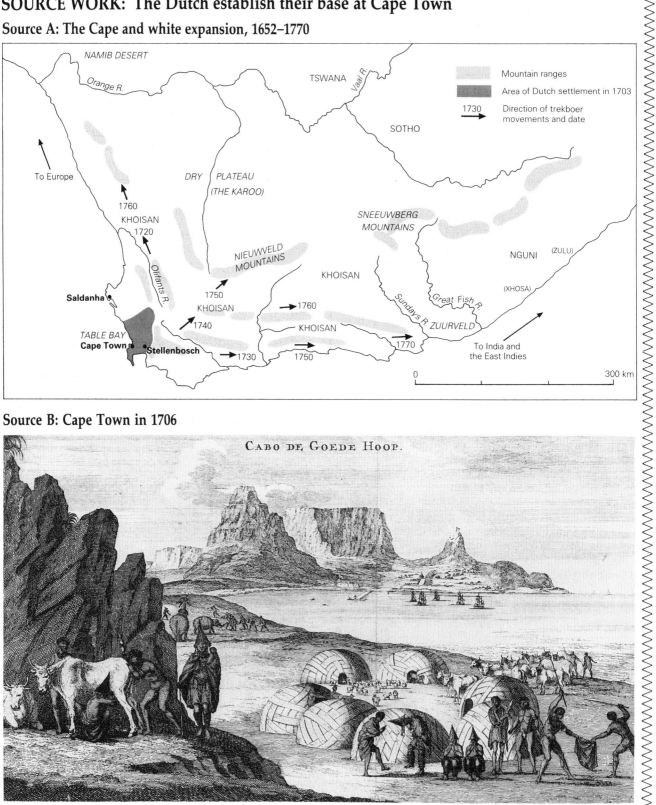

The 'Cabo de Goede Hoop' (Cape of Good Hope) drawn by the Dutchman Abraham Bogaert in 1706. Note the Khoikhoi settlement in the foreground and the white settlement across the bay

Source C: Jan van Riebeeck describes the first months at the Cape

'July 1652. 23rd... found all our hard work done in the garden completely flooded and spoilt... 24th As we were burying the surgeon's wife this afternoon we saw many large baboons... 27th Last night another soldier, named Hendrick Ertmann, died and was buried today. 28th, 29th, 30th Sunday with continual calm, warm and bright sunny weather. Much snow melted. During these fine warm days have again prepared some soil and have sown peas, turnips, carrots... During the past bad wet days about 8 to 10 persons have again gone sick. We can give them nothing better than a little warm wine, as to date we have not seen a single head of cattle or sheep. Hope however in the coming months the people of Saldanha will come down with their cattle and that we shall then be able to barter a good number from them for the refreshment of our men on land as well as those from the ships which are soon expected.'

Jan van Riebeeck's *Journal*, written in July 1652

1 Using Source A, explain why the Dutch chose Cape Town as their first base in South Africa and why it remained the most important town there for the next 250 years.

2 What does Source B tell you about (a) the Khoisan way of life? (b) the Dutch base of Cape Town?

3 Who were the people of Saldanha (see Source C) and why was Van Riebeeck so keen to meet them?

4 What were the main problems which Van Riebeeck faced in carrying out the instructions of the Lords Seventeen?

The whites and the Khoisan

The Khoikhoi

Van Riebeeck seems to have tried hard to keep to the VOC's policy which was to barter with the Khoikhoi for meat and to avoid fighting. Nonetheless, trouble soon came. The Khoikhoi would not trade as many cattle as the Dutch wanted. They accused them of stealing their animals while the Dutch, for their part, claimed that the Khoikhoi were stealing from them. In addition the buildings in the Dutch base and the nine new farms started in 1657 were a direct threat to the grazing lands which the Khoikhoi had used for generations.

Raids and ambushes led to open war, the first from 1659 to 1660, the second from 1673 to 1677. The Dutch won both after some setbacks. The Khoikhoi greatly outnumbered the whites but the way they organised themselves in small nomadic clans prevented them from making good use of their numbers. The whites with their muskets and horses were new and fearsome enemies and the Khoikhoi found their darts were of little use except in ambushes.

Diseases like smallpox and scarlet fever, against which the Khoikhoi had little immunity, further weakened them. A dreadful smallpox epidemic in 1713, caused by germs brought ashore in the laundry of ships visiting Cape Town, was followed by two other serious outbreaks in 1755 and 1767. The Khoikhoi population which historians estimate was about 100,000 when the whites first came may have dropped to as few as 10,000 in 1770. When in 1798 the first, not very reliable, government census was taken, the 'Hottentot' population was growing again and reckoned to be 14,447.

As more whites arrived so they took more of the Khoikhoi grazing lands. The Dutch farmers organised themselves into musket-bearing, horse-riding bands called *commandos* which they used to defend the land they had taken. In this situation, the Khoikhoi had three choices: to fight with little chance of winning, to move away into drier less fertile country, or to stay and work for the whites.

The San

The whites regarded the San hunter-gatherers as little better than wild animals. When they moved into the San hunting grounds and found that the San resisted by raiding their flocks, they sent out commandos to hunt them down. The commandos usually killed the adults and captured the children to work on their farms. Many of the Khoikhoi who lost their grazing lands and their herds became hunters once more and joined the San in their raids on the white farms. In the 1770s in the mountains of the Nieuwveld and the Sneeuwberg (see map, page 12), the Khoisan raids were so fierce that the trekboers were forced to retreat, but only for a short time. Muskets and horses won in the long run. The whites drove the San into the remotest mountains and deserts and their numbers greatly declined.

SOURCE WORK: Whites against the Khoisan

Source A: Jan van Riebeeck to the Lords Seventeen

Van Riebeeck is explaining why war with the Khoikhoi began in 1659.

> [The Khoikhoi complained] 'that our people... without our knowledge, had done them much injury, and also perhaps stolen... some of their sheep and calves etc. in which there is some truth... so that they think that they had some cause for revenge, and especially on people who had come to take and occupy the land which had been their own in all ages... we were at length compelled to say that they had entirely forfeited [lost] that right through the war that they had waged against us, and that we were not inclined to restore it, as it had now become the property of the Company by the sword and by the laws of war.'

Jan van Riebeeck's *Journal*, 1659

Source B: The displacement of the Khoikhoi

John Campbell, a Scottish missionary who travelled in the Cape in 1813, talks to some Khoikhoi (Hottentots).

> 'We came to a Hottentot kraal [settlement], where we would have halted for the night, but their fountain was all dried up... From their own account they had once a better place but a boor [Dutch farmer, usually spelt 'boer'] having asked permission first to sow a little corn, then to erect a mill, they allowed it; after which he applied to the government for a grant for the whole place, which they were promised not knowing that it was in the possession of these Hottentots; of course they were driven from it. An old Hottentot told us that he remembered the time when the boors were within five days journey of Cape Town and the country was full of Hottentot kraals; but they have gradually been driven up the country to make room for white people.'

John Campbell, *Travels in South Africa*, London, 1822

Source C: San against white farmers, around 1820

'Bushmen driving cattle up a kloof – Boers in pursuit': C. D. Bell, about 1820

Source D: A white raid against the San in the 1850s

Laurens van der Post (see page 7) describes a white raid against the San ('Bushmen') in his grandfather's time:

'My own people, thanks to their horses and guns, usually managed to keep out of range and fell only when ambushed. When they stormed a Bushman in his caves they usually moved behind a screen made from their saddle-cloths and thick duffle-coats.

The Bushman never stood a chance against them. His only hope lay in a compassion [pity] against which the hearts of Europeans at that brutal hour were firmly shut. Yet . . . he never asked for mercy . . . What could be prouder than the Bushman's reply to young Martin du Plessis, a boy of 14 who was sent into a great cave near my home where the Bushman was surrounded in his last stronghold by a powerful commando. The boy, almost in tears besought him to surrender, promising to walk out in front of him as a live shield against any treacherous bullets. At last, impatient that his refusal was not accepted, the Bushman scornfully said: "Go! Begone! Tell your chief that I have a strong heart! Go! Begone! Tell him that my last words are that not only is my quiver full of arrows but that I shall resist and defend myself as long as I have life left."'

Laurens van der Post, *The Lost World of the Kalahari*

1   For what reasons does Van Riebeeck (Source A) think that the Khoikhoi attacked the Dutch? Does he think that they were wrong to do so? Why will he not give them back their land?

2   List the stages described by Campbell (Source B) by which the Hottentots (Khoikhoi) lost their land to the white farmer. Why did the VOC not protect the Khoikhoi?

3   What is happening in the picture painted by C. D. Bell? How well does the scene fit in with what you know about the trekboers and the Khoisan?

4   In Laurens van der Post's account of the white raid (Source D), how did the white farmers defend themselves from the poisoned arrows of the San? Why will the 'Bushman' not surrender to the white farmers? Is the account a 'primary' or 'secondary' source of evidence? Is there anything about the story which seems to you at all curious?

Slavery and its effects

A major area of VOC trading was with the colonies in America and the Caribbean. Dutch merchants made large profits out of the slave trade, shipping human cargoes from West Africa to work on the sugar plantations. VOC officials in the Indies also had slaves themselves, copying the Asian princes with whom they traded. Van Riebeeck soon decided that his Cape settlement needed slaves, and, in 1658, persuaded the VOC to send him 400. By 1770, the Cape had about 8000 slaves, more in fact than it had whites. Some slaves, like the Malays who won a reputation as builders and craftsmen, came from the East Indies, but most were from Madagascar and East Africa.

The first slaves worked for the VOC either on building projects like Cape Town's fort, or as personal servants. The owners of the wheat and wine farms also used them to tend their fields and vines. The slaves had no legal rights. They were part of their master's belongings.

Owners kept control by savage punishments. A slave who stole or who raised his hand against his master faced death. The first attempt at escape meant a whipping; a second would lead to branding or the loss of a nose or an ear. Nonetheless many slaves did escape and travellers reported seeing the gleam of their fires on Table Mountain at night. Most were recaptured since the Khoikhoi seldom helped them and, without their help, food was hard to come by.

The position of the Khoikhoi worsens

The VOC always stated that the Khoikhoi were free and could turn to the Company law-courts if they had a complaint against the whites. However, as time passed, their position grew closer to that of the slaves. They lost their cattle and grazing lands; they depended on the whites for food and wages and they were forced to accept labour contracts which bound them increasingly tightly to white farmers.

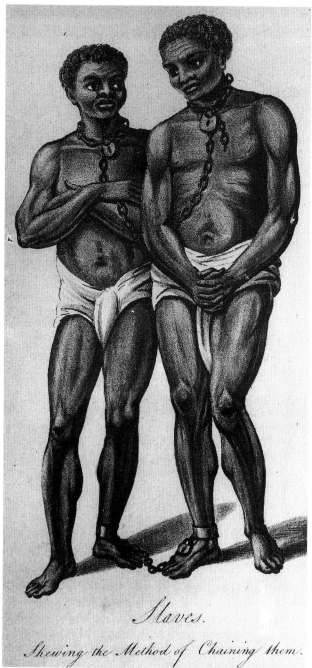

Slaves.

Shewing the Method of Chaining them.

Two slaves chained at the neck and ankles: a drawing from the Cape Archives

The white way of life increases racial prejudice

The Dutch colony at the Cape started as a place to provide fresh food for the VOC so most whites, of whom there were about 7200 by 1770, were farmers. The arable farms closest to Cape Town made the best profits from supplying the fleets. These farms made the greatest use of slaves. However, many whites were more attacted to trekboer pastoral farming which was cheaper to get started than arable farming.

Most trekboer families had a number of Khoikhoi labourers and servants. Nonetheless, the trekboer life was lonely and far from easy. There were no shops, doctors, chemists or schools inland. Pedlars might turn up with goods to buy but the trekboer and his family had to make most of the things they needed, like clothes, soap and candles, using their animals to supply raw materials such as leather and fat. For food they had plenty of meat but bread and vegetables were often scarce. Coffee and tea were their usual drinks. Sugar and wine were luxuries.

They had to spread themselves thinly to find enough grazing for their herds and the countryside was often dangerous. Wild animals like lions threatened their flocks and the Khoisan might make an unexpected raid. For these reasons, the men had to be expert horsemen and marksmen, and the wives had to be capable of bearing and bringing up children in isolated and sometimes frightening conditions.

By 1770, South Africa's whites had developed some forms of social life which marked them as different from the European Dutch. They began to call themselves *Afrikaners* (Africans) and to speak a language (the *taal*) which was noticeably different from Dutch. They looked at their farms, their crops and their herds, forgot that they had taken the land from the Khoisan, and told themselves that through their skill and courage they were taming the African wilderness.

Like many Europeans of the eighteenth century, they took it for granted that Christian whites were superior to non-Christian blacks and this sense of superiority was greatly strengthened by the fact that they made blacks do all their labouring and servants' jobs. They knew, too, that the blacks out-numbered them. If they were to remain the masters, the blacks must know their inferior place and stay there. Most whites needed to believe that the blacks were inferior to them and, as the eighteenth century drew to its end, the experience of the master–slave relationship, generation after generation, convinced them that whites were naturally superior.

SOURCE WORK: White attitudes to slaves and Khoisan

Source A: Vergelegen in the early eighteenth century

Vergelegen, near Cape Town, the farm of Governor William van der Stel, Cape Archives

Source B: A VOC inspector's view, 1748

Baron Imhoff visited the Cape in 1743.

'[Having] imported slaves every common or ordinary European becomes a gentleman and prefers to be served rather than to serve... The majority of farmers in this Colony are not farmers in the real sense of the word... and many of them are ashamed to work with their own hands.'

Source C: A Swedish scientist's view in the 1770s

Anders Sparrman, a Swedish scientist who visited the Cape in the 1770s, describes a thirty-day journey by a trekboer to the Cape Town market:

'...for such a journey every farmer has two or three Hottentots, one to lead the oxen, and either one or two to drive the spare team; besides which his wife often goes with him, either for the purpose of having her children baptised, or for fear of being attacked by the Hottentots in her husband's absence.'

Source D: The problems of being of mixed race in the 1780s

Le Vaillant, a French traveller in the Cape in 1783, notes the comments of a woman whose father was white and mother Khoikhoi:

'You know the profound contempt which the whites entertain [have] for the blacks, and even for those of mixed breed as myself. To settle among them was to expose myself to daily disgrace and affronts [insults].'

Source E: The colonists' views of non-whites, 1780

Governor van Plettenberg wrote this in a letter after a visit to the interior in 1780:

'It would take more than human efforts to persuade the colonists to accept Caffres [non-whites] as their fellow Christians, fellow men and brothers. The word heathen seems to be the device with which men like to give rein to their thirst for revenge and greed.'

1   Study Source A. William van der Stel would have been proud of his farm and sure that it had improved the lives of everyone who lived near it, Khoikhoi as well as white.
   (a) What points would he have made to support this claim?
   (b) What might the local Khoikhoi have thought of it?

2   What does Baron Imhoff (Source B) mean when he writes: 'farmers in this Colony are not farmers in the real sense of the word...'?

3   Put Source E into your own words to make its meaning clear.

4   Take each of the Sources A to E and explain what it shows about how the whites needed and/or misused the blacks.

5   Which important groups of people of eighteenth-century Cape society are not represented in the sources?

Chapter 3 The British at the Cape in the first half of the nineteenth century

The British take over the Cape

The decline of Dutch sea-power

The Dutch had built their Cape refreshment base when their navy was among the most powerful in Europe. During the eighteenth century it became much weaker. Two other European nations, France and Britain, overtook the Netherlands as sea-powers and fought each other bitterly to control the trade-routes to Asia and to the Americas. As a result of the Seven Years War (1756–63), Britain gained the upper hand and the victory of Trafalgar (1805) during the Napoleonic Wars began a period of nearly a century when the British navy ruled the oceans of the world.

Britain and the sea-route to India

The British first seized Cape Town in 1795 and the peace treaties of 1814–15 which ended the Napoleonic Wars gave Cape Colony to Britain. Like the Dutch, the British wanted South Africa because it was a useful staging post on the sea-route to Asia. India was the most important part of the growing British Empire and control of the Cape was vital to the safety of ships trading with India and the Far East. Like the Dutch, they did not expect to find riches in South Africa. Their main aim was to make sure that their ships calling in at Cape Town would get the refreshments and services they needed and that Cape Colony, which supplied the food and the services, was governed well and cheaply.

British attitudes

In other ways, however, British rule was quite different from Dutch rule. In 1806, Britain was in the middle of industrial changes which were to make her the most economically advanced and wealthiest nation in the world. British officials in South Africa were employed by the Colonial Office in London. They were more confident and firmer than those of the VOC. They also had more power to make people obey them. When they passed a law, they expected that law to be obeyed, even by the most distant trekboer. If they had trouble, whether with the trekboers or with the Xhosa, they could ship in regiments from their regular army whose firepower and training were much better than that which the VOC had had at its disposal.

British opinion was turning against slavery. Parliament made the slave trade illegal in 1808, which meant that slave-owning colonies could no longer receive fresh supplies of slave labour. In the next few years many British politicians turned against slavery itself. Their views were very often reinforced by reports from Christian missionaries working in the Caribbean, the

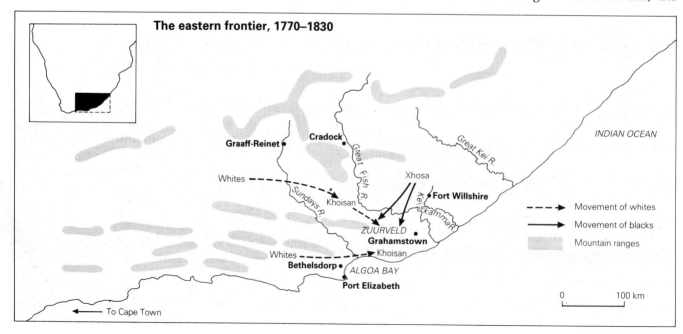

The eastern frontier, 1770–1830

Cape, and other colonies. In 1833 the British Parliament made slavery illegal within the British Empire.

Trouble on the eastern frontier

The trouble on the eastern frontier of Cape Colony had begun before the arrival of the British. It was here that whites met black Bantu-speaking farmers in large numbers for the first time. These blacks were a southern Nguni people, the Xhosa (see page 9). Almost at once blacks and whites found themselves enemies with pastureland for their herds the main cause of their conflicts.

The trekboers and their cattle began moving into the Zuurveld between the Sundays and Great Fish rivers in the 1770s (see map opposite). The Khoikhoi were already there. So too were the Xhosa whose growing population needed more space, particularly in years of low rainfall.

The Zuurveld was satisfactory grazing country but its mixture of sweet and sour pastures forced herdsmen to move their cattle according to the seasons. The sweet grasses of the valleys could be used all the year round, the sour grasses of the plains only in the spring and early summer. The shortage of good all-the-year-round pasture and the frequent movement of herds led to arguments between the different peoples. The trekboers thought that they could take and hold the grazing lands in the Zuurveld in the same way as they had taken other land from the Khoikhoi. They argued that the VOC had given them the legal right to the land and should defend them against the Xhosa. For their part, the Xhosa were also used to taking Khoikhoi land and to the Khoikhoi giving way to them. They believed that they should have the Zuurveld and expected the whites to give way to them too. The Khoikhoi, caught between two more powerful enemies, usually watched to see who was the more likely to win and then joined that side.

Arguments over land and thefts of cattle led to raids and counter-raids. The trekboers formed commandos (see page 13) and appealed to Cape Town for reinforcements. The first battle between the whites and the Bantu-speaking peoples took place in 1779.

The strength of black resistance

The Xhosa were more powerful than the Khoisan. There were many more of them and they fought better. They were more loyal to their chiefs and had greater resistance to European diseases. This last fact is central

The Eighth Frontier War, 1850–53. A detachment of the Second or Queen's Regiment is surrounded by blacks and Khoikhoi: painted by Thomas Baines

to the history of modern South Africa. If you read about the Aborigines in Australia, the Maoris in New Zealand or the Red Indians in North America, you will find that their experience of meeting the whites was like that of the Khoisan. They lost their lands and had weak resistance to European diseases. Their numbers fell and they were swamped by an increasing white population. The Bantu-speakers lost their lands but they did not die out. Though the white population of South Africa grew, the black one grew even more. The whites remained a minority.

The Frontier Wars, 1779–1878

In the first three 'Frontier Wars' (1779–81, 1793, 1799–1803) Boer commandos tried and failed to drive the Xhosa from the Zuurveld. In 1803, the Xhosa controlled more of the area than they had done in the 1770s, the Khoikhoi were prepared to fight alongside them and many trekboers had fled back towards Cape Town.

In the years that followed, more Xhosa moved across the Fish river but the British now ruled in Cape Town and with a well-equipped regular army stationed there, they were stronger than the Dutch. In the opinion of Sir John Cradock, who became Governor of the Cape in 1811, the lawlessness of the Xhosa was putting the meat supply of Cape Town in danger. In the next phase of the wars (the Fourth, 1811–12 and the Fifth, 1818–19) the British army drove the Xhosa back across the Fish river.

The 1820 settlers

The British government then tried to bring peace to this troublesome frontier by persuading more English people to come to settle in the Zuurveld. In 1820, 1000 British families arrived in the Grahamstown area. At that time many Britons were out of work so the government's offer of cheap and apparently fertile farming land in South Africa was very attractive.

As far as keeping the peace on the frontier was concerned the settlement plan failed since the plots of land sold to the 1820 settlers were much too small for them to earn a living, and after much suffering many of them moved into towns like Grahamstown and Port Elizabeth. Nonetheless most of them stayed in South Africa and became an important part of the English-speaking section of the white population which, though it never became as numerous as the Afrikaans-speakers, was to have great influence in economic and social matters.

More frontier wars

The fighting broke out again between black and white farmers in the 1830s. In the Sixth Frontier War (1834–35) the Xhosa invaded deep into Cape Colony (see map, page 18). British forces counter-attacked and their commander, Colonel Harry Smith, took possession of the land between the Kei and Keiskamma rivers. The Governor of the Cape realised, however, that the task of holding this conquest would be difficult and expensive, so, in 1836, he handed it back to the Xhosa, much to the disgust of the white farmers.

Yet no permanent peace followed. The Xhosa bought guns and raided white farms. The land was found to be ideal for sheep farming. The white farmers could get good prices for wool from the British woollen cloth industry, so they demanded more and more land. The Seventh Frontier War (1846–47) began after a Xhosa had been arrested for stealing an axe. After much destruction of cattle and crops, the British once more conquered the area between the Kei and Keiskamma rivers. This time they held on to it. Still the Xhosa fought on to prevent the whites gaining more of their land. The Eighth Frontier War lasted three years, from 1850 to 1853 and finally ended in a Xhosa defeat.

Xhosa cattle killing of 1856–57

The Xhosa despaired. Within seventy years they had fought eight major frontier wars, they had lost much of their land, their herds of cattle had been killed and their crops burned. Their chiefs were mocked by their white enemies who also criticised their whole way of life. In desperation they turned to their ancestors to save them.

In March 1856, Mhlakaza, a senior Xhosa councillor, was told by his niece that she had seen ghostly people and cattle. On going to investigate, he met, so he said, some of these people and his brother who had been dead for many years. 'Kill all your cattle, destroy your grain and sow no seeds,' said the ghosts. 'If you do this, the Russians [at that time Britain and Russia were on opposite sides in the Crimean War] will come and drive the English into the sea and the Xhosa will have all the cattle, grain, clothes, guns and ammunition they could possibly want.'

Chief Sarhili believed Mhlakaza and ordered the cattle to be killed and the crops destroyed. Most of his people obeyed him, slaughtering between 150,000 and 200,000 cattle before the end of 1856. As many as 20,000 Xhosa may have died of starvation and thousands more fled into Cape Colony in search of work and food.

After 1857 the Xhosa could do little to resist the whites. The British took full control of the land to the west of the Kei and, in one last frontier war, the Ninth, 1877–78, pushed the boundary of Cape Colony still further east, linking up with their second South African coastal colony, Natal (see map, page 31).

White missionaries

The missionary movement

Towards the end of the eighteenth century the various Christian churches of Europe found new energy. Growing numbers of men were ready to spend their lives trying to convert the non-Christian peoples of the world to Christianity. Some of these missionaries also believed in the new ideas of freedom, equality and justice which had helped to bring about the French Revolution in 1789 and which, in Britain, gave strength to the movement to abolish slavery.

Dr J. T. van der Kemp

One such missionary in South Africa was Dr J. T. van der Kemp, who worked on the Eastern Frontier from 1799 to 1811.

Van der Kemp was Dutch by birth but worked for the London Missionary Society. At Bethelsdorp near Port Elizabeth he started a mission station in 1799 where he not only taught the Khoisan the teachings of Christ but allowed them to farm independently of the whites. Moreover, since he believed that all people were equal in the sight of God, he fiercely questioned many of the practices of whites. First, he opposed the way they forced the Khoisan into military service and road-mending. Then he criticised them for their frequent cruel treatment of their Khoisan labourers. He also accused local officials of failing to protect the Khoisan in the law-courts.

Dr J. T. van der Kemp, Cape Archives

He taught that slavery was wrong. He married a coloured Malay slave, an act which upset his white neighbours and, most unforgivably of all as far as the local white settlers were concerned, he and other missionaries wrote to the British government in the Cape to complain about the ill-treatment of the Khoisan.

As a result, in 1812 the Cape government sent judges to check these complaints and found many trekboers guilty of cruelty. The whites were really shocked that their government could support the Khoisan against them and called the judges' visit the 'Black Circuit'.

Dr John Philip

In 1819 another strong-minded missionary arrived to champion the Khoisan and the Xhosa. Dr John Philip was superintendent of the London Missionary Society with powerful friends both in London and in Cape Town. He travelled widely in South Africa and in 1828 published a book called *Researches in South Africa* which gained much publicity.

Dr Philip loudly criticised the so-called Hottentot Codes, issued by the British colonial officials in the Cape in 1809 and 1812. These made the Khoisan carry passes and forced Khoisan children born on a white farm to work there from the age of eight to eighteen. In Philip's view they made the Khoisan little better than slaves.

The abolition of slavery and its effects

In 1828, by Ordinance 50, the Cape government abolished the Hottentot Codes and declared that all free citizens, whatever their colour, should be equal in the eyes of the law. Five years later, in 1833, the British Parliament abolished slavery throughout the British Empire.

Many Boer farmers strongly opposed the abolition, partly because they could see nothing wrong with the slavery which their Dutch ancestors had introduced to South Africa and partly because they stood to lose money. The British government paid only a third of a slave's value in compensation to the slave owners and would only make the compensation payments in London, not in Cape Town. South African slave-owners had, therefore, to pay fees to London agents to collect the compensation, which did not please them at all.

Ordinance 50 and the abolition of slavery gave the black people of South Africa important new legal rights and more freedom to work for whom they pleased. Nonetheless, social customs did not at once change greatly. Wherever the races mingled together, the blacks stayed the poor labourers, the whites the better-off employers.

SOURCE WORK: Missionaries and their work for the Khoisan: two views

Source A: 'Romance and Reality', a cartoonist's view of missionaries, about 1830

The cartoonist F. T. I'ons comments on the attitudes towards the Khoisan of missionaries like Dr John Philip

Source B: Dr John Philip's view

He is writing about his campaign for the Khoisan.

(i) In his Journal in 1822 while touring Cape Colony:

'...they [the Khoisan] could not travel half a mile to hear us preach without a written pass... The whole Hottentot nation...were compelled to be in service...any one of them neither in service nor in a [missionary] institution, might be had before a Field Cornet [local official] by any Boer, then committed to the service of his apprehender or to the Drostdy jail till he would go where he was sent...'

(ii) In his Journal in 1829:

'On my arrival in Cape Town [September 1829] I found the country full of alarm. It was asserted [said]...in all the pro-slavery journals that the Hottentots...were living by robbing their former masters and that the farmers and their families were trembling for their lives...

To ascertain [find out] the extent of the evils... I left Cape Town to visit the scene of the alleged disorder. In Cape Town we were told that it was at Hottentots Holland... At Hottentots Holland, it was at Swellendam. At Swellendam it was at George. At George it was at Long Kloof....'

(iii) In his Journal of 1832:

'When it was heard that I was to visit the Interior ...letters appeared in *De Zuid Afrikaan* [The South African] daring me to set foot in the country and threatening me... In my journey through the colony, my waggon was once set fire to...by one of the settlers.'

1 (a) Who was Dr John Philip?
   (b) Who were the Hottentots?
   (c) What was *De Zuid Afrikaan*?

2 What kind of treatment of blacks by whites is Dr Philip criticising in Source B(i)?

3 Which change in the law had been issued by the Cape government in 1828? Why did it alarm white settlers? How does Dr Philip view their alarm in Source B(ii)?

4 The I'ons cartoon (Source A) is divided in two. What does each section show?

5 Does I'ons sympathise more with the missionaries than with the settlers? Explain your answer.

6 What evidence is there that some white settlers deeply disliked the missionaries? Explain the reasons for this dislike.

Chapter 4   The Difaqane and the 'Great' Trek

The Difaqane (scattering of peoples)

Difaqane or 'scattering of peoples' is the Sotho-Tswana name for the nearly twenty years of war and destruction which laid waste much of the central plateau in the 1820s and 1830s. The Zulus called it the *Mfecane* or 'crushing', which is hardly suprising since the fearsome Zulu army attacked and eliminated surrounding chiefdoms.

Shaka

Towards the end of the eighteenth century some northern Nguni chiefs strengthened their armies and used them to fight more fiercely against each other. One of the most successful was Dingiswayo, the Mthethwa chief, in whose army a young Zulu warrior called Shaka made his name for his bravery. In 1816 Dingiswayo was killed in battle and Shaka became leader of the Zulus. In a space of three years he turned the Zulus from being one of a number of minor Nguni peoples into the most powerful of them all.

Shaka was an extraordinary person. He was born in 1797. His father was the chief of the Zulus but seems to have driven Nandi, Shaka's mother, from his home. Nandi appears to have been the only person for whom Shaka ever cared. He never had wives or children of his own. His passion was for his magnificent army and its wars of conquest.

Shaka was a brilliant military leader. He armed his warriors with short stabbing spears and trained them to fight with disciplined ferocity in great horn-shaped formations. As chief, he organised Zulu society so that he could wage war whenever he wished. Virtually all Zulu men up to the age of forty were divided into regiments to which he gave weapons and cattle. The women, who did most of the farming, belonged to regiments linked to the male ones. They could only marry and have children when Shaka decided that the regiment had fought enough. He also made his army fight more cruelly than had been the Nguni custom. Formerly wars had been glorified cattle raids with only a few human deaths. Now the Zulus killed the women and children of their enemies.

By 1818, Shaka had brought the independent Mthethwa chiefs under his control. Then in five days of fighting in 1819 he completely defeated his dangerous neighbours the Ndwandwe and forced them and their leader Zwide to flee northwards across the Pongola.

Shaka Zulu, about 1825. This portrait was engraved from a sketch by Lieutenant James King, a trader who knew Shaka. Cape Archives

He was now master of all the land between the Pongola and Tugela rivers but his appetite for conquest was far from satisfied. From 1821 to 1824 his war-machine laid waste a wide area of fertile land south of the Tugela. In 1822 it drove the Ngwane over the Drakensberg and in 1828 Shaka ordered it northwards in search of yet more victories.

Before the army returned, Shaka was dead. He had become a tyrant – his word had been law and his people had become terrified of him. White traders who first met him in 1824 reported how he had men killed for hardly any reason. When his mother died in 1827, he seems to have lost his balance and ordered deaths as if for enjoyment. His soldiers grew tired of the continuous fighting and, in 1828, two of his half-brothers stabbed him to death.

The results of Shaka's wars

By the time of Shaka's death, Zulu attacks had spread violence all over central southern Africa and northwards almost as far the Equator (see map, page 24). The Hlubi and Ngwane, fleeing from the Zulus, had to fight their way across the central plateau in search of food and a place to settle. In order to survive their attacks, a Sotho tribe, the Tlokwa, led by the warrior queen Mantatisi, also took to a travelling life of plunder. To the north east the Ndebele chief Mzilikasi fought his way across the Vaal. Once a favoured general of Shaka, he too fled from his anger.

The suffering in terms of deaths, destruction, hunger and fear was colossal. The Difaqane left large areas of land both along the coast and on the plateau almost empty of people and the black chiefdoms which survived were much weaker than before.

SOURCE WORK: The impact of Shaka's army in the 1820s

Source A: The Difaqane, 1820–40

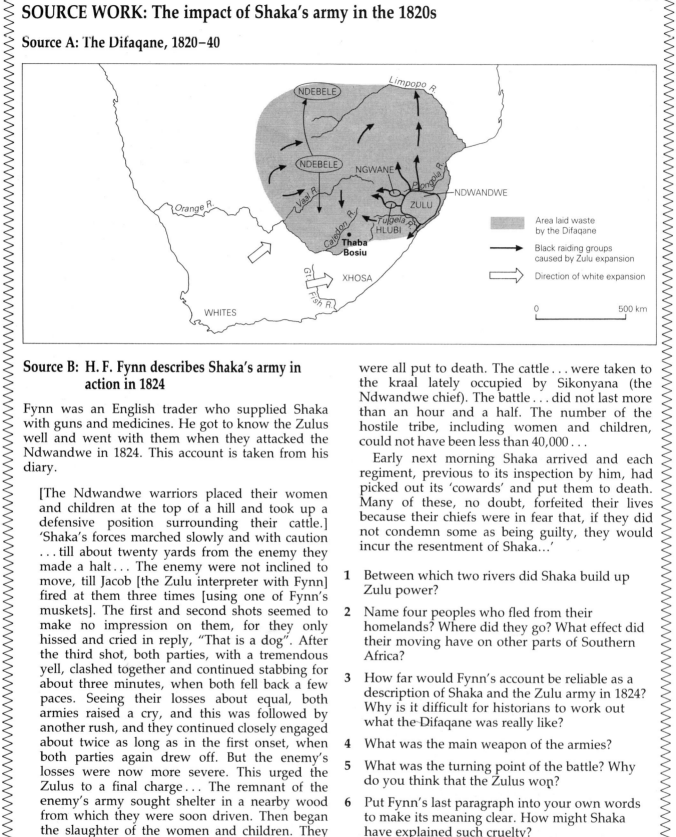

Source B: H. F. Fynn describes Shaka's army in action in 1824

Fynn was an English trader who supplied Shaka with guns and medicines. He got to know the Zulus well and went with them when they attacked the Ndwandwe in 1824. This account is taken from his diary.

[The Ndwandwe warriors placed their women and children at the top of a hill and took up a defensive position surrounding their cattle.] 'Shaka's forces marched slowly and with caution . . . till about twenty yards from the enemy they made a halt . . . The enemy were not inclined to move, till Jacob [the Zulu interpreter with Fynn] fired at them three times [using one of Fynn's muskets]. The first and second shots seemed to make no impression on them, for they only hissed and cried in reply, "That is a dog". After the third shot, both parties, with a tremendous yell, clashed together and continued stabbing for about three minutes, when both fell back a few paces. Seeing their losses about equal, both armies raised a cry, and this was followed by another rush, and they continued closely engaged about twice as long as in the first onset, when both parties again drew off. But the enemy's losses were now more severe. This urged the Zulus to a final charge . . . The remnant of the enemy's army sought shelter in a nearby wood from which they were soon driven. Then began the slaughter of the women and children. They were all put to death. The cattle . . . were taken to the kraal lately occupied by Sikonyana (the Ndwandwe chief). The battle . . . did not last more than an hour and a half. The number of the hostile tribe, including women and children, could not have been less than 40,000 . . .

Early next morning Shaka arrived and each regiment, previous to its inspection by him, had picked out its 'cowards' and put them to death. Many of these, no doubt, forfeited their lives because their chiefs were in fear that, if they did not condemn some as being guilty, they would incur the resentment of Shaka . . .'

1 Between which two rivers did Shaka build up Zulu power?

2 Name four peoples who fled from their homelands? Where did they go? What effect did their moving have on other parts of Southern Africa?

3 How far would Fynn's account be reliable as a description of Shaka and the Zulu army in 1824? Why is it difficult for historians to work out what the Difaqane was really like?

4 What was the main weapon of the armies?

5 What was the turning point of the battle? Why do you think that the Zulus won?

6 Put Fynn's last paragraph into your own words to make its meaning clear. How might Shaka have explained such cruelty?

The 'Great' Trek

Why did the Boers leave Cape Colony?

By the mid-1830s, many Dutch trekboers (who in the nineteenth century were generally called *Boers*) had had enough of British rule. In their opinion, Ordinance 50 and the abolition of slavery had done nothing but harm and was threatening their whole way of life. Nor did the Cape government seem ready to defend them from the Xhosa. In the Sixth Frontier War of 1834–35 more than 100 settlers had died, yet Governor D'Urban handed back to the Xhosa the land conquered by his army (see page 20). So they looked northwards across the Orange and Vaal rivers. Explorers returned in 1834 and 1835 with glowing reports of plenty of good farming country almost empty of people.

The first groups of *Voortrekkers* ('the people who travelled away'), as they became known, led their oxwagons across the Orange in 1835 (see map below). During the next ten years about 14,000 whites with a similar number of black servants followed them. Their chief desire was to get away from the British and in the words of Piet Retief, one of their leaders, 'to maintain such regulations as may suppress crime,...preserve proper relations between master and servant...[and] to lead a more quiet life than we have heretofore done'.

Events of the 'Great' Trek

This 'Great' Trek was a trekboer journey on a grand scale. The Voortrekkers travelled in groups of several hundred, the men on horseback, the women and children in the wagons pulled by yokes of oxen and the cattle and sheep herded by the servants.

The first group, which left Cape Colony in 1835, succeeded in reaching the Limpopo valley but many were killed by the Tsonga people while others died of disease. Only a few managed to reach the safety of the Portuguese settlement of Delagoa Bay.

A second group of Voortrekkers, led by Andries Hendrik Potgieter, was attacked by Mzilikasi, the Ndebele chief, as soon as it showed signs of settling in the Vaal valley. An Ndebele regiment, 5000 strong, caught them at Vegkop in 1836 as they retreated southwards, but they had time to form their wagons into a defensive circle (known as a *laager*) and, though greatly outnumbered, they managed to drive off their attackers. The Ndebele took their cattle, but Potgieter was able to get reinforcements from the Rolong chief, Moroka. After that, with the help of Moroka and other black allies, he rode against Mzilikasi twice in 1837. The Ndebele leader faced attacks from other black chiefs and the losses he suffered from the Voortrekkers and their allies made him decide to move northwards across the Limpopo. Left alone, the Voortrekkers now began to create farms for themselves, their main settlements being round Potchefstroom, just to the north of the Vaal, and Lydenburg, further to the east.

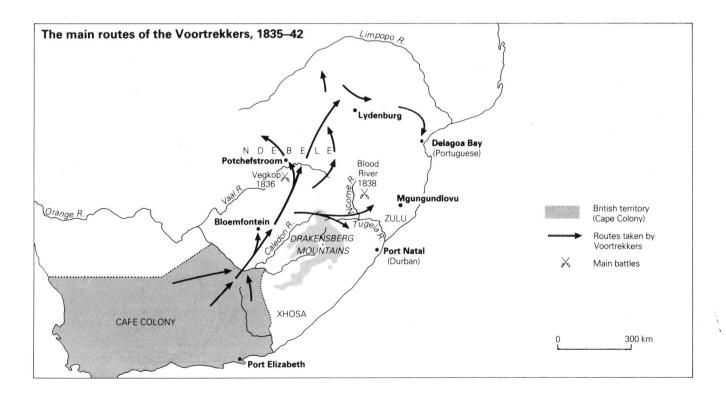

The main routes of the Voortrekkers, 1835–42

Dingane's capital, Mgungundlovu, built in 1829, drawn by J. J. Pierneef

The Voortrekkers and the Zulus

Towards the end of 1837, Piet Retief, leader of another Voortrekker group, descended through the Drakensberg to Mgungundlovu, the Zulu capital, with the aim of persuading Dingane, Shaka's successor, to give him land in the fertile coastal belt. Dingane seemed friendly. The Boers would get some land, he said, if they won back for him cattle stolen by a neighbouring chief. This they quickly did.

Also at Mgungundlovu were two whites, Wood, who acted as Dingane's interpreter, and Owen, an American missionary. Wood thought that Dingane was up to some mischief and warned the Boers to be on their guard. They ignored him and joined the Zulus to drink beer and watch a dancing display. Wood describes what happened next:

'The farmers had not been sitting for more than about a quarter of an hour when Dingane called out: "Seize them", upon which an overwhelming rush was made upon the party before they could get to their feet... The farmers were then dragged with their feet trailing on the ground, each man being held by as many Zulus as could get at him, from the presence of Dingaan [Dingane] who still continued sitting and calling out "Bulala amatakati" (kill the wizards).... When they had dragged them to the hill "Hlomo Mabuto" they commenced the work of death by striking them on the head with knobbed sticks, Retief being held and forced to witness the death of his comrades before they dispatched him.

It was the most awful occurrence and will never be effaced from my memory. The Rev. Mr Owen and I witnessed it, standing at the doors of our huts which faced the place of execution.'

The Battle of Blood River, 1838

Dingane's warriors then set upon the settler families who had confidently followed Retief down into Natal. They slaughtered between five and six hundred men, women and children.

These disasters struck the Voortrekkers in February 1838 but within ten months, a well-armed commando of 500 men, led by Andries Pretorius, rode into Zululand determined to destroy Dingane. On Sunday 9 December the commando stopped to rest and, during their prayers together, its members took a solemn vow that if God gave them victory in the coming struggle, they would build a church and keep the day of victory sacred forever.

On 16 December 1838, 10,000 Zulus attacked the laager which Pretorius had made on a strong defensive position beside the Ncome river. Once again spears, shields and bravery were no match for cannon, rifles, horses and equal bravery. Some 3000 Zulus died, while only three Boers were wounded. For the Boers, this Battle of Blood River, as it became known, appeared a miraculous victory. For Dingane, it was the end. His half-brother Mpande joined with Pretorius and drove Dingane into exile where soon he was murdered. Mpande became chief of the Zulus and agreed that Pretorius could found 'the Republic of Natalia', south of the Tugela river.

The British and the Voortrekkers

Yet, despite all the efforts of the Voortrekkers, Natalia was to last only three years. British traders already used its only port, Port Natal, and the British government was not prepared to have an anti-British Boer state overlooking the sea-route to India. In 1842, a British warship arrived at Port Natal (see map, page 25) and forced the Boers to surrender Natalia.

'We would rather go barefoot back over the Drakensberg to meet our independence or death,' declared Johanna Smit, sister of one of the Boer leaders, 'than bow down before a government which has treated us as the British has done.' And back over the Drakensberg onto the central plateau went three-quarters of the Boer settlers.

The British government was ready to leave the Boers alone once it had control of the South African coast. In the 1850s it signed two agreements, first with the Boers north of the Vaal (the Sand River Convention of 1852) then with those living between the Orange and the Vaal (the Bloemfontein Convention of 1854). By these agreements, the British, in return for a Boer promise not to re-introduce slavery, promised the Boers not 'to interfere in their affairs' and to supply them, but not 'the natives', with gunpowder.

The Orange Free State and the South African Republic

Though bitter personal rivalries divided the Voortrekker leaders, by the 1860s the Boers had established the Orange Free State and the South African Republic as independent republics run by them. The Boer farmers now had little difficulty in taking the best land. Because the Voortrekkers had defeated the Ndebele chief Mzilikasi, the South African Republic claimed that they owned all the land between the Vaal and the Limpopo by right of conquest. It ignored the fact that much of this land had belonged for generations not to the Ndebele but to peoples still living there, like the Tswana and the Pedi.

How later generations of Afrikaners used the events of 1838

Some historic events get exaggerated by later generations. At Waterloo in 1815, the British with vital help from the Prussians just managed to defeat the Emperor Napoleon of France. Even if the battle had been lost, Napoleon would soon have been defeated, because the forces combined against him were much too strong. Later generations of Britons, however, turned Waterloo into one of the world's most decisive battles. In the popular version, the overmighty French were outfought by the smaller British army, generalled, brilliantly of course, by the cunning Duke of Wellington. To keep the memory of such a victory alive, London's largest railway terminus was named Waterloo.

The French did much the same with the Bastille, a fortress prison which was captured by a Parisian crowd on 14 July 1789. The fortress was in a poor state of repair. It housed only seven prisoners and had only a handful of troops defending it. These were brutally murdered when they surrendered to the crowd. Nonetheless later French generations have celebrated the Fall of the Bastille as the moment when the cruel and unfair rule of the king and aristocrats began to collapse under the brave attack of the champions of liberty.

In a similar way, later generations of Afrikaners exaggerated the events of 1838. The advance of Piet Retief into Natal was in fact just one more example of whites moving into land where the blacks had lived for centuries. Dingane knew that wherever whites appeared they would try to take the best land for themselves and, if necessary, would fight and kill to win it. From his point of view the murder of Piet Retief and his party made good political sense.

Moreover, the Voortrekker settlement in Natal turned out to be much less important than those in the Orange Free State and the Transvaal, which became the foundation of Afrikaner power in modern South Africa. The British took control of Natal in 1841 and it was the British army of 1879–80, not Pretorius' commandos of 1838, which finally broke the Zulu impis.

Generations of Afrikaners learned a different, almost fairy-tale, version of 1838. In their school textbooks, the 'Great' Trek was described as the major turning point in the country's history, when the Afrikaner nation was formed, first by trekking to freedom from the bullying British and then by successfully defending, with God's help, civilised, Christian society from savage and treacherous blacks. Piet Retief's death, the Vow (Covenant) to God before the Battle of Blood River, and the Blood River victory itself were central to this national story. Officially known as the Day of the Covenant but by many white South Africans as Dingane's Day, 16 December became a national holiday.

SOURCE WORK: The 'Great' Trek and Afrikaner nationalism

Source A: Inside the Voortrekker Monument

The foundation stone of the Voortrekker Monument was laid in 1938 (see page 64). It is a stone building, on a hill near Pretoria, which looks like a vast burial chamber. In a sense that is what it is since its centrepiece is a stone slab on which is written 'We for You, South Africa', and on which at midday on 16 December (the date of the Battle of Blood River in 1838) the sun directly shines. Visitors who climb the steps towards the monument find themselves entering a wide circle surrounded by a high stone wall on which are carved the outlines of many ox-wagons. Round the interior of the monument are scenes carved in stone.

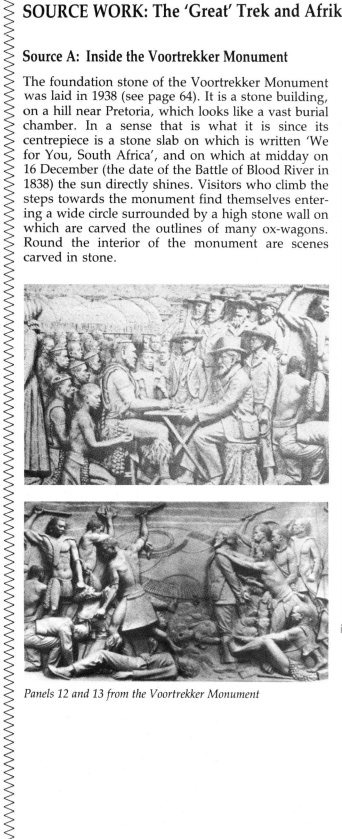

Panels 12 and 13 from the Voortrekker Monument

Source B: The Vow (Covenant)

The nearby Voortrekker Museum sells mementoes such as this, an English translation of the vow taken by Pretorius' commando in 1838 before the Battle of Blood River.

The Vow

My brethren and fellow countrymen, at this moment we stand before the holy God of heaven and earth, to make a promise, if He will be with us and protect us and deliver the enemy into our hands so that we may triumph over him, that we shall observe the day and the date as an anniversary in each year and a day of thanksgiving like the Sabbath, in His honour; and that we shall enjoin our children that they must take part with us in this, for a remembrance even for our posterity; and if anyone sees a difficulty in this, let him return from this place. For the honour of His name shall be joyfully exalted, and to Him the fame and the honour of the victory must be given.

The Vow

Source C: The Battle of Blood River

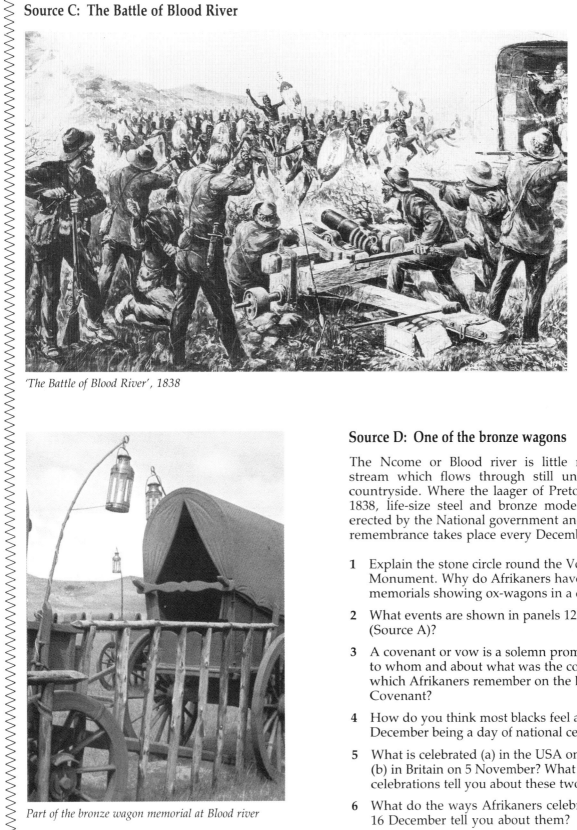

'The Battle of Blood River', 1838

Part of the bronze wagon memorial at Blood river

Source D: One of the bronze wagons

The Ncome or Blood river is little more than a stream which flows through still unspoilt rolling countryside. Where the laager of Pretorius stood in 1838, life-size steel and bronze models have been erected by the National government and a festival of remembrance takes place every December.

1   Explain the stone circle round the Voortrekker Monument. Why do Afrikaners have so many memorials showing ox-wagons in a circle?

2   What events are shown in panels 12 and 13 (Source A)?

3   A covenant or vow is a solemn promise. When, to whom and about what was the covenant made which Afrikaners remember on the Day of the Covenant?

4   How do you think most blacks feel about 16 December being a day of national celebration?

5   What is celebrated (a) in the USA on 4 July and (b) in Britain on 5 November? What do these celebrations tell you about these two countries?

6   What do the ways Afrikaners celebrate 16 December tell you about them?

Moshoeshoe and Basutoland (the land of the Sotho)

The most successful black resistance to white expansion between 1835 and 1870 was led by Moshoeshoe.

He was born about 1786, the son of a minor Sotho chief, and in 1824, during the chaos of the Difaqane, he moved his people to the mountain stronghold of Thaba Bosiu.

Thaba Bosiu

Thaba Bosiu is close to the valley of the Little Caledon river (see map, page 31). Its summit is 5 km square and has fresh water and pasture. The few passes to the top are easily defended and, though frequently attacked by both blacks and whites during Moshoeshoe's reign, it was never captured.

Moshoeshoe avoided fighting if he could and wherever possible bought off his most dangerous enemies by promises of friendship or by gifts. He kept his people together through the Difaqane and more and more Sotho asked for his protection. By 1840, he was the most powerful chief in the Caledon valley.

Fighting for the Caledon valley farmlands

His lands, however, bordered Cape Colony and the Orange Free State and he and the whites had frequent disputes about boundaries. In 1851 and again in 1852, Moshoeshoe defeated British forces and kept his freedom. He recognised, however, the strength of the British, and took care to keep on good terms with British officials. In the following years, his most dangerous enemy was the Orange Free State. The Sotho held the best land in the Caledon valley and the Boer farmers wanted it. The Boers attacked Thaba Bosiu in 1858 but were driven back with heavy losses. In 1865–68, they attacked again in greater numbers. They left alone the Sotho strongholds but seized their cattle and burnt their crops.

Becoming a British colony

Now an old man, Moshoeshoe knew that the Boers had become too strong for him so he turned to Britain for protection. Fearing that a Boer victory over the Sotho would cause continuing disorder on the borders of Cape Colony, the British government agreed to his request. In 1868, the new British colony of Basutoland came into existence. Moshoeshoe continued as chief until his death in 1870. Though part of the British Empire, the Sotho managed to keep more control over their affairs than most of the black peoples of South Africa.

Thaba Bosiu, Moshoeshoe's flat-topped stronghold

The limits to white settlement in 1870

As you can see from the map, in the 118 years since the Dutch had arrived at the Cape, white settlements had spread far. The British held two key ports, Cape Town and Port Natal (Durban), and the land around them (Cape Colony and Natal) to keep them safe and supplied with food. The Dutch (Boers/Afrikaners) had journeyed deep into the interior to set up their own independent republics.

However, it is easy to exaggerate the extent to which whites controlled South Africa in 1870. Most of them were farmers, spread very thinly across a huge area. Cape Town was the only town of any size. Many black peoples like the Sotho, Zulu, Pedi and Swazi ran their own affairs without much interference.

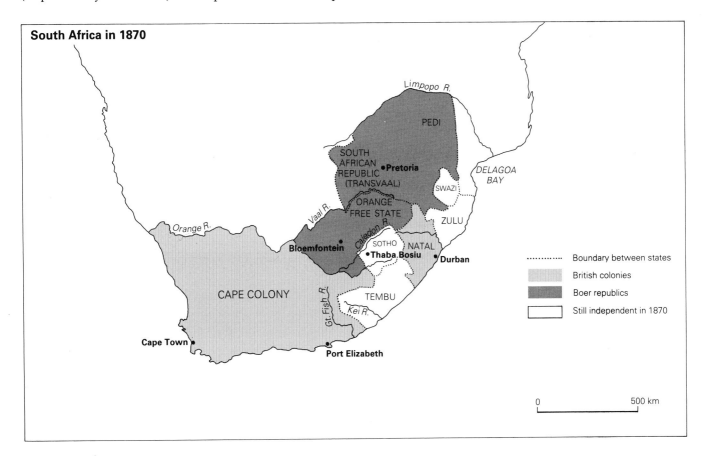

South Africa in 1870

Chapter 5   Mineral wealth and the growth of British power in South Africa

The importance of diamonds and gold

Diamonds are the hardest of all minerals. When cut by experts they shine with a special brilliance and are much prized as jewels. They are rare and very valuable. Gold is also rare and attractive. Since it neither tarnishes nor is easily damaged, people have used it from the earliest times for money, for jewellery or to display their wealth in other forms.

During the nineteenth century gold became more important to the trade of the world because the industrial countries increasingly used paper money and needed to hold enough gold to support the paper currency in circulation. In Britain, for example, the Bank of England kept the nation's gold and, if you look at a modern British banknote, you will find that to this day it carries the words 'I promise to pay the bearer the sum of £X' signed by the Chief Cashier of the Bank of England. This is a reminder of the times when people could actually change their notes into gold coins.

World trade, and with it the amount of paper money, grew fast between 1870 and 1914 so there was a strong demand for new supplies of gold to back up the paper money. That demand has continued in this century for, although many changes have taken place to the world's money system, gold still remains vital to it.

Rich diamond fields were found in South Africa in 1867 and less than twenty years later, in 1886, the world's richest goldfields. They brought enormous changes to the country, of which the following are among the most important:

● The world's businessmen, especially from Britain, Western Europe and the USA, started to spend huge sums to have the diamond and gold mines opened. They believed this 'investment' would make them large profits year after year, once the mines were working. Previously South Africa had not attracted much investment money since her main exports of wool, wine and ostrich feathers did not bring large and certain gains.

● The mines grew fast and as they did so other economic activities began to develop in the country. Railways were built to link the mines to the ports. Many farmers enjoyed a growing demand for their crops and animals. Villages grew into towns. New mining cities like Kimberley and Johannesburg mushroomed out of nothing.

● The mines also caused great changes to the lives of thousands, and eventually millions, of blacks. The whites provided the money and the technical skills to open the mines. They kept the ownership and the skilled, well–paid jobs to themselves. The blacks did the unskilled jobs and were strictly controlled by the 'compound' and 'migrant labour' systems (see page 34).

● Britain decided that these riches should be hers and fought both the blacks and the Boers to make sure that they were.

Together, these changes had a deep and lasting effect on the position of blacks. In 1867, despite the spread of the Boers and the British across South Africa, most blacks still lived under the rule of independent chiefs and worked as farmers on their own land. By 1914, the whites had defeated the chiefs and taken possession of 90 per cent of the land. More and more of the blacks worked as labourers in the mines or in the towns.

Diamonds at Kimberley

In 1867 two young brothers discovered the first diamonds on the banks of the Vaal river near where the Vaal meets the Orange. Others were found 40 km east of the Vaal; it was here that the mining town of Kimberley grew as miners, black as well as white, hurried to the Vaal and to Kimberley from all over South Africa and were joined by thousands more from overseas. Only ten years after the first discoveries, £60,000,000 worth of diamonds had been sold and Kimberley, with 30,000 inhabitants, was South Africa's second largest city after Cape Town.

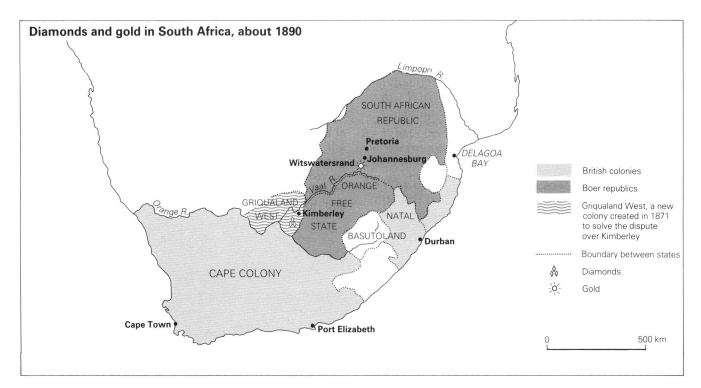

Diamonds and gold in South Africa, about 1890

British colonies

Boer republics

Griqualand West, a new colony created in 1871 to solve the dispute over Kimberley

.... Boundary between states

◊ Diamonds

☼ Gold

0   500 km

At first the digging was done by small groups of miners, working surface 'claims' of 3.7 square m. This method worked in the early days but, as the diggers pursued the diamonds deeper and deeper through the 'blue clay', the dividing walls between the claims frequently collapsed, sometimes killing the miners.

The diggers faced three other major problems. Firstly, the deeper the mines, the harder it was to drain them without expensive machinery. Secondly, since diamonds are small and valuable, they proved easy to steal. Thirdly, since they were thought of as rare luxuries, their price dropped rapidly if too many became available to the general public too quickly.

To solve such problems, some of the more successful miners joined with businessmen and formed companies to buy up blocks of claims and to install modern machinery such as water pumps. Backed by overseas bankers and other investors, a few large and powerful companies controlled diamond mining. To limit their losses through theft, they forced the black workers to live in closed compounds. The companies also began to co-operate to control the flow of diamonds to the public so that the price stayed at a level which gave them regular profits.

By the 1880s, Kimberley was dominated by two men, Cecil Rhodes and Barney Barnato, both of whose companies had millions of pounds from overseas invested in them. In the long run, Rhodes, who had the assistance of Alfred Beit, a clever German financier, proved too strong for Barnato. Rhodes's De Beers Company bought control of Barnato's Kimberley Mine in 1888 for £5,398,650. Today, more than a century later, De Beers

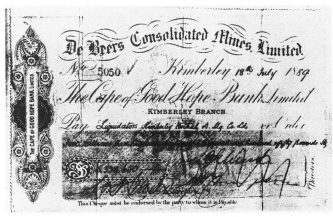

The De Beers cheque for over £5 million

remains the most powerful diamond company in the world.

Britain takes possession of the diamond fields

In 1867 it was far from clear in whose land the diamond fields lay. Waterboer, chief of the Griquas, a group of mixed European and Khoikhoi origin (coloureds), claimed them, so did three African chiefs, so did the Orange Free State, and the South African Republic. A special legal court presided over by R. W. Keate, the Lieutenant–Governor of Natal, was set up to decide the question of ownership. It awarded the lands to Waterboer, who asked for British protection against the Boers. The British then created a new colony, Griqualand West (see map above), and took control of the diamond fields. The Orange Free State considered itself

Kimberley mine, 1875, showing the network of steel ropes by which the diamond-bearing soil was carried to the surface

robbed but decided to make the best of a bad job by settling for a payment of £90,000 from Britain by way of compensation. The people of Griqualand West gained nothing. They found themselves losing their land to mine companies and farmers and, in 1878, rose in rebellion. Defeated after two months' fighting, they were left with little choice but to work either in the mines or on white farms.

The compounds and migrant labour

The big diamond companies began building compounds for their black workers in the 1880s. The first ones were cold and overcrowded and led to sicknesses, such as pneumonia. The later ones were warmer and less crowded (it was not profitable to have sick workers) but very similar to prison camps. They had entrance and exit tunnels to the mines and detention cells in which workers suspected of theft could be held for days on end. The companies succeeded in reducing theft and gaining a regular supply of unskilled labour but only by treating black workers in a way which whites would never have tolerated.

By this time blacks already travelled widely in South Africa, working for whites for a few months at a stretch before returning to their homes. In the 1860s and 1870s, many of these migrants were using their earnings to buy guns so that they could defend themselves better against white attacks. Many came to Kimberley to work as migrant labourers and before long, the big mining companies started to use the migrant labour custom to their own advantage. Since the worker's family was living a long way from the mines and seemed able to live within a chiefdom by farming, the companies kept wages down by paying their workers as if none of them had families to support.

In 1896, movement to and from the mining areas was controlled by the introduction of pass laws which forced blacks to carry an identity card. This pass gave them permission to be in a particular place for a stated length of time and stopped them moving about from employer to employer. Breaking the pass laws could be punishable by a fine or imprisonment.

They could do this as long as enough blacks wanted work in the mines. To keep up supplies of workers, the

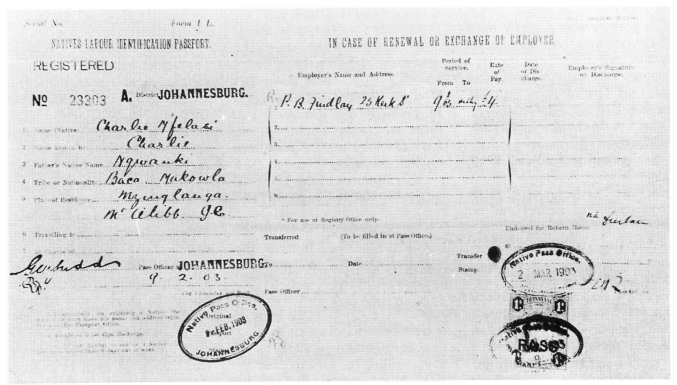

An identity card issued in 1903 to comply with the pass laws introduced in 1896

mining companies sent agents to encourage chiefs to send men to Kimberley. They also persuaded the white colonial governments to make laws which forced more blacks to work for whites. For example, in 1894, Cecil Rhodes, who by that time was Prime Minister of Cape Colony as well as a multi-millionaire, got the Cape parliament to pass the Glen Grey Act. This Act controlled the amount of land which blacks could hold in the Glen Grey area and it also made them pay an extra tax if they could not prove that they had worked at least three months each year away from home. Its aim was to increase the number of migrant workers available to white employers.

In addition, all the colonial governments made their blacks pay taxes, even if they worked only on the land. The taxes had to be paid in cash, which forced more and more of them to look for wage-earning work.

Gold on the Witwatersrand

Small groups of prospectors had come across gold in Southern Africa for many years but not in great quantities. They usually found it in river gravel and dug it out by using picks, shovels and pans in which they shook loose the gold from the other rocks.

The gold-bearing rock which the prospectors Harrison and Walker discovered in 1886 on the farm of Land-laagte on the Witwatersrand (ridge of white water) was quite different from the river gravels.

The Witwatersrand (usually shortened to Rand) goldfields were enormous. They stretched 65 km east to west and the gold-bearing rock layers ran down far below the surface. The gold, however, was thinly

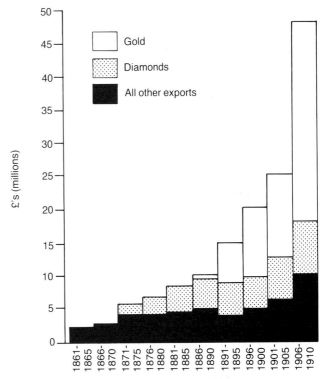

Exports of South African produce, 1861–1910

A single men's hostel for migrant workers, a more modern version of the early compounds

spread in the rock and hard to extract. It needed a completely different method of mining. It could only be separated by expensive methods of chemical engineering, such as the Macarthur-Forrest cyanide process, invented in 1887. The Rand, therefore, was not a place where individual diggers could strike gold and make a fortune overnight. From the start it was a place for big mining companies with the money to invest in machinery and workers on a large scale.

The big gold-mining companies and their workers

Diamond money got the goldfields started. Two leading Kimberley businessmen, Barney Barnato (see page 33) and J. B. Robinson, quickly set up gold-mining companies on the Rand and others followed, including Cecil Rhodes. Largest of all was Wernher-Beit & Eckstein which in fact owned two of the largest mining companies. Gold-mine company shares – called 'Kafirs' – captured the imagination of European investors. Money poured in from Britain, France and Germany. By 1895, more than £40,000,000 had been invested in seventy-nine gold-mines which employed 10,000 whites and 100,000 blacks. By then gold had overtaken

diamonds as the country's major export and Johannesburg, the bustling business centre of the Rand, which did not exist in 1886, was growing at a hectic pace. By 1903 it had 110,000 inhabitants.

The gold-mine companies were in business to make money for their owners who were the investors who had purchased shares in the companies. The price of gold was fixed by international agreement among the main trading nations so if the costs of producing it increased, because of the needs of new machinery for instance, the companies could not simply raise the price. They believed that they could only stay in profit by keeping down the amount they paid in wages. This was not easy with their white workers, who had vital technical skills and could move to other mining countries like Australia or the USA if pay and conditions in South Africa did not appeal to them. Black wages, therefore, were kept as low as possible.

As in Kimberley, the Rand mining companies used black migrant labourers whom they housed in compounds. They often co-operated together to recruit black workers and to pay them on an agreed wage scale. Many workers journeyed from Basutoland (Lesotho) and from the Eastern Cape, though the largest group came from nearby Mozambique after the companies had done a deal with the Portuguese colonial government. Working in the gold-mines might be dangerous and poorly paid and life in the compounds miserable, but it sometimes appeared better than struggling to survive in the shrinking areas of the countryside left for blacks to farm.

The Rand and the South African Republic

The Rand lay in the middle of the South African Republic (SAR), barely 64 km from Pretoria, the capital. Before 1886, the white population of the SAR was almost entirely Boer, widely scattered on their farms, living a life which had changed little since the eighteenth century. Their fathers had left the Cape and crossed the Vaal so that they could live independently of the British.

The men who made the gold-mining industry were quite a different breed. Most of them came from overseas, especially from Britain. They were miners, businessmen and adventurers, townsmen rather than farmers. They drank alcohol as much as coffee and went to bars, dance halls and gambling dens as often as to church.

The Boers called them *Uitlanders* or foreigners. They disliked their way of life and distrusted their Britishness. The government of the SAR and the Uitlanders soon found plenty of matters about which to disagree.

European imperialism, 1870–1914

The creation of a large, successful and white-owned diamond and gold-mining industry and the linked expansion of British power in South Africa took place at a time when many other European nations were also expanding their overseas empires. Historians often describe the years of the fastest expansion, 1870–1914, as the Age of Imperialism. By 1914, the British Empire was by far the largest, followed by the French, Dutch, Portuguese and German Empires.

The politicians and rulers of Europe encouraged the growth of their empires for a number of reasons. For one thing, the population of Europe was growing. Land was scarce in the countryside and the industrial cities were overcrowded. For another, European factory-owners needed new overseas markets for the goods which they made, while other businessmen were seeking products overseas, like diamonds and gold, which they could sell in Europe and America.

The empires also grew because the nations of Europe saw each other as competitors. They were ready to spend time, energy, money and lives on adding new lands to their overseas possessions, often for no better reason than to keep their rivals out.

Empire-building by Europeans was easier in the nineteenth century than ever before since the weapons their industries produced were so advanced in

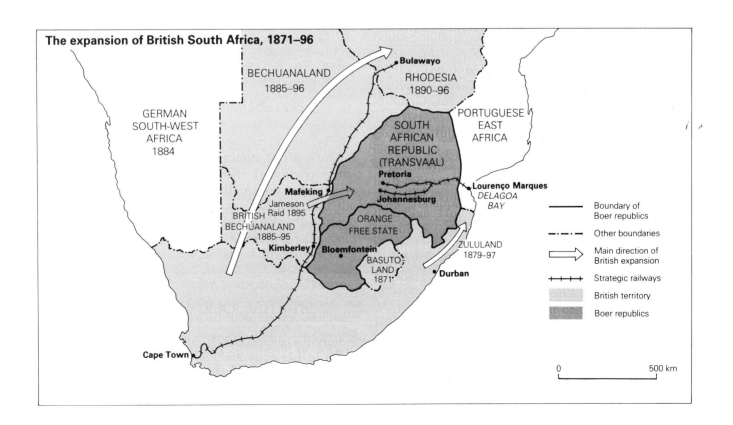

comparison to those of other peoples. Just as the Boers with rifles and cannon could defeat Dingane's Zulu regiments, so French and British iron-clad warships could smash wooden Chinese junks to matchwood.

British attacks, 1877–81

The two most powerful independent chiefdoms in South Africa were the Zulus, whose position on the south-eastern coast made them the neighbours of both Natal and the SAR, and the Pedi, who lived on the eastern borders of the SAR (see map, page 31). Their conquest by British armies between 1877 and 1881 is a good example of European empire-building in action.

Cetshwayo and the Zulus

After the defeat of Blood River and the death of Dingane in exile (see pages 26–7), his brother Mpande held the Zulus together by avoiding conflict with either the Boers or the British. Mpande's son Cetshwayo succeeded him in 1872. Like his father, Cetshwayo knew that he had to live at peace with his white neighbours if he possibly could. He mistakenly believed that Theophilus Shepstone, Natal's Secretary for Native Affairs, was his friend and allowed himself to be crowned by Shepstone at his coronation in 1873. He also trusted the British to defend him against the Boers who raided his people from the north. Nonetheless Cetshwayo was a warrior chief, who only succeeded Mpande because his regiments won a major battle against his brother's armies. He had 30,000 warriors itching 'to wash their spears' in the blood of an enemy, whom he could put into the field at a moment's notice. The white settlers in the region remembered Shaka and Dingane and, understandably, feared Cetshwayo.

Sekhukhuni and the Pedi

Sekhukhuni, the Pedi chief, also wished to live at peace with the whites, but, in the 1870s, there was increasing conflict between his people and the Boers over land and taxes. Sekhukhuni's brother Dinkwanyane, who was a Christian, left the mission station where he and his followers lived because of its high rents and because the missionaries made him pay SAR taxes. He said that the only chief he would obey was his brother and refused to pay the tax-collectors.

The Boers were worried since Sekhukhuni was becoming more powerful. The Pedi had strong fortifications in the mountains and their migrant workers returned home carrying guns. The President of the SAR Thomas Burgers decided that they must be defeated once and for all. He persuaded the Swazis to join an alliance against the Pedi and declared war in 1876.

The war of 1876 was a disaster for the Boers. The Swazis soon went home, complaining that their white allies were leaving the most dangerous fighting to them. The Boer farmer-soldiers had no stomach for the difficult attacks on Sekhukhuni's strongholds. President Burgers had to retreat, his reputation in tatters and his government bankrupt.

Lord Carnarvon's plan of federation

In Britain the Conservative Party, whose aim was to increase the size of the British Empire, won the 1874 general election. Benjamin Disraeli became Prime Minister and Lord Carnarvon the Colonial Secretary.

Carnarvon had ambitious plans for South Africa. He believed that the riches of the area could only be made safe for Britain if the Boer republics could be persuaded to join together with the British colonies, Cape Colony and Natal in a federation within the British Empire. (A federation is a nation, such as the USA or Nigeria, where a group of states join together with a single central government for matters like defence and the economy, but keep individual state governments for other things like education and the police.)

The white settler political leaders in Cape Colony and Natal were mainly against Carnarvon's federation plan. Nonetheless he pushed ahead using Theophilus Shepstone, Natal's Secretary for Native Affairs, and Sir Bartle Frere, whom Carnarvon appointed as Governor of Cape Colony. In 1877 Shepstone led a small British force into Pretoria to take over the SAR. The British excuse for this move was that the SAR government owed money to bankers in Cape Town. The Boer leaders of the SAR did not resist. They were still dismayed and divided by their failure to defeat Sekhukhuni. President Burgers resigned and the SAR became a British colony.

Shepstone and Sir Bartle Frere knew that white opinion would favour federation more if all the black chiefs were defeated. This would guarantee permanent peace and allow the federation to prosper. In the opinion of Frere and Shepstone, permanent peace was impossible if the Zulus and the Pedi stayed independent. They therefore set about provoking the Zulus and the Pedi into war.

War against the Zulus, 1878–79

In 1878 the wife of Sihayo, a Zulu chief, fled with her lover into Natal. Sihayo's sons crossed the frontier into the British colony, tracked her down and killed her. Frere used this raid as a reason for ordering Cetshwayo to disband his army. When, as Frere expected, the Zulu chief refused, the British army, commanded by Lord Chelmsford, marched into Zululand.

Lord Chelmsford's retreat from Isandhlwana the morning after the battle, in the Graphic, *a British illustrated magazine, 29 March 1879*

Things did not go as Chelmsford had planned. The main Zulu army shadowed the British army and in January 1879 cleverly ambushed one half of it in hilly country at Isandhlwana while Chelmsford, with the other half, was searching fruitlessly for the enemy elsewhere. The British could not get their tightly packed ammunition boxes open fast enough and the swift and deadly 'cow-horn-shaped' attack of the Zulus overwhelmed them. Casualties were 1500 British dead and about the same number of Zulus. British pride was only partly restored by the successful defence of the store and mission station at Rorke's Drift by 140 men, thirty of them wounded, against at least 3000 Zulus.

In the long run, his victory at Isandhlwana did Cetshwayo no good. The British government sent reinforcements with which Chelmsford won the battle of Ulundi in the heart of Zululand in July 1879. He then handed over to General Wolseley who captured Cetshwayo. The Zulu king ordered his warriors to stop fighting since, by this time, his people were starving.

The settlement of Zululand, 1879–87

Wolseley sent Cetshwayo to prison in Cape Town and divided Zululand into thirteen chiefdoms. This resulted in conflict among the chiefdoms and the divisions worsened when Cetshwayo was allowed to return in 1883. During 1883–84 there was civil war during which Cetshwayo died and Boers from the Transvaal moved into Zululand from the north-west. By this time the Germans, late-comers to empire-building, were actively seeking a foothold for themselves on the southern coast. In 1887, therefore, Britain turned Zululand into a full British colony.

The end of Pedi independence, 1877–81

In 1878 Shepstone led British troops against Sekhukhuni and the Pedis. Sekhukhuni fought them as successfully as he had resisted the Boers in 1876. Shepstone, however, had far greater resources than Burgers. He called in General Wolseley and reinforcements.

The Battle of Ulundi, 4 July 1879, in the Graphic, *23 August 1879*

Wolseley marched against the Pedi as soon as the Zulu War was over. He had with him more than 6000 of his own troops and, in addition, 8000 Swazis, who, once again, were ready to fight with the whites against their Pedi rivals.

Wolseley attacked Tsate, the Pedi capital, from the approaching valley, while the Swazis stormed in from the higher ground. The Swazi attack took the Pedi by surprise and they were defeated after heavy fighting. Modern weapons and military training made all the difference. More than 1000 Pedi died, including three of Sekhukhuni's brothers and nine of his children. The Swazis lost 500 or more, the British only thirteen. Sekhukhuni was captured and imprisoned in Pretoria. Meanwhile Wolseley shifted the Pedi survivors onto two reserves 80 km from their old capital. Pedi power was broken. When Sekhukhuni was released in 1881, he was murdered by one of his surviving brothers and the lands which he had defended so bravely became part of the Transvaal.

The first Anglo-Boer War, 1880–81

The British were unable to enjoy Wolseley's success for long. Their scheme for federation was breaking down because of divisions between the white peoples. Most Transvaal Boers hated British rule and, now the Pedi were defeated, were more confident in opposing it. Paul Kruger led them in rebellion and their commandos twice defeated British forces, first at Bronkhorstspruit near Pretoria in 1880 and again at Majuba on the Natal border in 1881. In Britain, a newly elected Liberal government led by William Gladstone had come to power. In contrast to Disraeli, Gladstone had little interest in empire-building where it cost money. He gave independence back to the Transvaal Boers and the SAR was reborn.

SOURCE WORK: British and black views on the British attacks

Source A: Sir Theophilus Shepstone

Shepstone sent this memorandum to the British government in 1878:

'At this moment the Zulu power is . . . a menace to the peace of South Africa . . . yet what other results can be looked for from a savage people, whose men are trained in youth to look upon working for wages and the ordinary labour necessary to advance the progress of a peaceful country to be degrading . . . and to consider the taking of a human life as the most fitting occupation for a man?'

Source B: Sir Bartle Frere

The Proclamation of the War was issued from Cape Town, 4 January 1879:

'The British forces are crossing into Zululand to exact from Cetshwayo reparation for violation of British territory committed by the sons of Sihayo . . .

When the war is over, the British Government will make the best arrangement in its power for the future good government of the Zulus in their own country, in peace and quietness, and will not permit the killing and oppression they have suffered from Cetshwayo to continue.'

Source C: Shepstone, 1878

'There are indications of the existence of a kind of common desire in the native mind in South Africa to try and overcome the white intruders . . . They are, however, incapable of precise combination and so long as we can roll one stone out of the way at a time, we shall be all right. Sekhukhuni is my first stone, confound him!'

Source D: Cetshwayo in exile

'Mpande did you no wrong, and I have done you no wrong, therefore you must have some other object in view in invading my land. It cannot be because of Sihayo's sons. The English have just crowned me. How is it that they crown me in the morning and dethrone me in the afternoon?'

Source E: Dinkwanyane to an SAR official in 1876

'Do you think that there is a God who will punish lying, theft and deceit? I ask you now for the truth . . . I also speak my whole truth. I say: this land belongs to us, this is my truth, and even if you become angry I will nonetheless stand by it . . . When I say your cleverness has turned to theft, I say in relation to the land, because you came to this country, you knew God's word but ate everything up . . . and said nothing to anybody, only flogged [people].'

Source F: The Pedi

During peace negotiations in 1878 the Pedi representatives said:

'We will never be subject to the English who make their subjects to build forts and to work for them; the English are liars, that rather than be in the position of subject tribes they will fight; we won't pay taxes before we have had a good fight for it.'

1 Who were Shepstone and Frere? What had been their main aim in 1877–78?

2 What reasons do Shepstone (Sources A and C) and Frere (Source B) give for going to war against the Zulus and the Pedi?

3 What were Britain's main reasons for fighting these black chiefdoms?

4 What does Cetshwayo mean when he says in Source D 'it cannot be because of Sihayo's sons'?

5 Who was Dinkwanyane? Why do you think that he twice mentions God in Source E?

6 What reasons do the blacks (Sources E and F) give for fighting the whites?

7 In this conflict with whom do you sympathise most? Give your reasons.

Chapter 6   The further expansion of the British Empire in Southern Africa, 1881–1902

An imperialist in action, Cecil Rhodes

Kimberley

Cecil Rhodes was born in England in 1853. As a youth, his health was poor and when he was seventeen his parents sent him to join his brother in Natal hoping that the South African climate would suit him better.

In 1871 he moved to Kimberley and in 1873, when he was still only twenty, he started a business selling water-pumping equipment which won a major contract in 1874 to clear the flooded mines. He quickly became quite wealthy and, with Alfred Beit, bought many claims, particularly in the De Beers mine. By 1880 he owned the majority of the De Beers claims and by 1887 the whole mine. The following year, he borrowed money from Beit and the Rothschild Bank to buy out Barney Barnato and gain a monopoly control of the diamond mines (see pages 32–3).

The imperialist ideas of Rhodes

Rhodes was an unusual mixture of businessman and

Cecil Rhodes photographed in the 1890s

dreamer. Between 1874 and 1881, while he was making himself a diamond millionaire, he studied from time to time at Oxford University. He persuaded himself that the Anglo-Saxon race had made England the strongest civilising force in the world; the growth of the British Empire, therefore, would benefit all peoples. In his first will, which he made when he was only twenty-four, he left his fortune to the Colonial Secretary to found a society to extend the British Empire and to win back the United States!

A bachelor who lived simply all his life, Rhodes liked money for the power which it gave him to pursue his imperial dreams. He used the money from his mining companies quite openly to pay for his empire-building adventures. He believed it was his destiny to make as much of Africa part of the British Empire as possible. A special ambition was to build a railway from Cape Town to Cairo in Egypt, which would run without a break through British colonies, the whole length of the continent. He knew that his health was poor (he died when he was only forty-nine) and he was always in a hurry to get things done.

Bechuanaland

While he was still in his twenties, he became a member of the Cape Parliament and he did his utmost to persuade the Cape Town and London governments to push British power northwards towards the Limpopo and Zambezi rivers where he was sure more fabulous mines would be found. He was worried lest the Germans, who by now had a foothold in South-West Africa, and the Boers, who wished to expand westwards across the Vaal, might block the route north. Partly because of his ideas, the British took possession of Bechuanaland in 1885 (see map, page 37).

Rhodesia

The main obstacle to his plans was the South African Republic. It had a tough anti-British President in Paul Kruger and after the discovery of the Rand goldfields it quickly got richer and stronger. In 1887, Rhodes heard that the SAR had its eye on the land of the Ndebele, north of the Limpopo (see map, page 37). Rhodes immediately took action. First, he tricked Lobengula, the Ndebele chief. Rhodes persuaded him to sign a treaty which Lobengula believed gave Rhodes' company, the British South Africa Company, the right to search for minerals. In reality it gave the company much greater land rights than Lobengula intended. Then, in 1890, Rhodes paid for a private expedition of settlers and soldiers which crossed the Limpopo and raised the Union Jack at a place which they called Salisbury in honour of the British Prime Minister of the time. (It is now called Harare.) The settler forces twice fought and defeated the Ndebele (in 1893 and 1896). In this way two new colonies were added to the British Empire, Southern Rhodesia (now Zimbabwe) and Northern Rhodesia (now Zambia). The British South Africa Company ran them in the name of the British government.

The causes of the Anglo-Boer War, 1899–1902

Rhodes's next target was the Rand goldfields. Whoever controlled the goldfields would in the long run control the whole of Southern Africa.

The British government wanted the gold because without regular gold supplies, it feared that London might lose its position as the centre of the world's money markets. It also feared that a rich SAR, supported by Germany and Portugal, might take over Britain's South African colonies and seriously weaken the whole British Empire.

Rhodes, who had become Prime Minister of Cape Colony in 1890, shared these views and had additional worries of his own. Rhodesia was proving a disappointment as far as new mines were concerned and his gold-mining company on the Rand was not doing as well as he had hoped. He realised too that if the SAR could build a railway to a foreign port like Delagoa Bay in Portuguese East Africa, his Cape Colony would lose valuable trade. A British take-over of the Rand would be greatly in the interests of his companies.

The map on page 37 shows how Rhodes managed to surround the Boer republics with British colonies to the south, west and north. Since he could not persuade the Portuguese to sell him Delagoa Bay, he began to look for ways of overthrowing the SAR government by force. The position of the Uitlanders on the Rand appeared to offer him his opportunity.

Kruger and the Uitlanders

The President of the SAR was Paul Kruger. As a boy he had taken part in the Boer Trek. As a young man he had led a commando to help his fellow Boers against Moshoeshoe and, in 1877 and 1878, he had voyaged to London to protest against Shepstone's take-over of the SAR in 1877 (see page 38).

He could hardly have been more different from Rhodes. He had little education but much common sense. Like his fellow Boers he was a farmer and a deeply committed Christian. His aim was to keep the SAR and the traditional Boer way of life as unchanged as he could. He saw no reason to trust either Rhodes or the British government and did all in his power to resist them.

The Uitlanders (see page 37) caused Kruger great problems. They came to the Rand in their thousands and, because they were making the SAR richer and paid taxes to the government, they expected to be able to vote in SAR elections. However, since Kruger believed that most of the Uitlanders were more loyal to Britain than to the SAR, he was reluctant to grant them the vote. The more political power the Uitlanders gained, he believed, the weaker the Boers would be.

The Uitlanders had other complaints against Kruger. Not only did he tax the mines but he sold the monopoly supply of dynamite and alcohol to friends who used their monopoly to sell to the mining companies at very high prices.

The Jameson Raid, 1895

With his friend Colonel Jameson, Rhodes decided to use the Uitlanders' anger against Kruger as a weapon to overthrow him. He plotted with Uitlanders to get them to organise a revolt in Johannesburg, while Jameson would come to their aid with an armed force paid for by Rhodes. Jameson would conquer the Rand, Kruger's government would be overthrown and the SAR would become part of the British Empire. The British Colonial Secretary Joseph Chamberlain had secret knowledge of the plan and supported it.

Jameson, with 500 armed horsemen, arrived as planned on the border but, from then on, nothing went right for the plotters. The Uitlander leaders lost their nerve. Rhodes tried to stop Jameson but the latter ignored his instructions and galloped rashly into the SAR. There he was soon surrounded and forced to surrender by a Boer commando.

The failure of the raid ended Rhodes's political career. He had to resign as Prime Minister and to appear before a Committee of Inquiry in London, which strongly criticised him for his part in planning the raid. He died in 1902 and was buried in a lonely but magnificant grave in the Matopo hills overlooking the lands which his private company had seized and called Rhodesia in his honour.

The Jameson Raid convinced Kruger that Britain would stop at nothing to win control of the Rand. He strengthened his army with modern weapons from France and Germany. He also continued in his refusal to grant the Uitlanders the political rights which they demanded, only allowing those who had lived in the SAR for fourteen years the right to vote.

The coming of war, 1897–99

Chamberlain, Britain's Colonial Secretary, remained convinced, however, that the Rand must come under British control and in 1897 appointed Lord Milner British High Commissioner in Cape Town with the task of using the Uitlander problem to provoke a showdown with Kruger. Milner told Kruger that all Uitlanders must have the right to vote after living in the SAR for five years and, in May 1899, rather than discuss the Boers' alternative suggestions, brought a conference at Bloemfontein to an abrupt end. After Bloemfontein, the Boers decided that they would have to fight if they were to keep their independence. Their only chance of victory lay in a swift success before Britain could bring in reinforcements by sea, so they declared war in October 1899.

The events of the Anglo-Boer War

The two sides

The contest looked completely unfair. On the one side were the two tiny Boer republics which in 1899 could put about 35,000 men into the field. This they raised to about 52,000 in 1900–01 using boys as young as nine

Paul Kruger as seen by the cartoonist of a Cape magazine in 1897

years old. On the other was the world's greatest empire which, though it had only about 27,000 troops in South Africa in 1899, was able to send in more than 400,000 reinforcements.

Nonetheless the Boers went to war in 1899 confident that they would win. They thought that the Boers in Cape Colony would rise in their support and that their well-armed, fast-riding commandos would sweep the scattered British regiments into the sea before the British navy could bring reinforcements. Should the war continue for more than a few months, some European rivals of Britain, for example, France or Germany, would surely come to the Boers' aid.

Early Boer victories, 1899–1900

At first the Boer confidence seemed well-founded. They invaded Natal and Cape Colony, laid siege to Kimberley, Mafeking and Ladysmith and handed out humiliating defeats to the poorly-led British armies at Modder River, Magersfontein, Stormberg, Colenso and Spion Kop (see Sources A–D). However, vital weeks were wasted in besieging the towns rather than in advancing on Cape Town and Durban, and the Boers' expectations of help were not realised. Few Boers in Cape Colony rose in rebellion and, although almost every nation in the world criticised Britain as a bully, none actually gave aid to the Boers. Britain appointed new generals, General Roberts and General Kitchener, and rushed in reinforcements. In 1900, General Roberts surrounded General Cronje at Paardeberg and forced him to surrender with 4000 men. Paardeberg was the decisive battle. From then on, Roberts's overwhelming advantage in numbers made his advance on Bloemfontein, Johannesburg and Pretoria unstoppable. He entered an undefended Pretoria in June 1900. President Kruger set sail for Europe in a vain search for help. The war seemed to be over.

Guerrilla war, 1900–02

The Boers, however, refused to give up. They changed to guerrilla warfare and, in small groups, used their skills as horsemen and their knowledge of the countryside to raid across a huge area. The commando leaders, Piet De Wet, Louis Botha and Jan Smuts in particular, amazed their enemy by their ability to appear quite suddenly, cause heavy casualties and then disappear as if into thin air. They lived partly off the land but they were also supplied by sympathetic Boer families.

Concentration camps and barbed wire

Such resistance greatly angered the British. It tied down a large number of troops, greatly adding to the costs of an already expensive war. To end it Kitchener did two things. Firstly, he cleared many Boer women and children from their farms into tented camps and then destroyed their crops and animals as well as the buildings. Secondly, he divided the countryside into huge sections of barbed wire and blockhouses. In these ways the food and shelter available to the guerrillas and their freedom of movement were lessened.

The moving of women and children into the 'concentration camps' brought disaster. The camps were hastily prepared, poorly supervised and dirty. They were swept by dangerous and highly infectious diseases. Within them more than 20,000 women and children died (see pages 48–9). Kitchener's methods, therefore, were strongly criticised in Europe and also, increasingly, in Britain. Nonetheless they had the intended results. Whereas in 1901 the Boer guerrilla leaders had refused to discuss any peace terms which did not include the Boer republics staying independent, in 1902, worn out by their own efforts and deeply worried for their families, they finally agreed, by the Treaty of Vereeniging, to come under British rule.

The blacks during the war

Both British and Boers agreed that their war should be a 'white man's war'. The Boers never forgot how hugely the blacks outnumbered the whites in South Africa and wherever possible prevented them from carrying guns. They would never, as Smuts put it, 'appeal for assistance to the coloured races'. The British government took the same line. Chamberlain told the House of Commons in 1902 that Britain had not used 'natives' as soldiers 'because in the peculiar circumstances of South Africa we believe that it would be bad policy'.

Nonetheless many blacks took part in the war, helping with transport, acting as scouts and police, and, in a few cases, mainly on the British side (despite what Chamberlain said), as soldiers. They also suffered greatly, though their suffering attracted much less attention at the time than did that of the Boers. At least 14,000 (11,000 of them children) died in concentration camps. Most of these were from the families of farm labourers whom the war had turned into refugees.

British newspapers were full of stories about the siege of Mafeking and the heroic leadership of the British commander, Colonel Robert Baden-Powell, who later became world famous as the founder of the Boy Scouts movement. What they failed to mention was the dreadful situation of the blacks there. While whites in Mafeking never really went short of food, for many blacks things were very different. When the London newspapers were telling their readers how Riesle's Hotel in the besieged town was still able to put on its famous nine-course Christmas luncheon, some of the black population had already died of starvation. Baden-Powell's aim was in fact to drive as many blacks as possible out of the town in order to reduce pressure on food supplies.

Some blacks who then tried to escape through the Boer lines were shot. Several were killed and the rest forced to return into the town. A white observer noted that it was all 'very hard luck on them, having no choice but that of two deaths, one being shot by Dutchmen, or that of staying here to slowly starve to death'.

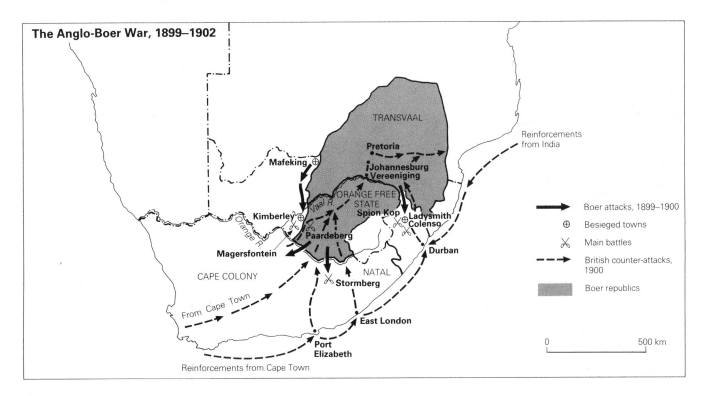

The Anglo-Boer War, 1899–1902

SOURCE WORK: Spion Kop, 23 and 24 January 1900

Source A: The position of Spion Kop and the Boer guns

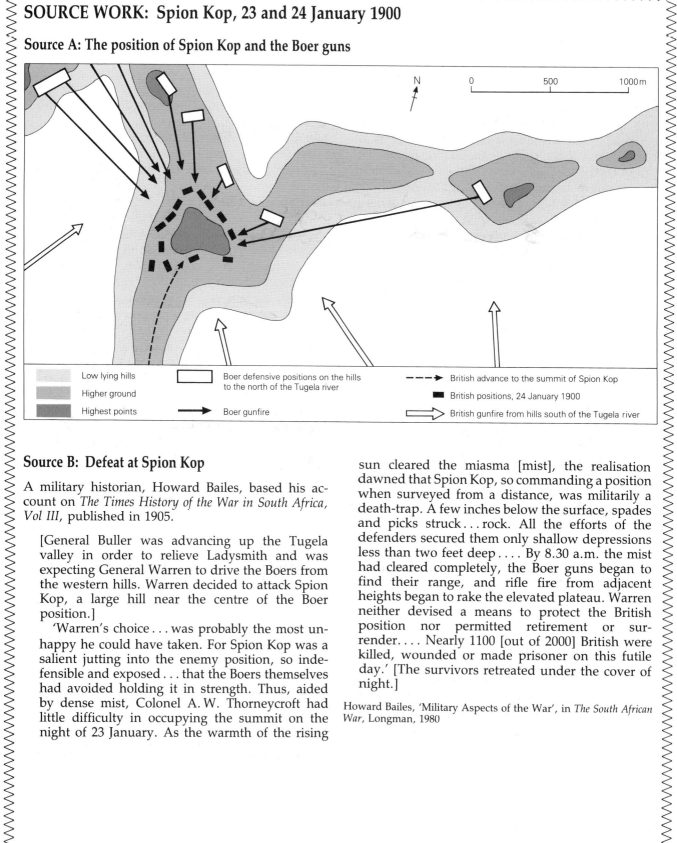

Low lying hills	Boer defensive positions on the hills to the north of the Tugela river	British advance to the summit of Spion Kop
Higher ground		British positions, 24 January 1900
Highest points	Boer gunfire	British gunfire from hills south of the Tugela river

Source B: Defeat at Spion Kop

A military historian, Howard Bailes, based his account on *The Times History of the War in South Africa, Vol III*, published in 1905.

[General Buller was advancing up the Tugela valley in order to relieve Ladysmith and was expecting General Warren to drive the Boers from the western hills. Warren decided to attack Spion Kop, a large hill near the centre of the Boer position.]

'Warren's choice...was probably the most unhappy he could have taken. For Spion Kop was a salient jutting into the enemy position, so indefensible and exposed...that the Boers themselves had avoided holding it in strength. Thus, aided by dense mist, Colonel A. W. Thorneycroft had little difficulty in occupying the summit on the night of 23 January. As the warmth of the rising sun cleared the miasma [mist], the realisation dawned that Spion Kop, so commanding a position when surveyed from a distance, was militarily a death-trap. A few inches below the surface, spades and picks struck...rock. All the efforts of the defenders secured them only shallow depressions less than two feet deep.... By 8.30 a.m. the mist had cleared completely, the Boer guns began to find their range, and rifle fire from adjacent heights began to rake the elevated plateau. Warren neither devised a means to protect the British position nor permitted retirement or surrender.... Nearly 1100 [out of 2000] British were killed, wounded or made prisoner on this futile day.' [The survivors retreated under the cover of night.]

Howard Bailes, 'Military Aspects of the War', in *The South African War*, Longman, 1980

Source C: The fight on Spion Kop

'The fight on Spion Kop' by F. J. Waugh, 1900

Source D: The account of a wounded officer of the 2nd Middlesex

'I crawled a little way with half my company ... It was impossible under the circumstances to keep regimental control ... We lay prone, and could only venture a volley now and then, firing independently at times when the shower of bullets seemed to fall away ... Everywhere however it was practically the same deadly smash of shells, mangling and killing all about us.

H. W. Wilson, *With the Flag to Pretoria*, Harmsworth, 1900

1 Using Source A, explain why General Warren attacked Spion Kop?

2 Why was Colonel Thorneycroft able to take possession of it so easily?

3 Why was Spion Kop a most unhappy choice as far as the British were concerned?

4 Compare the picture Source C with the written Sources B and D. Where might the artist have got his information for the picture?

5 Using the evidence available to you, describe the Battle of Spion Kop as it would have been seen by the Boer defenders on the surrounding hills (see Source A).

SOURCE WORK: The concentration camps

Source A: A panel from the National Women's Memorial, Bloemfontein

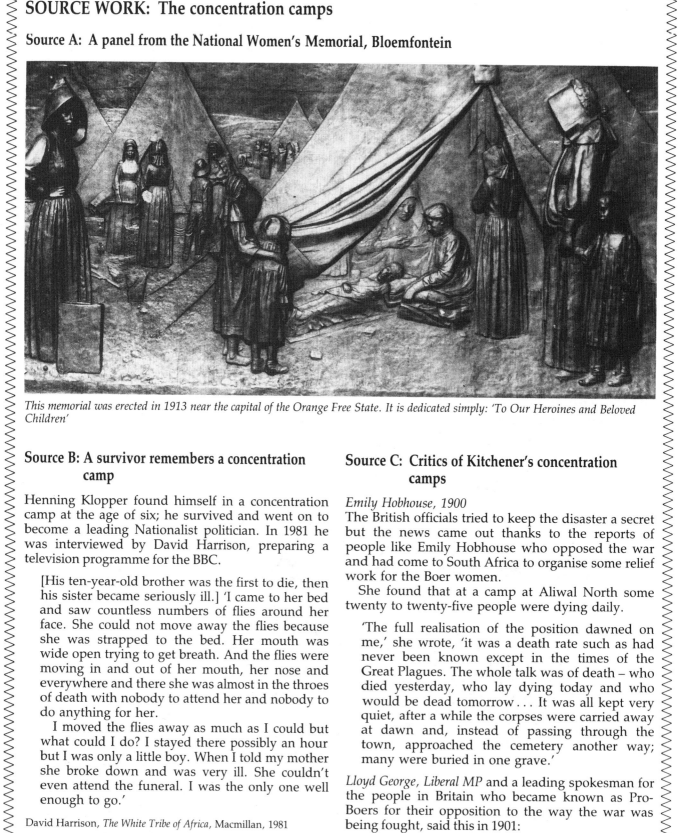

This memorial was erected in 1913 near the capital of the Orange Free State. It is dedicated simply: 'To Our Heroines and Beloved Children'

Source B: A survivor remembers a concentration camp

Henning Klopper found himself in a concentration camp at the age of six; he survived and went on to become a leading Nationalist politician. In 1981 he was interviewed by David Harrison, preparing a television programme for the BBC.

> [His ten-year-old brother was the first to die, then his sister became seriously ill.] 'I came to her bed and saw countless numbers of flies around her face. She could not move away the flies because she was strapped to the bed. Her mouth was wide open trying to get breath. And the flies were moving in and out of her mouth, her nose and everywhere and there she was almost in the throes of death with nobody to attend her and nobody to do anything for her.
>
> I moved the flies away as much as I could but what could I do? I stayed there possibly an hour but I was only a little boy. When I told my mother she broke down and was very ill. She couldn't even attend the funeral. I was the only one well enough to go.'

David Harrison, *The White Tribe of Africa*, Macmillan, 1981

Source C: Critics of Kitchener's concentration camps

Emily Hobhouse, 1900
The British officials tried to keep the disaster a secret but the news came out thanks to the reports of people like Emily Hobhouse who opposed the war and had come to South Africa to organise some relief work for the Boer women.

She found that at a camp at Aliwal North some twenty to twenty-five people were dying daily.

> 'The full realisation of the position dawned on me,' she wrote, 'it was a death rate such as had never been known except in the times of the Great Plagues. The whole talk was of death – who died yesterday, who lay dying today and who would be dead tomorrow ... It was all kept very quiet, after a while the corpses were carried away at dawn and, instead of passing through the town, approached the cemetery another way; many were buried in one grave.'

Lloyd George, Liberal MP and a leading spokesman for the people in Britain who became known as Pro-Boers for their opposition to the way the war was being fought, said this in 1901:

'When children are treated in this way and dying, we are simply ranging the deepest passions of the human heart against British rule in Africa . . .'

Source D: Henning Klopper again

'The only conclusion I could draw from the war is that Milner and Kitchener were out to break the backbone of the Afrikaner and their backbone consisted of their womenfolk. And to destroy as many women and children as they could. Otherwise you can't excuse a war campaign of this description.'

David Harrison, *The White Tribe of Africa*

Source E: A French cartoon, 1902

1 What does the scene in Source A show? Explain the tents and the person lying inside one.

2 What did Henning Klopper do when he grew up? What effect do you think his experience of the camp would have had on him?

3 What effect would you expect reports such as the one from Emily Hobhouse to have on public opinion about the war in Britain?

4 Why does Lloyd George criticise the camps' policy? Is there evidence in any of the other sources that he was right?

5 The caption of the French cartoon quotes Kitchener. What does the cartoon show? What is the attitude of the cartoonist?

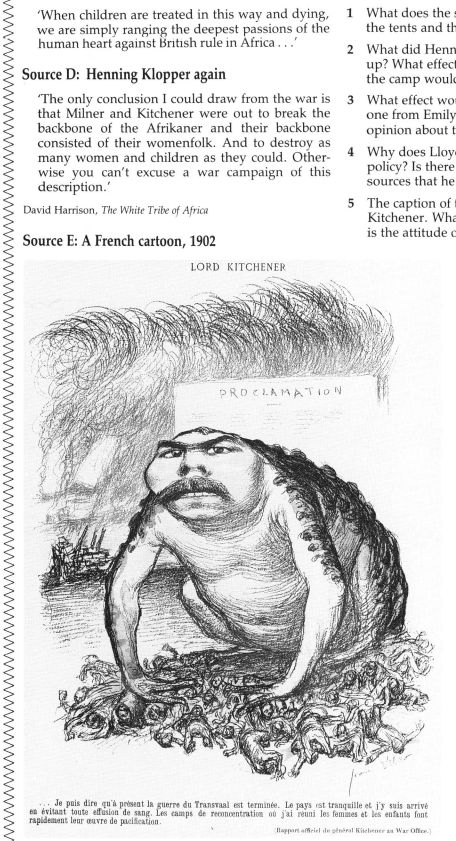

LORD KITCHENER

PROCLAMATION

. . . Je puis dire qu'à présent la guerre du Transvaal est terminée. Le pays est tranquille et j'y suis arrivé en évitant toute effusion de sang. Les camps de reconcentration où j'ai réuni les femmes et les enfants font rapidement leur œuvre de pacification.

(Rapport officiel du général Kitchener au War Office.)

Lord Kitchener as a monstrous toad, a French cartoon, 1902. The caption quotes Kitchener: 'The concentration camps where I have united together women and children are speedily doing their work of bringing peace.'

SOURCE WORK: Cecil Rhodes, for and against

Source A: A cartoon of Rhodes

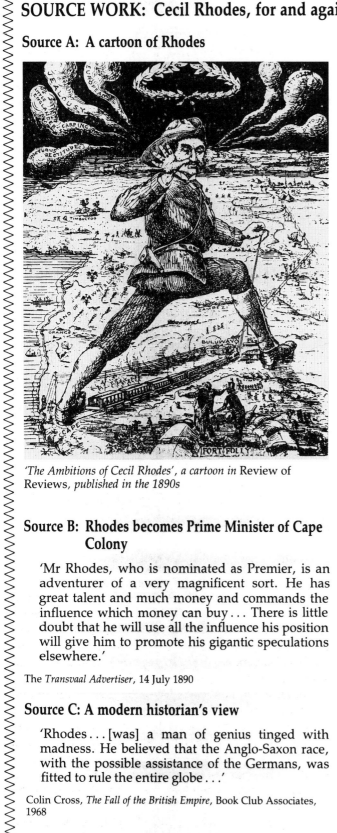

'The Ambitions of Cecil Rhodes', a cartoon in Review of Reviews, published in the 1890s

Source B: Rhodes becomes Prime Minister of Cape Colony

'Mr Rhodes, who is nominated as Premier, is an adventurer of a very magnificent sort. He has great talent and much money and commands the influence which money can buy... There is little doubt that he will use all the influence his position will give him to promote his gigantic speculations elsewhere.'

The Transvaal Advertiser, 14 July 1890

Source C: A modern historian's view

'Rhodes...[was] a man of genius tinged with madness. He believed that the Anglo-Saxon race, with the possible assistance of the Germans, was fitted to rule the entire globe...'

Colin Cross, The Fall of the British Empire, Book Club Associates, 1968

Source D: Lord Milner's view

Lord Milner, the British High Commissioner, 1897–1905, said:

'Rhodes is too self-willed, too violent, too sanguine [optimistic] and in too great a hurry.'

Source E: Rhodes speaking about the blacks

Speaking in the Cape Parliament about the Glen Grey Act (see page 35), Rhodes said:

'If you are really one who loves the natives, you must make them worthy of the country they live in, or else they are certain, by an inexorable [unavoidable] law, to lose their country. You will certainly not make them worthy if you allow them to sit in idleness and if you do not train them in the arts of civilisation.'

1   Compare Source A with the map on page 37. In which state is (a) Rhodes's left foot? (b) his right foot? (c) Fort Folly?

2   Why does the cartoonist use the name Fort Folly? Who is the man with his arms outstretched?

3   Explain the railway train.

4   What do you think is the cartoonist's opinion of Rhodes? Explain your answer.

5   The Transvaal Advertiser (Source B) writes in 1890 of Mr Rhodes's 'great talent'. What do you think the writer had in mind? Would you expect him to have changed his opinion by 1896?

6   What criticisms do Cross and Milner make of Rhodes? What evidence might they use to back their opinions?

7   Of Sources A, B, C and D, on whom can you (a) most rely, (b) least rely for a fair assessment of Cecil Rhodes? Explain your answer.

8   What does Rhodes suggest is the best way to help the blacks? Is it possible to argue that in fact what Rhodes is suggesting to be in the interest of the blacks is really in the interest of his mining companies? (See page 35.)

9   There is a statue of Cecil Rhodes on the northern slopes of Table Mountain in Cape Town looking out towards the Limpopo and to Cairo. Does he deserve a statue? Explain your answer.

Chapter 7 Afrikaner fears come to nothing: black hopes dashed

The Afrikaners: from total defeat to political power, 1902–10

Vereeniging, 1902

When the Boer generals signed away their independence at Vereeniging in 1902, they all regarded that day as one of the darkest in their lives.

'Brothers,' said General Smuts as he argued for surrender, 'we resolved to stand to the bitter end; let us admit like men that the end has come for us – has come in a more bitter form than we had ever thought possible.'

And the story goes that General De Wet, as he came outside from the hall in which he had signed the peace document, smashed his rifle in despair against a rock. What bleak future faced the Afrikaners, he must have thought, swallowed up in the huge and hated British Empire, with many of their women and children dead and their farms destroyed?

Yet only eight years later, their General Botha was Prime Minister of a united South Africa and Jan Smuts his second in command. Though the Union of South Africa remained within the British Empire, its government had plenty of freedom to act as it wished and, of the citizens with the right to vote, the Afrikaners had a clear majority.

The failure of Lord Milner's plans

This great change in the fortunes of the Afrikaners was certainly not what Lord Milner wanted. He had helped to cause the war so that the gold, the diamonds and the sea-routes of South Africa should become permanently British. His plan was to expand the goldfields, the industries linked to them and farming so that more Britons would emigrate to South Africa. Only when there were more British than Afrikaners should white South Africans be given their independence within the British Empire.

Things did not work out as he hoped. The country was hit by a terrible drought. The goldfields took longer than expected to get back to normal. Not nearly enough immigrants arrived from Britain.

A Liberal government in Britain, 1905

Lord Milner resigned and returned to England in 1905, the same year as the Liberal government took over from the Conservative government. Like many Britons, the Liberals felt guilty about the Anglo-Boer War. They believed that the best way forward for South Africa was through Britons and Afrikaners working more closely together as friends rather than as enemies and through the four colonies of the Cape, Natal, the Orange Free State and the Transvaal becoming united as one self-governing country within the British Empire. Though the Afrikaners would outnumber the British, the Liberals believed that they would soon come to understand the advantages of belonging to the Empire and stay loyal to it.

Botha and Smuts

The leaders of the main political party in the Transvaal were Louis Botha and Jan Smuts; both had been generals during the Anglo-Boer War. They too believed that the way forward for their people was through co-operation with the British. Smuts, who had studied at Cambridge University and had many English friends, visited London in the winter of 1905–06 and persuaded the Liberal leaders that co-operation between the Afrikaners and the British was possible.

The birth of the Union of South Africa, 1908–10

The National Convention, 1908–09

A National Convention representing white South Africans from the four colonies met first in Durban in 1908 and then in Cape Town in 1909. It produced a draft Act of Union. The British Parliament debated it in 1909 and it became law in 1910. Just eight years after the Boer surrender, the colonies were united in a self-governing dominion, the Union of South Africa.

Not all white politicians liked the idea of union and there were many disagreements at the National Convention. Where the capital of the new country should be was one cause of argument. Eventually it was agreed that Parliament should meet in Cape Town. Pretoria would be the seat of government and administration, and Bloemfontein would be the national centre of the law courts.

The question of what political rights blacks should have was obviously very important for the country's

There have been many strong differences of opinion between the " Federation " and " Unification " delegates to the South African Convention, which meets again, after an adjournment for the holidays, on Monday next, though it is hoped that unanimity will yet be secured. The figures in our portrait group are as follows :

Front Row (from left to right).—Hon. J. W. Sauer, Commissioner of Public Works, Cape Colony; Hon. J. X. Merriman, Premier, Cape Colony; Hon. M. T. Steyn, Vice-Pres. of Convention; Hon. A. Fischer, Premier, Orange River Colony; Rt. Hon. Sir J. H. de Villiers, Chief Justice, President of Convention; Rt. Hon. Gen. L. Botha, Premier, Transvaal; Rt. Hon. F. R. Moor, Premier, Natal; Sir W. H. Milton, Administrator of S. Rhodesia; Sir J. P. Fitzpatrick. Second Row.—Hon. E. H. Walton; Col. E. M. Greene, Minister of Railways and Harbours; Mr. H. C. van Heerden; Dr. J. H. M. Beck; Mr. G. H. Maasdorp; Mr. H. L. Lindsay; Hon. F. S. Malan; Gen. S. W. Berger; Hon. Dr. T. W. Smartt; Hon. Gen. C. R. de Wet, Minister of Agriculture, Orange River Colony; Rt. Hon. Dr. L. S. Jameson; Hon. H. C. Hull; Gen. J. B. M. Hertzog; Mr. C. F. Kilpin, Chief Secretary to Convention.   Third Row.—Gen. J. H. de la Rey; Mr. W. B. Morcom; Hon. A. Brown; Mr. T. Hyslop; Mr. J. W. Jagger; Hon. C. J. Smythe; Sir G. H. Farrar; Gen. J. C. Smuts, Colonial Secretary Transvaal; Mr. A. M. N. de Villiers, Secretary to Convention.   Fourth Row.— Mr. G. T. Plowman; Mr. W. E. Bok; Mr. G. R. Hofmeyr, Transvaal Secretary to Convention; Colonel W. E. M. Stanford; Hon. C. P. J. Coghlan.

WORKING FOR A UNITED SOUTH AFRICA: THE DELEGATES AT THE CONVENTION WHICH REASSEMBLES AT CAPETOWN ON MONDAY

The National Convention, 1909: Botha is front row, fourth from right; Hertzog is second row, second from right; Smuts is third row, second from right

future and caused much argument at the Convention since the colonies differed greatly in their practice. In the mainly Afrikaner Orange Free State and the Transvaal, blacks had no voting rights at all. In Natal, some blacks could in theory vote in elections but the rules were so complicated that in practice very few did. In Cape Colony, however, the franchise was colour-blind. Any man who earned £50 per year or owned property worth £75 or more could vote.

In the second half of the nineteenth century a new class of blacks had appeared. They were traders, peasant farmers, teachers, clerks, interpreters and priests, usually educated at mission schools. Many of them were wealthy enough to vote in the Cape and did so. There were not many of them but enough to make some white candidates in Cape elections take note of black needs.

Most of these blacks hoped that the Cape franchise would become the voting system for the new Union. The decision of the Convention however was to leave things as they were in each of the provinces after Union had taken place. The effect of this decision was to make the Cape franchise of less importance in the country as a whole, since the Cape made up only a part of the Union.

The position of the Afrikaners was improved by making both Dutch and English the official languages of the new Union, and by allowing the rural constituencies, which were mainly Afrikaner, to have 15 per cent less voters on average than the urban ones. Thus, in elections, the voting system worked in the Afrikaners' favour.

The General Election of 1910

The first general election showed how powerful the Act of Union made the Afrikaners, as long as they stayed united. The South African Party, for which most Afrikaners voted, won sixty-seven seats, the Unionist Party which had most of the English-speaking vote, only thirty-nine. Botha became Prime Minister and Smuts Minister of the Interior, Mines and Defence.

The blacks: disappointment and disillusion

Trust in the British

Most blacks had hoped for a British victory in the Anglo-Boer War. They knew that the Afrikaners could not be shifted from their belief that whites must be the masters and the blacks the servants in South Africa.

The British, the blacks thought, would be fairer and more ready to give them the chance to make better lives for themselves. They remembered how the British government had abolished slavery and how British missionaries had built schools and hospitals for them, as well as churches. The colour-blind Cape franchise gave them the hope that a future British-controlled South Africa would mean more of them gaining the right to vote.

In 1902, therefore, blacks expected the British victory to mean improvements for them: more land, better wages, less taxation, more freedom from the pass laws (see page 34) and more political power. They were quickly and deeply disappointed. The British government wanted South Africa to recover economically as quickly as possible after the destruction of the war. It knew that the mining companies and the farmers needed cheap labour so it gave the land back to the white farmers, helped them with grants and continued to encourage the migrant labour system through the pass laws and taxes. The main difference between the British government and the previous Afrikaner governments was that the British government was more efficient both in enforcing the pass laws and in collecting the taxes.

Blacks oppose the Act of Union

The black political leaders (see page 57) strongly criticised the plans of the whites-only National Convention and, when their suggestions for changes were ignored, sent their own delegation to London in 1909 to protest to the British Parliament against the draft Act of Union (see page 58). The group did have a meeting with a representative of the British government. It warned that the Act of Union would quickly make life worse for the black majority, but to no effect (see page 54).

The colour-bar in the mines

The warning of the black delegation to the London Parliament in 1909 proved correct. The first government of the new Union of South Africa immediately took action against the blacks. In 1911 it passed the Mines and Works Act which made the colour-bar in the mines legal. The skilled, well-paid mining jobs could only be done by whites, the unskilled, lower-paid ones were to be done by the blacks.

The destruction of black farming

More serious still was the attack on black farming. Between 1870 and 1900 some black farmers had made good profits. They were more skilful than most whites at raising herds and crops in the drier areas and they supplied growing towns like Kimberley and Johannesburg. Yet such farmers faced increasing difficulties. Many had been badly hit in the 1890s by the rinderpest epidemic which killed their cattle in large numbers. They also found themselves unable to compete with the wealthier white farmers who, helped by the government, introduced more scientific and profitable methods.

Despite these problems a number of blacks were buying farms for themselves. In 1912, for example, Pixley Seme, a successful Zulu lawyer and one of the leaders of black political opinion, had bought four farms in the Eastern Transvaal and had set up an association to buy more farms and teach modern farming methods. In addition many poor blacks were succeeding in making a living as 'share-croppers' or 'squatters'. They came to an agreement with a white farmer to cultivate a piece of his land and pay rent in the form of a share of the crop.

Share-cropping suited a few white farmers with large farms and land to spare. Many blacks liked it since it gave them some freedom, and, if they were successful, enabled them to have their own herds and farming equipment. It was certainly better than working as simple labourers on the low wages which most white farmers paid.

The Land Act of 1913

The majority of Afrikaner farmers wished to prevent Africans owning land or working as share-croppers, which cut down the numbers looking for labouring jobs. In 1913 their opposition to black farming led the Botha-Smuts government to pass the Land Act. The Act meant that blacks could no longer buy land from whites. The only land which they could own was in 'native reserves' which, mainly in the Transkei and Zululand, amounted to only 7 per cent of South Africa. The Act also forbade blacks to live on white farms except as full-time labourers. Share-cropping became illegal.

This law is important in the development of twentieth-century South Africa. Straightaway it caused great suffering to many black families who were driven from their homes unless they agreed to work as wage-earning labourers (see Source B, page 56). In the long run it became one of the foundation stones of the 'apartheid' system of the 1950s and 1960s (see pages 74–5). By stopping the blacks from owning land except in the reserves, the whites offered them a harsh choice. Either work in our areas (93 per cent of the country) as our servants and labourers or survive as best you can in your overcrowded reserves (7 per cent of the country). As the years passed and the Act took effect, independent black farming was destroyed and a supply of cheap black labour was created for white farmers and other white employers.

SOURCE WORK: Why did the British Parliament do nothing for the blacks?

Source A: Winston Churchill speaking in the House of Commons, 1906

Churchill was Under-Secretary for the Colonies in the Liberal government. He had also visited South Africa during the Anglo-Boer War as a journalist and had been captured by the Boers. The House of Commons was debating whether the defeated Boer republics should be granted self-government. Some MPs argued that the Boers' attitude to the blacks was wrong and that therefore they should not be allowed self-government. The Liberal government wanted the co-operation of the Boers and planned to give self-government to the Transvaal and Orange Free State. Here, Churchill tries to explain why the whites in South Africa feared the blacks.

> 'I would ask the House [of Commons] to remember for the moment the figure of the South African census...
>
> In the United States the proportion of white men to natives is 8 to 1 and even there I believe that there is something sometimes approaching to racial difficulties, but in South Africa the proportion is one white man to five natives. I ask the House to remember the gulf which separates the African negro from the immemorial civilisation of India and China. The House must remember these things in order to appreciate how the colonists feel towards the ever-swelling sea of black humanity upon... which they float. This black peril, as it is called in the current discussion of the day, is surely as grim a problem as any mind could be forced to face...
>
> We will endeavour as far as we can to advance the principle of equal rights of civilised men, irrespective of colour. We will not hesitate to speak out where necessary if any plain case of cruelty or exploitation [working too hard for too low wages] of the native for the sordid [dirty] profit of the white man can be proved...'

Source B: The Labour view

G. F. Barnes, a Labour MP, spoke in the House of Commons in 1909. He was unhappy about the way the proposed Act of Union abolished the right of blacks to stand for Parliament, a right which they had previously held in Cape Colony even if none had ever made use of it. He asked the House of Commons to support an amendment (a change) to the proposals which would have stopped this 'colour-bar' being created.

> 'We cannot forget what has been the record of South Africa in the past. It has been the hunting ground for monopolists, gold-seekers and financiers... who have gone in quest of wealth, and have been drenched with blood in the pursuit of it. We have today the opportunity of giving the country a new start on the basis of equal rights... and I think that we should avail ourselves of that opportunity...
>
> Absolutely the only argument put forward against this is that the Bill [the proposal for the Union of South Africa] will be wrecked if any amendment is carried. I refuse to think so meanly of people who carried themselves so well in the field of battle... At the twelfth hour I appeal to the government and to the [white] delegates from South Africa to take a more generous view of the situation...'

Source C: A Liberal disagrees with his leader

Asquith, the Liberal Prime Minister, spoke against the change suggested by Barnes. He regretted, he said, that there was any kind of 'colour-bar' in the proposed Act of Union. However, the main aim of the British government was to help Britons and Afrikaners to work better together. If the colour-bar sections were taken out of the Act, the Afrikaners would refuse to join the Union and the progress of co-operation between Britons and Afrikaners would be set back many years.

Ellis Griffith, a Liberal MP, supported Barnes in the same debate:

> 'We have heard a good deal about another deputation coming with great prestige from the four Colonies; but do not let us forget a more humble deputation whose expenses have been subscribed by 30,000 natives, to place their views before the people of England [the unofficial black delegation, see page 53].
>
> It has been said "Pass this and in a little time all will be right..." Is this very likely? I have here a review published the other day of the present Prime Minister of the Transvaal who said that no self-respecting man would sit in the same Parliament as a black man. If that be the view of colonial opinion, I think that there is a pretty slight chance of amendment.'

Sources A, B and C are from *Hansard*, the official record of debates in the British parliament

Barnes' Amendment was defeated by 155 votes to 55.

Source D: The *Eastern Province Herald*, 31 May 1910

1   To which event does the 'One Great Land' head-line refer in Source D? How can you be sure?

2   Why is Louis Botha shown at the top of the page in Source D? What had he been doing ten years earlier?

3   What does the word 'civilised' mean? How civilised does Churchill consider the Africans in Source A? Explain your answer.

4   In the third paragraph Churchill explains what he believed was the duty of the British government towards the blacks. Put this paragraph into your own words to make its meaning clear.

5   When Barnes (Source B) refers to 'monopolists, gold-seekers, financiers . . . drenched in blood', who has he in mind?

6   What evidence does Ellis Griffith (Source C) give to back up his argument that things were unlikely to improve for the blacks in South Africa if the Act was passed without any changes? What change did he and Barnes want the British government to make?

7   Asquith, the Liberal Prime Minister, argued against Barnes and Griffith and won the vote. What was his main reason for wanting the Act of Union passed unchanged?

8   What reasons can you think of to explain why the British were prepared to neglect the blacks who had supported them in the Anglo-Boer War in order to make friends with the Afrikaners whom they had defeated?

SOURCE WORK: British and Afrikaners unite at the expense of the blacks

Source A: 'Peace with Honour'

Laus Deo.

From the " Daily Graphic."

'Praise to God' – peace between Boer and Briton, a souvenir from the Daily Graphic *newspaper (London), June 1902*

PEACE WITH HONOUR!

Lord Kitchener to Secretary of State for War.

"PRETORIA, May 31st (11.15 p.m.).

"Negotiations with Boer delegates.

"The document containing terms of surrender was signed here this evening at 10.30 p.m., by all Boer representatives, as well as by Lord Milner and myself."

———

BUCKINGHAM PALACE, June 1st, 1902.

"The King has received the welcome news of the cessation of hostilities in South Africa with infinite satisfaction, and trusts that peace may be speedily followed by the restoration of prosperity in his new dominions, and that the feelings necessarily engendered by war will give place to the earnest co-operation of all his Majesty's South African subjects in promoting the welfare of their common country."

———

HOUSE OF LORDS, June 2nd.

"The Earl of Rosebery : I hope I may be allowed in a single sentence to express to his Majesty's Government my hearty, unstinted, and unreserved congratulations on the announcement of peace, which they have been at liberty to make, and to hope that to-day may mark the beginning of a new epoch of peace, prosperity, and commercial development throughout the Empire and South Africa."

(Cheers)

Source B: Sol Plaatje describes the effects of the Land Act

Plaatje, Secretary of the South African Native National Congress (see page 59), toured the farms of the Transvaal and Orange Free State to see what was happening to the share-croppers and squatters. He published what he found in *Native Life in South Africa*, in 1916. Here is the story of one squatter family.

'A squatter called Kgobadi got a message from his father-in-law in the Transvaal. His father-in-law asked Kgobadi to try and find a place for him to rent in the Orange Free State. But Kgobadi only got this message when he and his family were on their way to the Transvaal. Kgobadi was on his way to ask his father-in-law for a home for the family. Kgobadi had also been forced off the land by the Land Act.

The 'Baas' said that Kgobadi, his wife and his oxen had to work for R36 a year. Before the Land Act, Kgobadi had been making R200 a year selling crops. He told the 'Baas' he did not want to work for such low wages. The 'Baas' told Kgobadi to go.

So both Kgobadi and his father-in-law had nowhere to go. They were wandering around the roads in the cold winter with everything they owned. Kgobadi's goats gave birth. One by one they died in the cold and were left by the roadside for the jackals and vultures to eat.

Mrs Kgobadi's child was sick. She had to put her child in the ox wagon which bumped along the road. Two days later the child died. Where could they bury the child? They had no rights to bury it on any land. Late that night the poor young mother and father had to dig a grave

COME AND HEAR

Mr. SOL

PLAATJE

Of Kimberley, South Africa

Gives thrilling account of the condition of the Colored Folk in British South Africa.

A leading Negro writer and lecturer.

The story has gripped nearly a thousand audiences in England, Scotland, Canada & U.S.A

IT WILL THRILL YOU

Bethel A. M. E. Church

West 132nd Street, bet. Lenox and 5th Aves.

Sunday, March 13, 11 a. m.

THE BLACK MAN'S BURDEN IN SOUTH AFRICA

Friday, March 18th, 8 p. m.

THE BLACK WOMAN'S BURDEN IN SO. AFRICA

Interspersed with Quaint African Music sung in his own native tongue

Free Will Offering for Brotherhood Work among the South African Tribes

ADMISSION FREE

COME EARLY AND AVOID THE CRUSH !!

Dr. MONTROSE W. THORNTON, Pastor

Sol Plaatje speaks out in the USA against the Land Act: an advertisement for a meeting in 1919

where no-one could see them. They had to bury their child in a stolen grave.

Under the cruel workings of the Land Act, little children, whose only crime is that God did not make them white, sometimes have no right to be buried in the country of their ancestors.'

1 Describe what the *Daily Graphic* souvenir shows (Source A). What event was it celebrating? How can you tell? What does it tell you about the feelings of the British in 1902?

2 Who were Lord Kitchener and Lord Milner?

3 Which section of the South African population is missing from the picture? Why do you think the artist left them out?

4 Which government passed the Land Act of 1913? What were its aims?

5 The Land Act of 1913 was important in the development of South African society in the twentieth century. Why was this?

6 What is meant by 'Baas' in Source B? Kgobadi could have stayed where he was. Why didn't he?

7 The British government in London did not pass the Land Act and said that it was the business of the South African government. Sol Plaatje and other black leaders believed that Britain was largely responsible for their sufferings. How could they believe this?

8 What are the strengths and weaknesses of Plaatje's description as a source for the effects of the Land Act? List other sources which might be used to gain a full view of the Act and its results?

Black resistance, 1902–14

The Bambatha Rising in Natal, 1906

Blacks tried to resist the growing white demands upon them in various ways. In Natal, the government's taxes caused much anger. In 1906 two white policemen were killed. The culprits were shot by government troops (see page 58) who also burnt crops and homesteads in the area where the killings had taken place. Bambatha, a local chief, then led a small rebellion which caused the deaths of twenty-four whites. The Natal government's response was even more violent. Bambatha was hunted down, and his head cut off. Between three and four thousand of his followers were also killed.

The first black political associations

Bambatha was the last of the chiefs who tried to defend his people from the whites by leading his warriors into battle. As he was hunted down and his followers killed, a new kind of black leadership was trying out different methods of resistance which, in the long run, attracted many more supporters and made a more serious challenge to white South Africa.

The new black leaders were usually educated and Christian. They had been taught at missionary schools like Lovedale in the Eastern Cape and some had been to university in the USA or Britain. They were often teachers, priests or lawyers and, if they lived in Cape Colony, were educated and wealthy enough to vote.

They saw the sufferings of the black people. Often they themselves had been badly treated or insulted by whites. Selope Thema, for example, joined a political party after he had been knocked off his bicycle and kicked by a white policeman for not taking his hat off to him! They knew that blacks in other parts of the world, especially in the USA and the West Indies, were beginning to create trade unions and political organisations. Consequently they were drawn together into a movement, the aim of which was to win political and social equality for all blacks in the land of their birth.

The first black political association was founded in the Eastern Cape in 1880. In 1884 the first black newspaper, *Imvo Zabantsundu* (African Opinion), edited by J. T. Jabavu, was published. Many others formed political groups, including the African Political Organisation (APO), founded in 1902 led by Dr Abdullah Abdurahman, which spoke for the Cape coloured people. The Natal Indian Congress was founded by M. K. Gandhi in 1894. There were about 100,000 Indians in Natal, most of whom had come to work on the Natal sugar plantations since 1860.

Gandhi, who later became world famous for the part he played in leading Indian resistance to British rule, led a number of campaigns to improve the position of the Indians in Natal and tried out the methods of mass passive resistance which he later used so successfully in India. By the time he left South Africa in 1914, he had gained some improvements for the Indian community in Natal but he campaigned quite separately from the blacks. By contrast, Dr Abdurahman and the APO worked closely with black leaders.

Action, 1902–14

Black anger against the British government grew between 1902 and 1910. The black leaders believed that when Lord Milner promised the Boers at Vereeniging in 1902 that he would disarm the blacks and prevent them gaining the franchise in the near future, he was in fact breaking a promise which he had made to them the previous year, that their political rights would be increased.

They thought that if the British king and Parliament heard their case, they would come to their aid. In 1906, the Transvaal Native Congress wrote to the British Parliament complaining about the pass laws. The letter was ignored. In 1909 black leaders from every province

'Paying the penalty for muder' by F. Dadd. A white view of the Bambatha Rising. The two men found guilty of murdering two policemen are executed by government troops

met at Bloemfontein to complain about the terms of the Act of Union which the all-white National Convention was discussing. First the National Convention, then the British Parliament took no notice of their carefully argued and peacefully presented protests.

The Foundation of the South African Native National Congress, 1912

The Act of Union and the election of the Botha-Smuts government in 1910 made the blacks realise that they must become better organised and more united. In January 1912 hundreds of representatives from all over the country met at Bloemfontein and set up the South African Native National Congress (SANNC). Its mastermind was P.K.I. Seme, a lawyer who had just returned from Britain and the USA. He was elected Treasurer. J.I. Dube, who had completed his education in the USA and had raised money there to build an industrial school in Zululand, became President; and

S.T. Plaatje, a journalist, became Secretary. The SANNC, which changed its name to the African National Congress (ANC) in 1923, has proved to be the longest-lasting and most important black political organisation in South Africa.

Early methods of the SANNC

Its first campaign was against the 1913 Land Act. Having protested strongly but unsuccessfully against the Act in South Africa, it sent a delegation to Britain, which though winning some support in the newspapers, got nowhere with the government. Yet despite their shabby treatment both at home and in London, the SANNC leaders stayed moderate and patient. They believed that their case was so strong that if they continued to put it reasonably and calmly and, if they protested peacefully, they would eventually persuade the whites to see the justice of their cause and win the reforms for which they asked.

The SANNC delegation to Britain in 1914. From left to right: Dr W. Rubusana, T. Mapikela, Rev J.I. Dube, S. Msane and Sol Plaatje

Chapter 8   From the Act of Union to the Second World War, 1910–39

Economic and social trends, 1910–39

Economic growth, 1910–20

The Botha–Smuts government took South Africa into the First World War (see page 129) on Britain's side. The gold price rose and, since goods from Europe became much harder to get, local manufacturers did well with products such as clothing and engineering goods. The mining companies were short of labour to meet the new demands and began to employ blacks in semi-skilled jobs which hitherto had been for whites only. These better conditions lasted until 1920 when world trade declined and South Africa could no longer get war-time prices for her gold and agricultural products.

The Rand Rebellion, 1922

The Rand mine-owners, who acted together as the Chamber of Mines, faced two major problems in 1920.

Not only was the gold price falling but many of their black miners were striking for better wages and working conditions. At that time the wages bill for 21,000 white miners was more than that of 181,000 black miners. The answer of the Chamber of Mines was to try, in December 1921, to reduce the total wages bill by employing fewer expensive white miners and offering their semi-skilled jobs to blacks but at much lower rates. This led to an outburst of protests from white miners who demanded that the colour-bar (reserving some jobs for whites only) should remain. 'Workers of the world unite and fight for a White South Africa' read some of the banners of the demonstrating miners. The *Johannesburg Star* reported how the white miners 'shot and bludgeoned unoffending Coloured men as though they were engaged in a rat hunt', their aim being to frighten them away from the Rand and their jobs.

The white miners went on strike in January 1922. Smuts, who had become Prime Minister on Botha's

The black miners' strike, 1920. Police confront workers at the compound gate

THE RAND REVOLT: 6000 PRISONERS; THE CAPTURE OF FORDSBURG.

PHOTOGRAPHS BY C.N.

" UPWARDS OF 6000 PRISONERS HAVE BEEN TAKEN ": A TYPICAL GROUP OF REBELS, WITH THEIR HANDS UP, SURRENDERING TO THE SOUTH AFRICAN GOVERNMENT FORCES.

The Rand Rebellion, 1922. This picture and caption appeared in the Illustrated London News, *8 April 1922*

death in 1919, decided to give to the mine-owners the full backing of the police and the government's defence force, which he himself commanded. The miners formed their own commandos and talked of turning the Rand into an independent republic.

Violence began in February when the white miners tried to stop 'scab' labour from entering the mines, and also tried to release gaoled miners. From 10 to 17 March a small-scale war took place in Johannesburg and near-by towns. By the time the defence force overcame the miners with the aid of heavy guns and aeroplanes, more than 200 people were dead and 500 wounded. 5000 miners were arrested, 1000 put on trial and four of the leaders hung for treason.

The defeat of the rebellion allowed the mine-owners to reduce their wages bill by sacking white miners and relaxing the colour-bar; but only for a short time. General J. B. H. Hertzog (see page 63) won the 1924 general election and put the colour-bar back.

The poor whites

The bitterness of the white workers on the Rand had been fuelled by the growing number of 'poor whites', mainly Afrikaners, who were coming into the cities in search of jobs which did not exist. Before the Anglo-Boer War they had worked on the farms of other Afrikaners but the increase in the white population, the damage done to many farms by the Anglo-Boer War, drought, diseases like rinderpest and a change to more commercial farming drove them off the land. In the 1920s, between 2000 and 3000 Afrikaners, about a fifth of the Afrikaner population, could not earn a living and depended on charities like the mayor's soup kitchen in Cape Town where for an hour each day soup was doled out from four big stock pots into the bottles, jam jars and sweet tins of the passing queue of hungry whites.

A commission, paid for by the Carnegie Foundation of the USA, made a careful study of the 'poor white' problem from 1929 to 1932. Hertzog's government helped to improve the situation for the whites by making jobs previously done by blacks (for example, on the railways) for whites only, and many Afrikaner employers made a point of putting Afrikaners first when it came to filling job vacancies. By 1939, a general improvement in the economy was making the 'poor white' problem a thing of the past, but it had been solved at the expense of black workers. As far as the government was concerned, unemployed black workers could return to the rural areas. The reality was increasing poverty, hardship and starvation in those areas.

Economic growth in the 1930s

The Wall Street Crash of 1929, which began the worst economic depression of modern times, started to hit South Africa hard in 1931. Mine-owners' and farmers' profits from diamond and wool exports fell drastically. Other countries, like Britain and Australia, devalued their currencies so that their goods would be cheaper in the world's markets. Hertzog's government delayed devaluation. A major financial and political crisis followed in 1932. Hertzog had to agree to devalue the South African currency in 1932 and to go into a new 'fusion' or coalition government in 1934.

In 1933, the South African economy entered a period of rapid growth which was to last without serious interruption for forty years. In the lead were the mining companies which profited from a large rise in the gold price. They reorganised into larger units and continued to attract investment from overseas. The largest was the Anglo-American Corporation (AAC). Sir Ernest Oppenheimer, a successful diamond buyer from Kimberley, had created the AAC in 1917 with mainly American backing. By 1929, he had won control of De Beers and of a number of Rand goldfields. During the 1930s AAC opened up new mines in Central Africa. Oppenheimer, a Smuts supporter, was MP for Kimberley and a man of great political as well as economic power. In 1932, he simply ignored the request of Hertzog's government that he should keep some diamond mines open which were losing money and refused to give evidence to the inquiry which the government set up to investigate his actions.

Simultaneously, manufacturing industry grew fast. Hertzog's government created the Iron and Steel Corporation (ISCOR) in 1927 which helped it to bring into being other metal-working businesses. During the 1930s, many new factories were built, mainly on the Rand and near Port Elizabeth, but also in Cape Town and Durban. By 1939, there were 20,000 new jobs in mining and 50,000 in manufacturing.

The black experience

Although there was no public outcry, the daily experience of most blacks was worse than that of the poor whites. Like the whites, the blacks moved in growing numbers into the towns and cities. In 1904, 340,000 (10 per cent) were town dwellers, by 1936, 1,150,000 (19 per cent). A higher proportion of the newcomers were women seeking permanent homes for their families close to the employment of their menfolk and themselves.

Some city councils built municipal townships like Johannesburg's Western Native Township. These housed only a small proportion of blacks. They were not attractive, often being sited near sewage farms and rubbish tips and other places where the whites did not wish to live. Many blacks lived more freely in leasehold or freehold townships like Johannesburg's Sophiatown or in urban slum yards. Most bachelor 'migrant' workers continued to be housed in compounds and hostels.

The Rand mines provided many jobs though they recruited more than half the black miners from outside South Africa, in particular from Mozambique. Manufacturing industry became a major employer. A very large number of blacks, men as well as women, worked as servants for the whites and many others survived through prostitution or the illegal brewing of alcohol.

The wages paid by the mines set the standard for black workers generally and between 1919 and 1939 the Chamber of Mines held wages down. It was able to do so because of its success in recruiting migrant black workers from outside South Africa. It survived a major twelve-day strike of 70,000 black miners in 1920 by improving working conditions, not by raising wages. By 1939, the average black was 10 per cent worse off (compared to 1919) because prices had risen while wages had stayed the same. The average white was 10 per cent better off.

White governments, 1910–39, and 'segregation'

The Botha–Smuts governments, 1910–24

In the first Parliament of the new Union of South Africa in 1910 when all-white MPs were elected by a virtually all-white electorate, except in Cape Province, the South African Party (SAP) held sixty-seven seats, the Unionist Party thirty-nine and the Labour Party four. The Afrikaner majority had voted heavily for the SAP, the British for the Unionists, and the white miners on the Rand for Labour. Louis Botha was Prime Minister, Jan Smuts, Minister of the Interior, Defence and Mines and J. B. Hertzog, Minister of Justice.

A major aim of Louis Botha and Jan Smuts (the SAP leaders) was to lessen the enmity between the British and the Afrikaners. They made it clear that they would keep South Africa within the British Empire and played down the differences between the two white groups. In contrast, Hertzog emphasised the differences. He feared that the Afrikaner way of life would be swamped by British influences and that South Africa's real needs would be lost within the vast British Empire. 'South Africa first' was his motto and he argued for the white groups to develop as two separate streams with their own language, schools and churches. In 1914 he broke from the SAP and founded the National Party. Soon afterwards the First World War broke out in Europe.

Botha and Smuts immediately led South Africa into the war on Britain's side and prepared to invade the German colony of South-West Africa. The Nationalists, however, opposed the war and some ex-commandos, formed for the Anglo-Boer War, rose in rebellion, hoping with German help to drive the hated British out of South Africa. More than 11,000 men joined the rebellion, which lasted from September to December 1914, and 322 died in the fighting, while many of the rebel leaders were put in prison. One, Japie Fourie, was shot by firing-squad.

Afrikaners turned to the Nationalists and away from the SAP. In the 1915 general election the SAP held on to only fifty-nine seats, though it remained the largest party, the Unionists forty while, in their first election, the Nationalists won twenty-seven. The swing to the Nationalists continued after the war. In the 1920 election, they won the most seats, forty-four against the SAP's forty-one, the Unionists' twenty-five and Labour's twenty-one. To stay in power, Smuts persuaded the Unionists to merge with the SAP and in another election in 1921 the SAP gained a clear majority (SAP seventy-nine, Nationalists forty-five, Labour nine). Smuts, however, had lost a lot of support. He was seen increasingly to be the friend of the mine-owners of the Rand and of the British Empire. The tough action he took in 1922 against the Rand Rebellion was not popular. In the election of 1924, the Nationalists won sixty-three seats, the SAP fifty-three and Labour eighteen.

The Hertzog years, 1924–39

The 1924 election brought Hertzog to power as Prime Minister. He governed with Labour support until 1928 and in the 1929 election won an overall majority (Nationalists seventy-eight, SAP sixty-one, Labour five). However, the great economic crisis of 1932–33 convinced him that a government of national unity was needed and he merged his National Party with Smuts's SAP. He stayed on as Prime Minister and Smuts became Deputy Prime Minister and Minister of Justice.

The 'fusion' of the two parties was completed in 1934 when the leaders declared themselves members of the new United Party. Most of the former Nationalist and SAP members of Parliament believed that national unity was urgently needed and warmly supported this 'fusion' of parties. However, nineteen Nationalist MPs, led by D. F. Malan, thought that Hertzog had betrayed the Afrikaner people and had sold out to Smuts and British interests. They refused to join the United Party and formed their own Purified National Party.

In the 1938 election, the United Party won a large majority, 111 against twenty-seven for Malan's Nationalists. However, Malan was becoming more and more attractive to Afrikaner voters so Hertzog and Smuts had to depend more on the British vote.

The outbreak of the Second World War in Europe split the United Party leadership. Hertzog wished to keep South Africa neutral but Smuts wanted to fight alongside Britain. By a small majority, Parliament backed Smuts. Hertzog resigned and Smuts replaced him as Prime Minister, a position he was to hold until 1948.

This anti-Smuts cartoon shows him being warmed by the sun of the British Empire with his cigar-smoking friend Hoggenheimer, a symbol of English-Jewish ownership of the Rand gold mines

SOURCE WORK: The new Afrikaner nationalism of the 1930s

D. F. Malan, who broke with Hertzog in 1934 (see page 63), believed that the Afrikaners were a special people with a mission to guard white Christian civilisation in South Africa. They would only survive if they held together as a single people and took pride in their Afrikaner language, history and way of life. For him the experiences of the Afrikaner 'poor whites' in the new industrial towns and cities which were run by the British and in his view flooded by blacks proved that the Afrikaners were doomed unless they followed the 'pure nationalism' which he offered. A secret and very influential group of Afrikaners, the *Broederbond* (band of brothers), worked with Malan to give to Afrikaners this strong sense of nationality. The economic sufferings of many Afrikaners in the 1920s and 1930s made them ready to turn to this brand of nationalism in much the same way as high unemployment in Germany in the 1930s made many Germans ready to follow the Nazis.

Source A: Who became a member of the Broederbond?

Henning Klopper (see page 48), became first chairman of the Broederbond in 1918. He talked to David Harrison in 1981 about the sort of people needed in the Broederbond:

> 'We did not want weaklings with us to be helped. We wanted people who could help... We wanted people with sufficient courage to make their own way through life... What we said to people was: "Look, wherever you work you must be the best worker in that office, in that area, so that no one can stop your promotion. And even a man of a different political opinion to you should promote you in his own interest." Then we should have... men who would be worthy of carrying a nation.'

The members decided to become a secret society in 1921. They organised themselves into cells, between five and twenty in number, known only to each other and to headquarters. People would be invited to join only after careful inquiries about their abilities. They had to be Afrikaans-speakers, Protestants, financially sound and present or future leaders of their communities.

David Harrison, *The White Tribe of Africa*

Source B: The centenary of Blood River, 1938

The appeal of Afrikaner nationalism became clear in the enthusiastic celebrations of the centenary of the 'Great' Trek (see page 25). Two ox-wagons modelled on those used in 1838 and accompanied by men and women in Voortrekker dress left Van Riebeeck's statue in Cape Town in August and arrived at the site of the Voortrekker monument near Pretoria the following December. Wherever they went, huge crowds gathered. Gideon Roos reported for the South African Broadcasting Corporation:

> 'You have no idea what emotion it caused. I saw people in tears because of this wave of intense patriotism, crystallised around the pride in this romantic page in our history. We never had a symbol before; the ox-wagon became that symbol.'

Source C: The 1938 centenary programme

The cover of the 1938 Centenary Programme. It shows the ox-wagon laager beside Blood river surrounded by Zulu spears

Source D: The aims of the Broederbond

Professor J. C. van Rooy, chairman of the organisation, wrote this in a secret message to members in 1932 which became public in 1935:

> . . . the Afrikaner Broederbond will have to devote its attention to the political needs of our people. And here the aim must be a completely independent, genuine Afrikaans government for South Africa.'

Source E: 16 December 1949

The doors of the Voortrekker Monument being pushed open by Afrikaner youth, 16 December 1949. Note that the young people are dressed in Voortrekker costume and 16 December is the anniversary of Blood river

Source F: The anti-Semitism and anti-communism of the Nationalists

Solly Sachs was General Secretary of the Garment Workers Union. Though himself a Jew and a Communist well-known for his opposition to the government's policies of racial segregation, most of his members were Afrikaner women so he wrote to the centenary celebration organisers and asked that his union could send a delegation to the celebrations. This is part of the reply he received:

> 'The Afrikaner nation is busy uniting, to mobilise its forces against you and your sort. The thousands of Afrikaner daughters which you have in your clutches will settle with you . . . Our people do not want anything to do with Communists and Jews, the high priests thereof, least of all. The day when we Afrikaners begin to settle with you Jews, you will find that Germany is a Jewish paradise compared with what South Africa will be . . . You . . . who all day long organise and address kaffirs, will you dare bring them along also to the celebrations? They are your fellow workers and "Comrades".'

1   Using Sources A and D, explain what sort of people joined the Broederbond and what they hoped to achieve?

2   What do you think (a) Malan and (b) Smuts thought of the Broederbond? Explain your answer.

3   What happened in 1838? Why do you think that Malan's Purified Nationalists (see page 63) celebrated it on such a large scale?

4   What are Sources B, C and E? What parts of their history did the Afrikaner nationalists want their people to remember?

5   In Source F, explain
(a) what the organisers were accusing Solly Sachs of;
(b) how they were threatening him and other Jews.

SOURCE WORK: Smuts and race relations

Jan Smuts was the most famous South African of his time. He had been a brilliant student, first at Stellenbosch, then at Cambridge. The British came to respect him, first as a courageous enemy during the Anglo-Boer War, then as a good ally during the First World War. His advice was so valued that he became a member of the British war cabinet in London in 1917–18 and, in 1919, helped to found the League of Nations. He wrote books on philosophy and was much in demand as a lecturer. But for all his ability and political experience, he had great difficulty in deciding what was the best way forward for the various races of his country.

Source A: A Boonzaier cartoon

Smuts as seen by the Afrikaner cartoonist, Boonzaier

Source B: Writing about voting rights in 1906

'...it ought to be the policy of all parties to do justice to the Natives and to take all wise and prudent measures for their civilization and improvement. But I don't believe in politics for them.'

Source C: A letter from an old friend in 1906

H. J. Wolstenholme, an old Cambridge friend, wrote to him in 1906:

'The native question is, I know, a very thorny one, but I cannot help regretting that you do not see your way to the cautious and gradual granting of the franchise to such natives as in education etc... show themselves capable of exercising it. No class of subjects with any degree of intelligence and ambition... has ever obtained justice from a ruling class; and no such class will ever be content to remain in such subjection.'

Source D: Speaking at the Imperial Institute, London 1917

'...In land ownership and forms of government we are trying to keep them [blacks and whites] apart, and in that way laying down in outline a general policy which it may take a hundred years to work out, but which in the end may be the solution to our Native problem. Thus in South Africa you will have in the long run large areas cultivated by blacks and governed by blacks... while in suitable parts you will have your European communities, which will govern themselves separately...'

Source E: Speaking to the Institute of Race Relations, Cape Town, 1942

'The high hopes which we had of [segregation] as a policy have been sadly disappointed... A revolutionary change is taking place among the Native peoples of South Africa through the movement of the country to the towns... Segregation tried to stop it. It has, however, not stopped in the least. The process has accelerated. You might as well try to sweep the ocean back with a broom.'

Source F: Writing to a friend

Smuts wrote this just before the election of 1943:

'Of course the Natives are not without a case... I am going to do whatever is politically possible... But I dare not do anything which will outpace public opinion too much on the eve of an election...'

1   In Source A what sort of person is the cartoonist making Smuts out to be?

2   In 1906 (Source B) what did Smuts believe that the whites should do for the blacks? What, in his opinion, should they *not* do?

3   What was the main difference of opinion between Wolstenholme (Source C) and Smuts (Source B)? Why did Wolstenholme believe that the blacks should be given the vote?

4   Describe how Smuts had changed his mind between 1917 (Source D) and 1942 (Source E).

5   What reason did Smuts give in Source F for not making too many changes too quickly?

6   How powerful was Smuts between 1910 and 1939? What did he do in these years to help the blacks?

7   How fair a comment on Smuts' treatment of the blacks is Source A?

Segregation laws, 1910–39

In these years most whites believed that the races should live apart. They also believed that towns were for white people. If blacks wished to work in the towns, they should only come for as long as the whites needed them and then return to their rural homes. Such beliefs led to the segregation laws that the Botha, Smuts and Hertzog governments passed. As more and more blacks moved to the towns and more of their labour was needed permanently, the more suffering these laws caused and the harder they were to enforce.

By the Mines and Works Act of 1911, the SAP government placed a colour-bar on jobs in the mines. Hertzog strengthened the colour-bar by the Mines and Works Amendment Act of 1926. Similarly, in 1936 by his Native Trust and Land Act, Hertzog continued the SAP policies of the 1913 Land Act which prevented blacks from owning any land outside their reserves, though he increased the size of the reserves from 7 to 13 per cent of the country.

By the 1923 Natives (Urban Areas) Act, Smuts linked an urgently needed plan of slum clearance with the building of segregated black 'locations' well away from the town centres. In 1937, Hertzog aimed to control the number of blacks living in towns by the Native Laws Amendment Act. This Act set limits on the numbers of blacks who could live in an urban area at any one time and was intended to keep blacks working on white farms as much as to prevent them moving into towns in larger numbers.

These Acts were backed up by pass laws which strictly controlled the movement of male blacks. The pass laws became the main focus of black demands for fairer treatment and more political rights but, because they were so central to its policy, the white government refused to change them.

Hertzog went even further when he reduced the very limited political rights remaining to the blacks of Cape Province. In 1936, he removed from them (but not from the coloureds) the right to vote alongside whites in national and in provincial elections. In future they could only vote separately for their own members of Parliament and provincial councillors – and these members would be white. Simultaneously Hertzog created a Natives' Representative Council (NRC). It was chaired by the Minister for Native Affairs and had seventeen black members (twelve elected and five appointed) and five white members. The NRC had no powers; it could only advise the minister.

Black opposition and protest, 1910–19

The African National Congress (ANC)

We have seen in Chapter 7 how the blacks opposed the Act of Union, how they founded the South African Native National Congress (SANNC) in 1912, and how the SANNC leaders spoke out against the 1913 Land Act, both in South Africa and in Britain. After the First World War, the SANNC, which changed its name to the African National Congress (ANC) in 1923, continued its opposition. In 1919 it sent a group to Versailles, near Paris, where the world leaders were working out the peace settlement, in the vain hope of winning more political rights for South Africa's blacks. The ANC leaders were, for the most part, teachers, lawyers and clergymen, respectable, well-educated and religious. They continued to believe that peaceful methods would persuade the whites to give them a better deal and that more violent protest should be avoided. However, many black workers lost patience with their caution and moderation.

The Industrial and Commercial Workers Union (ICU)

The most popular black political movement of the 1920s was the Industrial and Commercial Workers Union (ICU). Its main leader was Clements Kadalie. The ICU started in Cape Town where its members organised a

Clements Kadalie

strike of dock-workers against high food prices. Although the strike collapsed, the ICU rapidly increased its membership not only among urban workers but in the countryside too. By 1926 it claimed to have 100,000 members. Kadalie invited British trade unionists to advise him and also tried to have the ICU recognised internationally. However, between 1928 and 1930, the ICU collapsed. Kadalie was a fine public speaker but not a good organiser. He never made up his mind whether the ICU was mainly a trade-union movement which should concentrate on getting better wages and working conditions, or a broader political protest movement. He quarrelled with George Champion, the powerful leader of the Natal ICU, and also with the Communists within the organisation who wished to encourage strike action. And he failed to bring into the movement the most important group of black workers, the miners of the Rand.

The Communists

The successful Communist revolution in Russia in 1917 attracted many people throughout the world to communism. The aim of the Communist Party of South Africa (CPSA) was to work towards the overthrow of white business and government through workers' strikes, demonstrations and, one day, a revolution. CPSA numbers were never large but its members were active within the ANC and the ICU and also within

trade unions. One of its members, Johannes Nkosi, led an anti-pass demonstration in Durban in 1930 and was shot dead by the police as he spoke to the crowd. However, neither the ANC nor ICU leadership agreed with the Communists' aim of overthrowing the system of government and their influence was small.

Anti-pass law demonstrations

Perhaps the most successful protests were those by women against the pass laws. In 1913, women in the Orange Free State publicly dumped their passes in the centre of Bloemfontein, risking arrest and imprisonment. In 1920 Charlotte Maxeke, leader of the SANNC's Women's League, led a similar campaign on the Rand. The law requiring women to carry passes was withdrawn and it was not until 1956 that the government again forced all black women to carry passes.

Black churches

Many blacks found that the white mission churches had little understanding of the needs of black Christians. White priests seemed unable to share in the music and prayers which blacks used to express their faith. White congregations did not show the same Christian love and friendship towards their black brothers and sisters as they did to each other. Blacks began to found their own churches. The biggest breakaway was led by Mangena Mokone who founded the

A demonstration against the pass laws being broken up by police and black 'collaborators', 1919

Ethiopian (African) Church in 1892 which linked up with a similar movement in the USA.

In 1920, the 'Israelite' movement, believing that the end of the world would soon come and that they were obeying the laws of God, settled on common land at a place called Bulhoek. They refused to obey police instructions (and SANNC advice) to move. Eventually they fought a full-scale battle with the police and 163 of them were killed and 129 wounded.

In 1925, a preacher named Wellington Buthelezi travelled round the Transkei telling huge audiences that the day of judgement of white South Africa would soon come. Black Americans, he said, would arrive in aeroplanes and free their black brothers. Those who wanted to be freed should kill their pigs and paint their houses black. Hertzog's government was worried enough by Buthelezi's fame to banish him from the Transkei.

The weakness of the black opposition

Black protest was frequent and widespread but it was usually local and short-lived. No organisation was able to co-ordinate black protest nationally or continuously. The ANC leaders, mainly Christian and middle class, could not work with the ICU nor the Communist Party, nor give an effective lead to the black industrial workers. The ICU and the CPSA also quarrelled.

By the standards of its successors, the white government dealt mildly with the black opposition, but it did take action which weakened it. Between 1927 and 1930 the white government banned black political meetings and limited the movements of some of the ICU and Communist leaders. The police also acted forcefully against strikers and political demonstrations, as in Port Elizabeth in 1920 and Durban in 1930. The pass laws and the other powers which the police held to control black movement made mass black protest very difficult to organise.

The political weakness of the blacks showed clearly in 1936. The ANC used its usual methods of peaceful protest against Hertzog's new segregation laws, but with no success. A new political organisation, the All-African Convention, was formed to fight the proposed laws. It met Hertzog and sent a complaint about his plans to the London Parliament, to no effect. Both the ANC and AAC agreed to co-operate with Hertzog's new Natives' Representative Council, but by 1939, support for the AAC was dwindling away and the ANC desperately needed new leaders.

SOURCE WORK: Anti-pass law demonstrations in the Orange Free State, 1913

Sol Plaatje described the demonstrations in his book, *Native Life in South Africa*, first published in 1916:

'A crowd of 600 women, in July 1913, marched to the municipal offices in Bloemfontein and asked to see the mayor. He was not in, so they called for the Town Clerk. The Deputy Mayor came out, and they deposited before him a bag containing their passes and politely signified their intention not to buy any more passes (which cost a shilling a month).

At Jagersfontein there was a similar demonstration, led by a jet-black Mozambique lady. She and a number of others were arrested and sentenced to various terms of imprisonment. The sentences ranged from three weeks to three months, and the fines from 10s to £3. They all refused to pay their fines . . .

We went on Sunday morning to visit the prisoners at the jail. A severe shock burst upon us . . . It was an exceptionally cold week and our hearts bled to see young women of Bloemfontein who had spent all their lives in the capital and never knew what it was to walk without socks, walking the chilly cemented floors and the cold sharp pebbles without boots. Their own boots and shoes had been taken off, they told us, and they were, throughout the winter, forced to perform hard labour barefooted. Was ever inhumanity more cold-blooded?'

1   Who was Sol Plaatje? Why did he write *Native Life in South Africa* (see page 56)?

2   For what reasons did the provincial government of the Orange Free State wish black women to carry passes? Why did they object to doing so?

3   What happened to the demonstrators at Jagersfontein?

4   Who was Plaatje accusing of being cold-blooded and inhuman?

5   How reliable do you think Plaatje's evidence is for the anti-pass demonstrations in the Orange Free State in July 1913?

6   What sort of reasons might the magistrate at Jagersfontein have given to Plaatje if asked to explain why he had sent the women to prison?

Chapter 9   The Second World War and its effects

South Africa and the war

South Africa fought with the Allies (Britain, the USA and the USSR) against Germany and Italy. Two hundred thousand whites, half of them Afrikaners, volunteered to fight. One hundred and twenty-five thousand blacks joined them as drivers, labourers and servants since they were not allowed to carry arms. At first the South African army fought in East and North Africa, but then invaded Sicily and mainland Italy as part of the Eighth Army.

White opposition to the war

Both Hertzog and Malan opposed the war. As the cartoon below shows, Hertzog left the United Party and rejoined the Nationalists. Some Nationalists hoped for a Nazi victory since the defeat of Britain would make it easier for them to turn South Africa into an Afrikaner-controlled republic. Some of them agreed with Hitler's racial ideas but said they disliked his dictatorship and use of violence. A few, who founded a secret society called the *Ossewabrandwag* or Ox-wagon Sentinel, used sabotage to weaken the war effort. Some of its leaders, including B.J. Vorster (see page 96), were arrested and imprisoned by the Smuts government.

Economic advance

Mining and manufacturing had already been doing well before the war. Being cut off from European supplies caused the manufacturing industry to expand

The split in 1939 between Smuts on the one hand and Hertzog and Malan on the other. Smuts takes the Empire road towards European war, while Malan and Hertzog follow the sun-lit South African road: a cartoon by Boonzaier

faster still. With the mines and factories working flat out and many men away at the war, more and more blacks were needed in the cities. Simultaneously, in the countryside, conditions were bad for many blacks. The population was rising continuously. Years of drought caused widespread starvation in 1942 and 1943 and white farmers, by making greater use of machinery, needed fewer labourers. Between 1936 and 1946, the number of blacks living in towns doubled. The Smuts government relaxed the job colour-bar and stopped enforcing the pass laws so strictly.

The changing mood of the blacks

The Atlantic Charter

In August 1941, America's Franklin Roosevelt and Britain's Winston Churchill met on board a battleship off the coast of Newfoundland. There they produced the Atlantic Charter, a statement of their basic principles, which they would defend to the end against Nazi Germany. In brief, the Charter stated that the Allies were fighting the war to save freedom, democracy and peace from Hitler's tyrannical dictatorship.

Black South Africans who fought in Africa and in Europe knew what the Charter said. Blacks within South Africa also read about it and heard whites talking about the virtues of freedom and democracy. They knew that Smuts was greatly respected by the Allies and, towards the end of the war, was playing an important part in setting up the United Nations, the main principles of which were those of the Atlantic Charter. As the war drew to its close, their own hopes for greater freedom and democracy within South Africa rose and they took action with the aim of turning their hopes into reality.

The revival of the ANC

Of the black political organisations, the ANC was the most active. The Rev J. Calata had held it together in the late 1930s when black opposition was at its weakest. Dr A. B. Xuma, President from 1940 to 1949, gave more decisive leadership. He strengthened the Central Committee, reduced the power of the chiefs within the organisation and looked out for new younger talent. During the war, new energetic young members joined, including Walter and Albertina Sisulu, Anton Lembede, Nelson Mandela and Oliver Tambo. They set up the Youth League which opposed the white government with growing fierceness.

Yusuf Dadoo, President of the Transvaal Indian Congress, addressing a meeting in Johannesburg in 1945. Nelson Mandela is behind the microphone

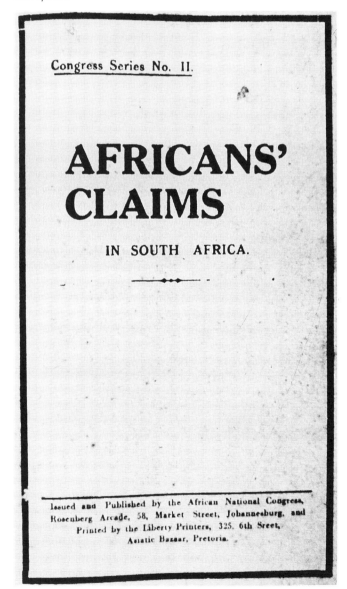

Congress Series No. II.

AFRICANS' CLAIMS

IN SOUTH AFRICA.

Issued and Published by the African National Congress, Rosenberg Arcade, 58, Market Street, Johannesburg, and Printed by the Liberty Printers, 325, 6th Sreet, Asiatic Bazaar, Pretoria.

The ANC made its aims clear in this document published in 1943

In 1943 the ANC published *Africans' Claims* which made clear how determined it was to achieve genuine democracy, freedom and equality for all races. Above all, there should be no advantages or disadvantages based on race. This the government ignored.

In 1944 the ANC led a series of large demonstrations against the pass laws, although it failed to achieve its target of a million signatures on a petition for the permanent abolition of the pass laws.

The government and the Natives' Representative Council, 1946

One of the few ways by which black leaders could talk regularly to the government was through the Natives' Representative Council (NRC) which Hertzog had set up in 1936 when he took Cape Africans off the common voting roll (see page 67). In 1946 the NRC supported the ANC in its anti-pass law campaign and strongly criticised the government for the way it was handling the miners' strike of 1946.

Black miners were on strike for higher wages and the right to form a trade union. They had brought the gold mines to a halt. The mine-owners, backed by the government, set about breaking the strike by force. Six strikers were killed and more than 400 injured. When the NRC met in Pretoria in August, the black elected members expected to meet the Minister for Native Affairs and to discuss the mines' crisis. Only the minister's deputy turned up and would not have mentioned the strike if the black members had not insisted that he did so. This treatment was the last straw for the black members who fiercely criticised Smuts's government (see Source work, page 72).

The Nationalist government replied by abolishing the NRC in 1951. Although black leaders had clear ideas about the best way forward for the country, the white government now ended the only legal way they had of expressing them.

SOURCE WORK: The protests of the NRC members, 1946

Source A: The Atlantic Charter, 14 August 1941

Clause 3: 'They [Roosevelt and Churchill] respect the right of all peoples to choose the form of government under which they live; and they wish to see the sovereign rights and self-government restored to all those who have been forcibly deprived of them.'

Source B: Albert Luthuli, writing about the NRC meeting in August 1946

Albert Luthuli, who later became President of the ANC, attended the August 1946 meeting of the NRC as representative for Natal. In his autobiography, *Let My People Go*, published in 1963, he discussed the meeting:

'Away from home, the world was torn by a war fought in the interests of human freedom. We could not but be aware of the contradiction between Smuts' behaviour on the world stage and his behaviour at home. On the world stage he was vocal about freedom, human liberty and Western values. At home he denied us these things... A great number of Africans realised, perhaps with some surprise, that South Africa was not the world, and there were alternatives to white South Africa's ingrained ways of doing things.'

Albert Luthuli, *Let My People Go*, Fontana, 1963

Source C: Speaking at the NRC meeting, August 1946

(i) *14 August*: Councillor Mosaka:

'The experiment [of the NRC] has failed because the Government... has never bothered itself for one single moment about the Council... We have been fooled. We have been asked to co-operate with a toy telephone. We have been speaking into an apparatus which cannot transmit sound and at the end of which there is nobody to receive the message...'

(ii) *15 August*: Councillor Moroka bitterly attacked the government's segregation policies and persuaded the NRC to agree to the following motion:

'The Council therefore in protest against this breach of faith towards the African people in particular and the cause of world freedom in general, resolves to adjourn this session, and calls upon the Government forthwith to abolish all discriminatory legislation affecting non-Europeans in this country.'

Extracts from the minutes of the NRC meeting

Source D: Albert Luthuli describes the government's answer to the NRC protest

'At this time Smuts was away so it fell to the Acting Prime Minister, J. H. Hofmeyr, to answer us... The government could accede [agree] to none of our requests, and the laws which we considered discriminatory were really in the best interests of "the native".'

Albert Luthuli, *Let My People Go*

1 What was the NRC (see page 71)?

2 Read Sources A and B. What was the Atlantic Charter? How did black leaders believe that the ideas it contained could be used to help their campaigns?

3 In Luthuli's opinion in what way did Smuts seem to contradict himself?

4 How did the Second World War change black attitudes within South Africa?

5 What did Councillor Mosaka mean when he talked about a toy telephone (Source C(i))? Why was the NRC so angry with Smuts's government? What were the main changes it demanded? What action did the NRC take?

6 What then did Smuts's government do? What eventually happened to the NRC?

The 1948 election

The shock of the Nationalist victory

'Smuts: Sensation in London' was one of the headlines of the *Cape Times* the day after the 1948 election (see opposite). No one in London expected Smuts and his United Party to lose to Malan's Nationalists. Nor did Smuts and most of white South Africa. He was, after all, internationally famous. He had guided South Africa successfully now through two world wars. Only recently he had made what seemed a triumphal tour of his country, accompanying the British royal family on their state visit of 1947.

Smuts's problems

However, 1945 to 1948 had been difficult years for his government. Smuts was by now an old man of seventy-nine and he had lost touch with the changing mood of many Afrikaners. He had angered the Indian community in Natal by stopping them buying land in 'white' areas. In the new United Nations, India led a strong attack on South Africa's racial policies and questioned whether the white government should be trusted any longer to look after the inhabitants of South-West Africa. There were economic difficulties and some servicemen felt that they had had a rough deal when they returned from the front.

Above all loomed the country's racial problems. The large numbers of blacks moving into the cities and the mushrooming of the overcrowded shanty towns worried the whites, many of whom thought that they were earning less when the blacks were getting more. Moreover, the blacks were striking and demonstrating as never before and their leaders spoke with growing confidence. Smuts did not seem to have any solutions. Although he had driven the NRC and ANC to defiance (see page 71), he gave an impression of muddle. Hofmeyr, his Deputy, was widely believed among whites to be too soft on the blacks.

The Fagan and Sauer Reports

Smuts's government appointed a commission in 1946 to inquire into the problems caused by the movement of blacks into towns. The findings of the commission, the Fagan Report, were published in 1948 just before the election. Fagan reported that the idea of total segregation could never work; that industry and commerce needed a permanent settled black urban population; and that it was quite impossible for all the present black townspeople ever to return to the reserves which were already overcrowded. He recommended that migrant labour be discouraged and black families be encouraged to settle in locations in a carefully controlled way. Smuts's United Party accepted the Fagan Report and fought the 1948 election upon it.

The Nationalists had their own commission which published the Sauer Report, also in time for the election. Sauer argued that 'apartheid' or the separate development of the different races of the country was the only way forward. Equality and mixing would mean the suicide of the white race. The reserves were the true fatherland of the blacks. The flood of blacks into the cities in recent years was a dangerous development and urban blacks must continue to be treated as visitors without political rights and their numbers strictly controlled. The migrant labour system should continue and the black locations kept clearly separate from the white towns.

Reasons for the Nationalists' success

The Nationalists were united and well organised and the 'apartheid' plan of the Sauer Report proved a vote-winner amongst white voters. Farmers and white workers on the Rand who had voted UP in 1943 voted NP in 1948. Furthermore, Malan did a deal with Havenga's Afrikaner Party which won him vital seats. Nonetheless, Smuts won more than 50 per cent of the votes cast against Malan's 40 per cent. He lost because fewer votes were needed to win the rural, mainly Nationalist seats, compared to the urban ones.

The 1948 election, the Natal Mercury's *headline, 28 May 1948*

Chapter 10   The first stages of apartheid, 1948–61

The meaning of 'apartheid'

'Apartheid' means 'separateness' and is the word used to describe the ideas about racial separation which the Nationalists put into effect after 1948. These ideas had been developed by Afrikaner professors, writers and politicians who had led the revival of Afrikaner nationalism in the 1930s. They were contained in the Sauer Report (see page 73) and helped Daniel Malan to victory in 1948.

Laws passed by earlier white governments had made South Africa a segregated country in many ways. What apartheid did was make segregation more far-reaching and racial inequality more obvious just at the time when the rest of the world was turning away from such practices.

The Nationalists were sure that the way forward for South Africa could not be by mixing or integrating the races. In their view, the history of South Africa (and other parts of the world like Australia and North America) proved that the different races could not live at peace in the same areas. They believed one group would always push the others about and close contact would cause fear and hatred. If, however, the groups lived apart and developed their ways of life separately, there could, they said, be peace and progress for all races. As far as possible the blacks should live as separate peoples – for example, Xhosa and Zulu on separate reserves – and there develop their own ways of life. Some blacks would need to work in white areas on a temporary basis but their permanent homes and the place where they had political rights would be in the reserves. The Nationalists never forgot that the blacks outnumbered the whites five to one.

A detailed plan: the Tomlinson Report (1950–55)

In 1950 Malan appointed Professor Tomlinson to chair a commission 'to carry out an investigation into the comprehensive rehabilitation (improvement) of the black areas of South Africa with a view to the development of their own national structure, based on effective socio-economic planning'. In other words, Tomlinson was to decide how apartheid would work in practice.

The Tomlinson Commission reported in 1955. Separate development would work, the commission agreed. The government should add land to the reserves and

divide them into seven clear areas or 'homelands' (see map, page 85). It should also spend £104,000,000 over ten years to improve farming in the reserves and to set up factories on the 'homeland' borders to provide jobs for those blacks who could not make a living from farming. If that investment took place, the commission argued, the reserves would be able to support the majority of the blacks, even though their number was growing. The intention was that over the years many blacks would be moved out of white areas so that the white and black populations in the white areas became roughly equal. Such measures would mean that whites need not fear being drowned by a flood of blacks, while most blacks, in due course, could lead their lives as they wished in their reserves.

The next thirty years proved Tomlinson wrong. His commission greatly underestimated the growth in the numbers of blacks and the National government would not spend money on the reserves as he advised. As a result, the reserves could not begin to support the numbers which the government required and became more and more crowded and poverty stricken. The main employment was in the cities so it was there that blacks needed to live. The government used the Tomlinson Report to claim that such a need was only temporary when in fact it was permanent.

'When I ask you for proof, I mean your identity card!' This cartoon by David Marais appeared in the Cape Times, 24 November 1959

One view of the Separate Amenities Act of 1953: a cartoon by Abe Berry

Apartheid laws, 1948–53

Between 1948 and 1953, Malan's government passed many laws which began turning its 'apartheid' theory into practice and satisfied the wishes of Nationalist voters for rigid control of the blacks.

The Prohibition of Mixed Marriages Act (1949) made marriages between people of different colour illegal.

The Population Registration Act (1950) put every South African into a particular 'racial' group. If Nationalists were to succeed in forcing 'races' to develop separately, then it followed that all South Africans had to be told to which racial group they belonged. However, in many cases this was impossible to do accurately since so many mixed marriages had taken place in the previous three hundred years, between whites, Khoisan and blacks. One aim of the government was to prevent the Cape coloureds from being treated as whites and it was coloured families who suffered the most from these laws (see page 92).

The Group Areas Act (1950) increased the powers of the government to force the different racial groups to live separately from each other and to move them from their homes if they were in the 'wrong' racial neighbourhood (see page 93).

The Suppression of Communism Act (1950) banned communism in South Africa and also any political group 'which aimed at bringing about political, industrial, social and economic change within the Union (of South Africa) by the promotion of disturbances or disorder...' The government used this act to silence or imprison thousands of its opponents, very few of whom were actually Communists.

The Native Laws Amendment Act (1952) gave the government control over the movement of blacks to all urban areas and gave local authorities the power to remove 'idle or undesirable natives'.

The Abolition of Passes Act (1952), despite its name, tightened up the pass laws and made all black men, and eventually all black women, carry a reference book without which employment and living in a 'white' area were illegal. Its main aim was to control the movement of blacks in the towns and cities. It was strictly enforced and particularly hated by the blacks for the great suffering which it caused to individuals and to their families.

The Separate Amenities Act (1953) divided public services like post offices, trains and buses and public spaces such as beaches and picnic-areas between the races (see illustrations opposite). Visitors knew immediately that they were in South Africa from the 'Europeans Only' and 'Non-Europeans Only' signs which appeared in every public place.

The Bantu Education Act (1953) brought black education more completely under government control. Primary schoolchildren would be taught in their own ethnic language and black pupils would follow different courses from whites. The aim was to educate them for separate development in the mainly rural 'homelands'; they were not to be part of the white urban world.

In 1951, the Nationalists began a long battle to take the coloured voters off the common voting roll. Eventually, after bitter opposition inside and outside Parliament, the Separate Representation of Voters Act was passed in 1956. It ended the right of the Cape coloured to vote alongside whites in general and local elections. In future they had to vote separately for four representatives (white) in the House of Assembly.

Peaceful opposition to apartheid, 1948–56

The ANC and its Youth League, 1948–49

In 1948 the ANC was divided. Its Youth League, impatient for action, no longer respected the older, more cautious leaders. They disagreed too over whether Africans should work with people of other races who shared the same aims or whether they should work alone to win their freedom. So, even though the Indians in Natal were protesting strongly against the way they were being treated by the whites, and within the United Nations India was turning international opinion against the white government, Indian and ANC leaders in South Africa did not co-operate.

In 1949, there was terrible rioting in Natal between Africans and Indians which only ended when the police and army moved in. More than 140 people were killed and another thousand were injured. Shops and homes (mainly Indian) were looted and destroyed. This tragedy made the black leaders realise that Indians and Africans had to work more closely together.

Major changes took place within the ANC in 1949. Walter Sisulu of the Youth League was elected Secretary-General while Dr Moroka, the Youth League's candidate, became President. The 'Programme of Action', drawn up by the Youth League, of strikes, demonstrations and no co-operation with the government, became the official policy of the ANC.

A National Day of Protest in June 1950 was one of the first demonstrations of this new programme.

The Defiance Campaign, 1952

A much bigger campaign, the Defiance Campaign, was planned for 1952, the three hundredth anniversary of

NATIONAL DAY OF PROTEST
MONDAY, 26TH JUNE, 1950
Begins the all out struggle for Freedom.

Dr. J. S. Moroka, President-General of the African National Congress, supported by Leaders of the South African Indian Congress, and African Peoples' Organisation calls upon all South Africans to REFRAIN FROM GOING TO WORK ON THIS DAY.

• DEFEAT THE SUPPRESSION OF COMMUNISM AND THE GROUP AREAS BILLS WHICH WILL TURN OUR COUNTRY INTO A POLICE STATE.
• DON'T ALLOW MALAN GOVERNMENT'S OPPRESSIVE FASCIST MEASURES TO CRUSH OUR LIVES & LIBERTIES!
• FIGHT FOR FREEDOM — PASS LAWS AND POLICE RAIDS MUST GO! LAND, VOTES AND DECENT WAGES FOR ALL!

'Tis better to sacrifice all in the struggle for Freedom rather than live as slaves.

African, Coloured, Indian and European Democrats—FREEDOM NOT SERFDOM!

Black protest, June 1950: an ANC poster

the arrival of Jan van Riebeeck at the Cape (see page 11). The government planned to celebrate this event all over the country, so the blacks decided to use the occasion to show the whites in South Africa and the whole world how wrong apartheid was and how black patience was running out.

The Defiance Campaign was a peaceful mass protest against the apartheid laws. It began in June in the Eastern Cape where volunteers, wearing ANC armbands, ignored 'Europeans Only' signs and allowed themselves to be arrested. In the next few months, thousands of similar incidents took place all over the country, with the Eastern Cape as the most active area. The ANC leaders believed that their protests would be most effective if they stayed peaceful and made it as easy as they could for the police to arrest them. More than 8000 arrests took place. However, in October, rioting broke out and both blacks and whites were killed. The government introduced new laws which added whipping to fines and imprisonment as punishments for defiance and up to three years in gaol, instead of a month or two, for leading a protest. In the autumn of 1952, ANC membership rose from 7000 to nearly 100,000 members but the harsh measures taken by the government brought the campaign to an end.

The Freedom Charter, 1955

One of the most important political documents in the years after 1948 was the 1955 Freedom Charter. The Defiance Campaign gave confidence to the leaders of the resistance – Indian, coloured, white and black – that a mass protest movement could bring their hoped-for political changes to South Africa. They believed that they, like other revolutionary movements, needed a manifesto, with a clear statement of the aims of all those taking part. That was what the Freedom Charter was intended to be.

On 25 and 26 June in the open air at Kliptown, a village on the Rand, representatives of the ANC, the South African Indian Congress, the South African Coloured People's Organisation and the white Congress of Democrats met together. They called themselves a Congress of the People. Of the 3000 delegates, about 2000 were black, and between 200 and 300 each Indian, coloured and white. The Special Branch police were present in force and confiscated any papers they could find.

The first act of the Congress was to present prizes to three leaders of the opposition to apartheid: Father Huddleston, the English priest who had done his utmost to prevent the destruction of Sophiatown, Dr Dadoo, the Indian leader, and Chief Luthuli. Only Father Huddleston could be present since the other two were banned from taking part in politics.

SOURCE WORK: The Congress of the People adopts the Freedom Charter, 1955

THE PEOPLE SHALL GOVERN!

Every man and woman shall have the right to vote for and stand as a candidate for all bodies which make laws...

ALL NATIONAL GROUPS SHALL HAVE EQUAL RIGHTS!

All apartheid laws and practices shall be set aside.

THE PEOPLE SHALL SHARE IN THE COUNTRY'S WEALTH!

The national wealth of our country, the heritage of all South Africans, shall be restored to the people;

The mineral wealth beneath the soil, the banks and monopoly industry shall be transferred to the ownership of the people as a whole...

THE LAND SHALL BE SHARED AMONG THOSE WHO WORK IT!

Restriction of land ownership on a racial basis shall be ended, and all the land re-divided among those who work it, to banish famine and land hunger;

The state shall help the peasants with implements, seed, tractors and dams to save the soil and assist the tillers...

ALL SHALL BE EQUAL BEFORE THE LAW!

No one shall be imprisoned, deported or restricted without fair trial...

ALL SHALL ENJOY HUMAN RIGHTS!

The law shall guarantee to all the right to speak, to organise, to meet together, to publish, to preach, to worship and to educate their children...

Pass laws, permits and all other laws restricting these freedoms shall be abolished.

THERE SHALL BE WORK AND SECURITY!

All who work shall be free to form trade unions...

Men and women of all races shall receive equal pay for equal work;

There shall be a forty-hour working week, a national minimum wage, paid annual leave, and sick leave for all workers, and maternity leave on full pay for all working mothers...

THE DOORS OF LEARNING AND CULTURE SHALL BE OPENED!

Education shall be free, compulsory, universal and equal for all children...

THERE SHALL BE HOUSES, SECURITY AND COMFORT!

Rent and prices shall be lowered, food plentiful, and no one shall go hungry; free medical care... shall be provided...slums demolished...the aged, orphans, the disabled and sick cared for by the state...

Fenced locations and ghettoes shall be abolished, and the laws which break up families shall be repealed.

THERE SHALL BE PEACE AND FRIENDSHIP!

Let all who love their people and their country now say, as we say here:

THESE FREEDOMS WE SHALL FIGHT FOR, SIDE BY SIDE, THROUGHOUT OUR LIVES UNTIL WE HAVE WON OUR LIBERTY.

1 Who agreed to the principles set out in the Freedom Charter?

2 Why did they think it important to publish it in 1955?

3 What South African laws of 1955 would have to have been abolished if the National government had agreed to paragraphs 4, 5, 6 and 8?

4 Which principles of the Freedom Charter do you (a) agree with, (b) disagree with, (c) are not sure about? Which principles if any would the National government have accepted?

5 If conservatism supports free enterprise, the private ownership of business and individual freedom; if socialism supports some public ownership of business, human rights and individual freedom; and if communism gives priority to public ownership and to the common good rather than individual freedom, is the Freedom Charter best described as conservative, socialist or communist? Explain your answer.

Then the Freedom Charter was read out, paragraph by paragraph, and approved. 'It was,' said Chief Luthuli, in a written message to the Congress, 'a torchlight in whatever dark skies overcast the path to freedom.' And a torchlight it has remained to the following generations of blacks (see page 77).

The 'Treason Trials', 1956–61

The Congress of the People got much attention from the white newspapers and the government soon took action against its leaders. In 1956, 156 people were arrested, including almost all the ANC leaders and South African Indian Congress leaders, and charged with high treason. In long, drawn-out trials the government lawyers tried to prove that the Freedom Charter was communist and that the black leaders were plotting violent revolution.

The government could not make its case stick. Sixty of those arrested were released in 1958, another sixty in 1959. The last thirty, who included the black opposition leaders Nelson Mandela, Walter Sisulu, Helen Joseph and Lilian Ngoyi (see page 82), were finally found not guilty and freed in 1961. However, if the government did not win its case and prove that the accused had committed treason, it kept the best-known resistance leaders on trial for nearly five years and so greatly weakened the opposition.

Black opposition leaders

Albert Luthuli

The President-General of the ANC from 1953 until it was banned in 1960 was Albert Luthuli. His father was a Christian missionary, his uncle a chief in the Groutville area of Natal. The young Albert was educated at the Groutville mission station and became one of the first black lecturers at the Adams Teacher Training College in Natal. He was also an active member of the local Methodist Church. Although he loved teaching, he agreed to become chief at Groutville on his uncle's death in 1935. He was able to travel abroad, first to India and then to the USA, and slowly began to get involved in national politics. By 1948 he was a member of the NRC (see page 71). In 1951 he became President of the Natal branch of the ANC and in 1953 succeeded Moroka to become national President.

Luthuli won the admiration of the blacks but also gained the respect of many whites. He was a dignified Christian gentleman and wrote and spoke well. He argued that there must be non-violent solutions to South Africa's problems, and whites could have a fine future by sharing the country's riches with all its citizens.

The 'Treason Trials', the accused are cheered as they are taken from prison to appear in court

He was an eloquent opponent of apartheid and the government dismissed him from his post as chief when he refused to resign from the ANC. In 1953, following the Defiance Campaign, he was 'banned' which made it virtually impossible for him to be an active president. He could not attend the Kliptown meeting (see page 76) which approved the Freedom Charter. Nonetheless he was one of the accused in the 'Treason Trials', and, having been found 'not guilty' in 1959, was banned again. When, in 1960, he publicly burned his pass, he was put in prison for five months.

Despite such treatment, he continued to work for peaceful co-operation among the different peoples of South Africa and, in 1961, he was awarded the Nobel Peace Prize. Though the government allowed him to go to Oslo to receive the prize, it otherwise restricted him to the Groutville area where he died in 1967.

Walter Sisulu

Sisulu was Secretary of the ANC. The son of a Transkeian village headman, Sisulu moved to Johannesburg at the age of sixteen. He worked in the mines for some years and educated himself privately. In 1940, he set himself up as an estate agent and joined the ANC.

He was good organiser, if hot-tempered. He was one of the founders of the ANC's Youth League and among the authors of its Programme of Action. When Moroka was President, Sisulu was the real driving force of the ANC. He led the Defiance Campaign, was brought to trial and sentenced to nine months' imprisonment, suspended for three years.

During 1953, he travelled in Europe, in the Soviet Union and in China. On his return, the government

Nelson and Winnie Mandela celebrating the end of the Emergency in 1960

ordered him to resign from the ANC and included him among those accused in the 'Treason Trials'. Though he was acquitted, he was soon placed under 'house arrest'. By now the government had declared the ANC an illegal organisation and put him on trial for 'furthering its aims'. This time he was found guilty and sentenced to six years in prison, but, in 1963, during his release on bail, while appealing against this sentence, he took the chance to go underground with *Umkonto we Sizwe* (see pages 88–9). Caught by the security police at Rivonia later that year, he was sentenced to life imprisonment which he served with Nelson Mandela first on Robben Island, then at Pollsmoor, near Cape Town.

He was released in 1989 by the government of F. W. de Klerk.

Nelson Mandela

Nelson Mandela was born into a noble family of the Transkei. He was educated at a mission school and at Fort Hare College, where he was expelled for taking part in a student strike. He fled to the Rand in order to avoid a forced marriage, and became a mines' policeman while working, with Sisulu's help, for a law degree. He then set up a law firm with Oliver Tambo, joined the ANC and became President of the Youth League in 1950.

The Defiance Campaign brought him to the government's attention. He received a nine-month suspended prison sentence and was forbidden to leave Johannesburg for six months. The government ordered him to resign from the ANC and included him in the 'Treason

Nelson Mandela in gaol after his arrest in 1962

Trials'. By this time Mandela had emerged as the strongest personality in the ANC, a natural leader who won the respect of all his colleagues. He was a physically powerful man and his clear thinking, backed by his legal training and eloquent speaking, caused him to dominate both the 'Treason Trials' and the 'Rivonia Trials' (see pages 88–9).

Eventually found 'not guilty' at the end of the 'Treason Trials' in 1961, Mandela soon went underground to plan a more violent campaign of sabotage. For seventeen months he travelled widely in South Africa and visited other African countries before being captured

Oliver Tambo, President of the ANC, speaking in exile, February 1981

by the security police in 1962. He had already been sentenced to five years' imprisonment when the police raid on the Rivonia farm (see pages 88–9) brought to light documents which the government used to bring charges of high treason against him as well as those arrested during the Rivonia raid. His speech at the 'Rivonia Trial' in 1964 (see page 90) was an impressive statement of black suffering and of the ANC's hopes for the country's future. Like Sisulu, he was sentenced to life imprisonment. As time passed, more than any of the black leaders, he came to symbolise the black cause.

When he was released in 1990, as part of de Klerk's reform programme, many experts on the South African situation said that he alone could lead the country peacefully to black majority rule.

Oliver Tambo

Oliver Tambo came from a Pondoland peasant family. His school fees were paid by his stepbrother and two local Englishwomen. A good school pupil, he won a scholarship to Fort Hare College, from where, like Mandela, he was expelled for his political activities. He taught science for a while and then, with the help of

Women against passes: a demonstration outside the City Hall, Johannesburg, 1955

Sisulu, joined a law firm in Johannesburg. A member of the Youth League, he became close friends with Sisulu and Mandela. He took part in the Defiance Campaign and was one of the accused at the 'Treason Trials'. He was found not guilty and became Deputy President of the ANC in 1959.

In 1960, the ANC leaders realised that the government might soon declare the ANC to be illegal and chose Tambo to go into exile to build up the organisation outside South Africa. This he did successfully and, with the other major leaders of the ANC either dead, in prison or banned, became the undisputed leader of the movement, as long as Nelson Mandela remained in prison.

In 1989 he suffered a stroke which reduced his political activities.

Women's resistance

Anti-pass law demonstrations

In 1955, the government announced that African women as well as African men would have to carry passes. Major demonstrations like those described in Source A and shown in the photographs opposite and below followed.

In the continuing women's campaign against the pass laws, Albertina, wife of Walter Sisulu, played an important part. She led a demonstration in Market Square, Johannesburg, which ended with passes being burned. For this she was arrested and imprisoned. As soon as she was released, she again began to criticise the government in public and was 'banned' for seventeen years. A mother of five children and a full-time nurse, she was also, in 1963, the first woman to be held

Police baton charge a peaceful meeting of women protesting against the pass laws in Pretoria

in prison without trial under the 90-day law (see page 91). The government arrested her eldest son Max at the same time. Her husband, Walter, was then in hiding from the police, so the four younger children were cared for by a fourteen-year-old cousin.

White and black women work together

Of the white critics of the government, some of the fiercest were women. In the 1940s, Margaret Ballinger, one of the white native representatives in the Assembly, never rested in her defence of black interests, nor did Helen Suzman in the 1960s and 1970s.

Ruth First, journalist and member of both the ANC and Communist Party, was an early victim of the infamous '90-day' law. She was arrested in 1963, in connection with the Rivonia plot, held for ninety days without trial in solitary confinement, released and immediately arrested again even though she was the mother of three young children. Finally after 117 days she was set free without being charged. She later left South Africa and worked at the Centre for African Studies at Maputo University in Mozambique. There she was killed in 1982 by a letter bomb sent by the South African secret service.

Apartheid placed heavy burdens on African women. The system of migrant labour took their husbands away from their homes for months on end and left the women and the elderly to care for the crops and animals as well as the children. In the towns, the 'Section 10' laws, as Section 10 of the Black (Urban Areas) Act of 1945 was known, forbade blacks to live in 'white' urban areas unless they has been born there, they had lived there continuously for fifteen years, or they had worked for the same employer for ten years. Without Section 10 qualifications blacks could stay in 'white' areas for only seventy-two hours. Being married to someone with Section 10 rights was not accepted as a reason for staying in a 'white' urban area. The result was that the law split many families.

The Black Sash organisation

A group of white women founded this organisation in 1955 to fight the National Party's plans to remove the voting rights of the coloureds. The members organised demonstrations and later gave practical help to urban blacks–for example, free legal advice on Section 10. The organisation also made surveys of the effects of apartheid on black families.

In 1956, the Federation of South African Women, whose President was Lilian Ngoyi and Secretary Helen Joseph, organised a gathering of women in the heart of white Nationalist power, the Union Buildings in Pretoria. Twenty thousand women came, each carrying letters of protest against the apartheid laws, especially the hated pass laws (see Source A).

SOURCE WORK: Women against apartheid

Source A: The protest organised by the Federation of South African Women, 9 August 1956

Helen Joseph describes the protest in her book, *Side by Side*, published in 1986:

'We took those letters of protest into the Union Buildings, to the offices of the Prime Minister, Johannes Strijdom. He was not there. We flooded his office with them and returned to the thousands of women, waiting for us packed tightly together... Lilian Ngoyi called on them to stand in silent protest. As she raised her right arm in the Congress salute, 20,000 arms went up and stayed up for those endless minutes. We knew that all over South Africa, women in the cities and towns were gathered in protest. We were not just 20,000 women, but many thousand more...

At the end of that half hour, Lilian began to sing, softly at first, "Nkosi Sikelele" ("Lord, give strength to Africa!"). For the blacks it has become their national anthem and the voices rose, joining Lilian, ever louder and stronger. Then I heard the new song, composed specially for the protest, "Wathint' a bafazi, wa uthint' imbolodo uzo kufa" ("You have struck a rock, you have tampered with the women, you shall be destroyed!"). It was meant for Strijdom...'

Helen Joseph and Lilian Ngoyi are reunited after ten years of separation through banning

Source B: Lilian Ngoyi and Helen Joseph

Both women were 'banned' for their political activities. Not only could they no longer be active politically, but they were forbidden to see each other, though they were close friends. The Federation of South African Women collapsed as a result of government action against its leaders. Both also served prison sentences for a time as well.

Source C: Ellen Kuzwayo describes her experiences of prison in 1976

Ellen Kuzwayo was a social worker in Soweto, the huge black township with more than two million inhabitants, near Johannesburg. During the troubles of 1976, she was a member of the Committee of 10, a group set up by the Sowetan residents during the riots to find some solutions to those troubles. She was arrested by the government and held without trial in Johannesburg Fort for five months.

'During my detention I... was surrounded by the perpetual pain of the young girls, who were detained under Section 6 of the Terrorism Act [for taking part in the Sowetan demonstrations] and who were separated from me by just the wall which divided our... cells... I myself was detained under Section 10... under Section 6 you are open to severe interrogation at the hands of the security police...

These young girls could not be visited by their parents...; they were refused fresh food and garments; they could not read a book or a newspaper, except the Bible on request... [Their] interrogation, more often than not, was accompanied by severe assaults, restricted diet and painful isolation.'

Helen Kuzwayo, *Call Me Woman*, The Women's Press, 1985

1 Describe how apartheid affected black women particularly badly?

2 How did the white government treat (a) Ruth First, (b) Albertina Sisulu, (c) Helen Joseph, (d) Lilian Ngoyi (e) Ellen Kuzwayo (f) the young girls from Soweto? What, in the view of the government, had they each done wrong?

3 Which white women and organisations helped the blacks? How did they give that help?

4 The great demonstration of 20,000 women in Pretoria had no effect on the government. In fact, Strijdom, the Prime Minister, never actually received the petition which Helen Joseph and Lilian Ngoyi gave to his officials. Why do you think that they achieved so little?

Chapter 11   Verwoerd, the 'Bantustans' and increased black opposition

Apartheid's main architect: Hendrik Verwoerd

In Britain for the Commonwealth Conference, Dr Verwoerd with Duncan Sandys, a British minister, 6 March 1961

Verwoerd's early career and personality

Hendrik Verwoerd, more than anyone else, was the man who turned apartheid from the old-style segregation of the Smuts-Hertzog years into a system which aimed to deal with every aspect of relations between the races in South Africa.

He was born in the Netherlands in 1901 but his parents emigrated to South Africa when he was two. His father was a missionary of the Dutch Reformed Church and eventually settled in Brandfort in the Orange Free State where he opened a religious bookshop.

The young Verwoerd was an outstanding student at the University of Stellenbosch where he became a lecturer in pyschology, sociology and social work. His interest in the 'poor white' problem (see pages 61–2) brought him into politics as an enthusiastic Nationalist and he joined the Broederbond early in the 1930s. In 1937, he became editor of an important Afrikaner newspaper, *Die Transvaler*. He criticised Smuts's decision to fight alongside Britain in the Second World War and hoped for a German victory.

In 1950, after the National Party had come to power, Malan made him Minister of Native Affairs. This was a vital job if apartheid was to succeed. Verwoerd held it for eight years, greatly to the satisfaction of the Nationalists. When Johannes Strijdom, Malan's successor, died in 1958, Verwoerd became Prime Minister.

He was unusually energetic, hard-working and determined. He had a vision of a safe, prosperous and Christian white South Africa and believed that he had the God-given task of bringing it about through separate development. He was completely self-confident, never suffering, as he himself put it, from 'the nagging worry of self-doubt'.

Few doubted Verwoerd's many talents but they were used for a miserable cause. The only people to benefit from his 'vision' were white racists and those whose only interest was to enjoy the riches of white South Africa. In the eyes of the blacks he was an evil tyrant. 'If any man is remembered as the author of our calamity,' wrote Chief Luthuli, 'it will be he.'

The 'Bantustan' plan

As Minister of Native Affairs, he introduced the Bantu Authorities Act (1951) which set up new forms of local government for the reserves and for the townships. Where possible, power was given to traditional chiefs, closely supervised by white officials. Verwoerd seems to have believed that the blacks would have a better life if they lived apart from the whites and that, logically, separate development must mean independence for them in the long run. He argued that the blacks of South Africa were not one people but separate 'tribes' which should in time develop into several small, separate 'nations'. The Promotion of Bantu Self-Government Act (1959) which led to the creation of eight 'Bantu National Units', or 'Bantustans' as they were often called by their critics, was based on these ideas.

Verwoerd's government encouraged chiefs in the reserves to become more self-governing with the aim in the future of gaining independence. In 1963, the Xhosa reserve of Transkei became self-governing. Mantanzima was elected Prime Minister by the Transkeian Assembly in which chiefs appointed by the South African government held the majority. The Transkei moved to 'independence' in 1976, as did Bophuthatswana in 1977, Venda in 1979 and Ciskei in 1981. Their 'independence', however, was in name only since no other country recognised them and their leaders needed the support of South African money and security police to stay in power. However, the 'Bantustans' made it possible for the South African government to claim that it was giving blacks the chance to run their own affairs in their own new nations and to tell the blacks in the white urban areas that they had a country elsewhere to which they properly belonged.

The faults in the apartheid plan

Verwoerd believed that his apartheid design was sound. All it needed was a strong government and plenty of time – sometime beyond the year 2000 – to bring permanent peace between South Africa's different racial groups. However, even if you were ready to accept that separating the races was a sensible idea, which most blacks and some whites did not, Verwoerd's apartheid had built into it a number of major faults which grew more obvious as time passed.

Its most striking flaw was the smallness of the black reserves, just 13 per cent of the total area of South Africa. This amount of land was hardly enough for the black people living in the reserves in the early 1950s.

To make matters worse the Tomlinson Commission greatly underestimated how much the black population would rise during the next thirty years. Using the 1950 Census, it predicted a black population in the year 2000 of between 16,000,000 and 21,000,000, half of which would need to work in white areas. In fact by 1980, the black population had already reached 19,000,000 and was expected to rise to between 30,000,000 and 34,000,000 by 2000 with well over half the working black population employed in white areas. These population changes meant desperate overcrowding and poverty in the 'Bantustans' and millions of blacks still in the white areas with no secure future to look forward to. The

police, enforcing the pass laws, constantly harassed them.

The apartheid system worked against the economic changes taking place in South Africa. Industry and business continued to expand rapidly in the 1950s and 1960s and to need black labour. Yet the government refused to put money into creating new jobs in the 'Bantustans' at anything near the level the Tomlinson Commission had recommended. Most of the new jobs appeared in the 'white' areas, notably on the Rand and round Port Elizabeth. Instead of helping to push the races apart, economic growth pulled blacks into the 'white' cities.

The most serious weakness of all was the hatred which, not surprisingly, most blacks had for apartheid which grew rather than lessened as it took effect. It caused great and growing hardship and humiliation. It was carried out for their benefit, the government said, but without any serious attempt to discover their opinions. As the government dealt with their opposition using unusually violent and ruthless methods (see page 91), black opposition increased.

White support for the National Party increases, 1948–61

The table below shows the general election results from 1948 to 1961. The National Party steadily increased its share of the votes at the expense of the United Party, though not until 1958 did it win an actual majority of the votes cast. This was because, as in 1948, fewer votes were needed to elect an MP in the less populated rural, mainly NP constituencies than in the more densely populated, mainly UP urban ones.

The UP, which by now had become a party mainly supported by English-speaking whites, had difficulty in finding a good leader to succeed Smuts who died in 1950, and in working out a policy on race relations which was clearly different from apartheid. In 1959 eleven of its MPs broke away to form the Progressive Party. They fought the 1961 election with a new plan for a multi-racial franchise based on educational and wealth qualifications. The white voters, in the year after the Sharpeville crisis (see pages 87–8), were not impressed. Only one of the eleven, Helen Suzman, was re-elected.

Year	Parties National	Afrikaner	Labour	United	Progressive	Others
1948	70	9	6	65	–	–
1953	94	–	4	57	–	–
1958	103	–	–	53	–	–
1961	105	–	–	49	1	–

SOURCE WORK: Verwoerd and the 'Bantustans'

Source A: Hendrik Verwoerd

(i) Speaking to the Senate, the Upper House of Parliament, in 1948:

'South Africa is a white man's country and he must remain the master here. In the reserves we are prepared to allow the Native to be the masters: we are not the masters there. But within the European areas, we, the white people in South Africa, are and shall remain the masters...'

(ii) As Minister of Native Affairs, speaking to the Senate in 1953:

'I will reform [Native education] so that the Natives will be taught from childhood to realise that equality with Europeans is not for them... What is the use of teaching the Bantu mathematics when he cannot use it in practice? The idea is quite absurd... The school must equip the Bantu child to meet the demands which economic life will impose on him... There is no place for him above the level of certain forms of labour...it is of no avail for him to receive a training which has as its aim absorption in the European community...

(iii) A message to the people of South Africa on becoming Prime Minister in 1958:

'I am absolutely convinced that integration in a country like South Africa cannot possibly succeed ... I am seeking justice for all groups... The policy of separate development is designed for the happiness, security and stability provided by their home language and administration for the Bantu as well as the Whites.'

Source B: The 'Bantustans' showing the Tomlinson Consolidation proposals and the actual 'Bantustans'

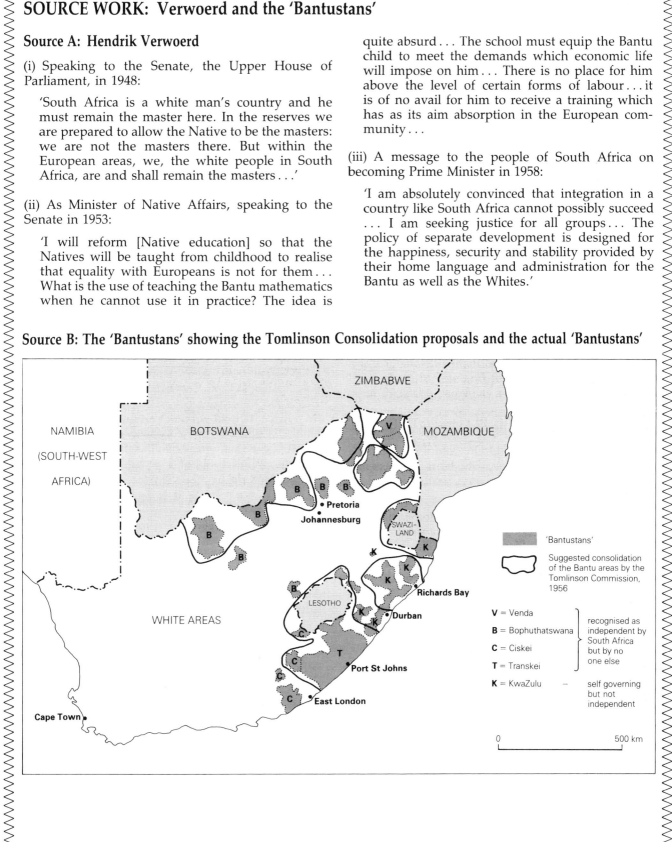

Source C: The Transkei gains 'Independence'

B. J. Vorster for South Africa and Kaiser Matanzima sign the 'independence' papers, 1976

Source D: Albert Luthuli

In his autobiography, *Let My People Go*, Albert Luthuli (see page 98) wrote:

'The Bantustan Act [the Promotion of Bantu Self-Government Act of 1959] divides South Africa neatly, horizontally. At the top there is an upper-crust white parliament. Beneath the upper crust there is... one man, the Minister of Bantu Administration and Development... This man is in effect no longer answerable to the white parliament. He is the absolute controller henceforward of all African affairs...

Inside this closed world [of the Bantustans] there is no hint, not the remotest suggestion, of democratic rule... The modes [methods] of government proposed are a caricature. They are neither democratic nor African. The Act makes our chiefs, quite straightforwardly and simply, into minor puppets and agents of the Big Dictator.'

Source E: A white official

The Chairman of the Bantu Affairs Commission, speaking in Cape Town in 1968. He was a senior white official responsible for the Bantustans:

'The Government does not view the Bantu as one single people, but the Bantu are in fact divided by language, culture and tradition into several peoples or nations... Fortunately for each of [the] peoples or nations, history left to them large tracts of land to serve as their homelands. The Government's policy is therefore not racial policy based on the colour of skin of the inhabitants of the Republic, but a policy based on the reality and the fact that within the borders of the Republic there

are found the White Nation and several Bantu nations... The Government's policy is a policy of differentiating on the grounds of nationhood of different nations, granting to each self-determination within the borders of their homelands – hence the policy of separate development.'

1 In Source A(i), what does Verwoerd mean by 'Natives' and 'reserves'? What does he say is the main aim of 'we', the National government?

2 In Source A(ii), what does he consider to be the main aims of Bantu education? How do his ideas about Bantu education fit in with his ideas of white control and of separate development? Why did most blacks hate the Bantu Education Act?

3 In Source A(iii), what does he mean by 'integration' and why did most whites agree with him 'that integration in a country like South Africa cannot possibly succeed'? What does he mean by separate development and how can he argue that it is designed for 'the happiness, security and stability of the blacks'?

4 Comment on these views of the Chairman of the Bantu Affairs Commission (Source E):
   (a) 'Fortunately... history has left to each of the black peoples large tracts of land to serve as homelands.'
   (b) 'The policy of separate development is not a racial policy.'

5 Who is Luthuli talking about when he uses the phrase 'Big Dictator'. What does he mean when he says that the Bantustans are neither democratic nor African? How much popular support does he think the chiefs will have?

From the Sharpeville killings to the 'Rivonia Trial', 1960–64

Black leaders question non-violent tactics

'Who will deny,' said Luthuli in his speech in 1961 accepting the Nobel Peace Prize, 'that thirty years of my life have been spent knocking in vain, patiently, moderately and modestly at a closed and barred door? What have been the fruits of moderation? The past thirty years have seen the greatest number of laws restricting our rights and progress, until today we have reached a stage where we have almost no rights at all.'

Luthuli never gave up his faith in non-violence and in South Africans of all colours working together in a common cause. Within the ranks of the ANC, however, bitter arguments broke out about its lack of success, its caution against risking violence, and, once again, whether it should be for Africans only. In 1959, Robert Sobukwe led a break-away group to found the Pan-African Congress (PAC). The PAC had an entirely African membership and was ready to risk violence by new campaigns of protest and defiance.

Sharpeville and Langa, 1960

Both the PAC and the ANC decided to hold new anti-pass-law demonstrations in 1960. The PAC intended to invite arrest and to fill the gaols until they overflowed.

Early on the morning of Monday 21 March, Robert Sobukwe began the campaign by marching with some supporters to the police station of Orlando township, near Johannesburg, where he was immediately arrested. At Sharpeville township near Vereeniging, 56 km from Orlando township, thousands of demonstrators gathered outside the police station. A young policeman lost his nerve and shot into the crowd, as did his colleagues. They fired more than 700 rounds, killing sixty-nine people and wounding 180. Of the dead, fifty-two died from shots in the back. Meanwhile, at Langa in the Cape, the officer in charge of the police ordered the demonstrators to leave and then baton-charged them. They replied by throwing stones; the police responded with bullets. Two blacks were killed and forty-nine were injured.

Sharpeville and Langa shocked both world opinion and South Africa. The world was united in its criticism of apartheid and demanded immediate changes. White businessmen asked themselves whether the country had any chance of a peaceful future and the consequent lack of business confidence caused a serious financial crisis. For a few days the government did not know what to do. It suspended the pass laws, then put them into force again and declared a state of emergency.

On 30 March one of the largest black political demonstrations in the history of South Africa took place in Cape Town. A young PAC leader, Philip Kgosana, led 30,000 marchers through the centre of the city to Parliament to demand the release of recently arrested demonstrators. Cape Town had seen nothing like it. Was this the beginning of the revolution which would bring black liberation?

After the Sharpeville shootings

It was not. Kgosana was double-crossed. He believed the promises of the Minister of Justice that genuine negotiations would begin once the demonstrators had returned peacefully to their homes. As soon as Kgosana had led the demonstration back to the townships, he was arrested.

The government decides on repression, not reform

The government now decided on total repression. It called out its reserve army, the Active Citizen Force, and arrested thousands of the leading anti-pass-law campaigners. On 8 April, it declared the ANC and PAC illegal organisations. Defiance and rioting came slowly to an end. The confidence of white business returned and the financial crisis ended.

For most of the black leaders, Sharpeville and Langa were the end of the road of peaceful protest. Oliver Tambo had already left the country to lead the ANC in exile. Mandela went underground to form a new fighting group – *Umkhonto we Sizwe* (the Spear of the People). *Umkhonto*, or MK as it was often called, started to sabotage public buildings and power supplies. Simultaneously the PAC formed its own fighting wing, *Poqo* (we go it alone). *Poqo*, unlike 'the Spear of the People' which aimed at property, also included policemen and informers amongst its targets.

Electricity pylons destroyed by Umkhonto *saboteurs 1961*

Mandela 'underground', 1961–62

As soon as he was found not guilty at the end of the 'Treason Trials' in 1961, Mandela went 'underground'. Since both the ANC and PAC were now illegal organisations, it was the only way that he could keep the black protest movement going. The government issued a warrant for his arrest but for months he toured the country, dodging the security police.

In 1962, Winnie Mandela was working for the Child Welfare Society in Johannesburg. She was having problems with her car and got a message at her office saying that, if she were to drive it to a certain corner, a mechanic would be there to put it right. At the corner was a tall man in blue overalls, whom she did not at first recognise. It was in fact Nelson Mandela. He drove her to a garage, bought her a new car, drove her back into the city and, at a stop sign, quickly said goodbye and disappeared into the pavement throng. In such ways did Mandela keep in touch with his family and friends while 'underground'.

A regular meeting place for both the Mandela family and *Umkhonto* was Lilliesleaf Farm in the Rivonia suburb of Johannesburg. Here the group planned the first acts of sabotage. On 16 December bombs exploded in Johannesburg, Port Elizabeth and Durban.

A month later, in January 1961, Mandela slipped out of the country. He spoke to the Organisation of African Unity in Ethiopia and then toured North and West Africa before flying to London with Oliver Tambo to meet the leaders of the Labour and Liberal parties. Then he was back in Central Africa, seeking support to continue the struggle within South Africa. Home again, he reported to *Umkhonto* in Johannesburg, then decided, against the advice of some of his friends, to visit Luthuli in Natal so that 'the Chief' was up to date with his activities. On his way back to Johannesburg, his car was stopped by three cars full of security police.

Mandela arrested, 1962

They seemed to have been given a vague tip-off that someone important to them would be travelling that day and they recognised Mandela instantly. He was arrested and taken to Johannesburg Fort.

His trial took place in the autumn of 1962. At that time the government did not know that *Umkhonto* existed so Mandela was tried on the relatively minor charges of 'incitement to strike' and of 'leaving the country without permission'. He was given a five-year prison sentence.

Meanwhile *Umkhonto* continued planning sabotage at Lilliesleaf Farm. Somehow, in July 1963, the security police found out about the group. Perhaps someone had betrayed them, perhaps they were simply careless. Nine were arrested, including Sisulu, and among the papers found were a number which made it clear that Mandela was one of *Umkhonto's* leaders.

The 'Rivonia Trial' lasted from December 1963 to June 1964. The main charge was 'recruiting people for training in sabotage and guerrilla warfare for the purpose of violent revolution'. The prosecution demanded the death penalty. Mandela, Sisulu and six others were found guilty and sentenced to life imprisonment.

Nelson Mandela and Walter Sisulu prisoners on Robben Island in Table Bay, 1966

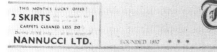

The end of the 'Rivonia Trial' as reported in the Cape Argus, *12 June 1964*

SOURCE WORK: The 'Rivonia Trial', 1963–64

Source A: Mandela's statement at the 'Rivonia Trial'

The National government has always claimed that Mandela is a communist and the ANC a communist-directed organisation. Mandela commented at his trial:

'...I am not a communist and have never been a member of the Communist Party...

The most important political document ever adopted by the ANC is the Freedom Charter. It is by no means the blueprint for a socialist state... The ANC has never... advocated [been in favour of] a revolutionary change in the economic structure of the country, nor... ever condemned capitalist society...

It is true that there has often been close cooperation between the ANC and the Communist Party. But cooperation is merely proof of a common goal... not of a complete community of interests.'

Source B: The final part of Mandela's statement

'Africans want to be paid a living wage. Africans want to perform work which they are capable of doing, and not work which the government declares them to be capable of. Africans want to live where they can obtain work, and not to be endorsed [forced] out of an area because they were not born there. Africans want to own land in places where they work... and not be obliged to live in rented houses which they can never call their own... African men want to have their wives and children to live with them where they work, and not be forced into an unnatural existence in men's hostels. African women want to be with their menfolk and not be left permanently widowed in the reserves.... We want to travel in our own country and to seek work where we want to and not where the Labour Bureau tells us to. We want a just share in the whole of South Africa. We want security and a stake in society.

Above all, we want equal political rights, because without them or disabilities will be perma-

nent. I know this sounds revolutionary to the whites of this country, because the majority of voters will be Africans. This makes the white man fear democracy. But this fear cannot be allowed to stand in the way of the only solution which will guarantee racial harmony and freedom for all. It is not true that the enfranchisement of all will result in racial domination. Political division, based on colour, is entirely artificial, and when it disappears, so will the domination of one colour group by another. The ANC has spent half a century fighting against racialism. When it triumphs, it will not change that policy....

This then is what the ANC is fighting for. Their struggle is a truly national one. It is a struggle of the African people, inspired by their own suffering and their own experience. It is a struggle for the right to live.

During my lifetime I have dedicated my life to this struggle of the African people. I have fought against white domination, and I have fought against black domination. I have cherished the ideal of a democratic and free society in which all persons live together in harmony, and with equal opportunities. It is an ideal which I hope to live for and to achieve. But, if needs be, it is an ideal for which I am prepared to die.'

1   How did Mandela come to be on trial for his life in 1963–64?

2   What was his attitude to communism?

3   What did he mean by 'equal rights'?

4   What does he mean when he says 'the ANC has spent half a century fighting against racialism... I have fought against white domination... I have fought against black domination...'?

5   Why did the National government sentence him to life imprisonment?

6   How could this speech be used to explain why Mandela gained the respect of most blacks in South Africa and many people in other countries?

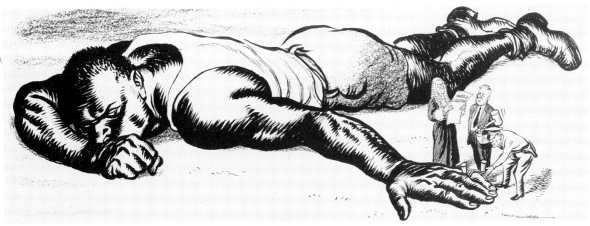

A British cartoonist reacts to the sentence of life imprisonment on Nelson Mandela

An apartheid police state: methods of controlling the opposition

The whites were determined to stay in control and took ruthless action against any blacks (or whites) who opposed them. Bannings and detentions were the measures which they most commonly used in the 1950s and 1960s, though the more extreme step of declaring a state of emergency was taken in 1960.

Bannings had begun to be used widely in the 1950s. A banning order, signed by the Minister of Justice, prevented the named person from attending meetings, writing, broadcasting or being quoted, or leaving a particular district without permission from a magistrate. In some cases, the banned person had to report regularly to the police or was forced to stay at home from 6 p.m. to 6 a.m. Banning orders were normally for two or five years.

Any gathering which, in the opinion of the Minister of Justice, might 'seriously endanger the public peace' could also be banned. Political organisations like the ANC and PAC were banned. Bannings made it impossible for black resistance leaders to carry on their political work legally and drove many of them underground or into exile.

Detention without trial was first used on a large scale during the Sharpeville crisis of 1960, when 11,700 people were detained under the state of emergency. At first detention was limited to twelve days, then to ninety and then to 180. In exceptional cases, like that of Robert Sobukwe, the PAC leader, it could be extended indefinitely by a decision of the Minister of Justice. People suspected of 'terrorism' could be held for up to thirty days in the first instance, and for longer if the Minister of Justice gave his approval.

Detention could mean not just the loss of freedom but torture and death. At least sixty-nine people died in detention in South Africa between 1963 and 1985.

Among the officially stated causes of death were 'suicide', 'slipping in the showers' and 'falling from the tenth floor window while being questioned'. There seems little doubt that the security police tortured many detainees and murdered some.

Other political opponents of the government were murdered and their killers never found. In 1978, for example, a Natal university teacher, Rick Turner, was shot through his front door and died in the arms of his fourteen-year-old daughter. He was under a banning order at the time because of his writings criticising the government. In 1981 Griffiths Mxenge, a lawyer well known for his courageous defence of blacks being prosecuted by the state, was stabbed to death and four years later his wife Victoria was shot outside her home in Durban. Victoria was herself a lawyer and was trying to track down her husband's killers. In 1989 a friend of Rick Turner, David Webster, was shot as he was out jogging with his girlfriend. He was a teacher at Wits University in Johannesburg and had just finished a book on political murders in South Africa.

These murders were never solved. The killers were certainly government sympathisers and may have been supported secretly by the security police.

The English language press in South Africa had, for many years, a good reputation for its independence. However, even in the 1950s and 1960s it could not quote banned persons and, in the 1970s and 1980s, it was further harassed and restricted by the government. The government successfully prosecuted Laurence Gandar, the outspoken editor of the *Rand Daily Mail*, for the critical articles which he published about South Africa's prison conditions, and it banned the *World* newspaper in 1977. It went further still during the 1985 state of emergency, forbidding journalists under pain of a £10,000 fine or up to ten years' imprisonment for reporting without official permission any unrest or action by the security police. It controlled television through the South African Broadcasting Corporation.

SOURCE WORK: Apartheid: the cost in human suffering

Source A: Victims of the Population Registration Act of 1950 (see page 75)

The Du Proft family lived in Cape Town. The account comes from David Harrison's research for the 1981 BBC programme about the Afrikaners, *The White Tribe of Africa*.

'In 1950, just after the government introduced . . . its new rules . . . Raymond du Proft was serving in the police force . . . He was twenty when he met a waitress named Diane Bassick . . . They fell in love, but since she was classified Coloured . . . they could only meet in secret.

Du Proft remembered how scared they were that they would be found out . . . but before long they took a chance and started to live together. When their first son was born they found a house in an Afrikaans-speaking district and passed themselves off without difficulty as a white married couple. Eventually they had five children, all of whom were classified Coloured . . . Regularly they applied for Diane and the children to be reclassified and just as regularly they were refused. So marriage remained out of the question. When their eldest boy, Graham, was nineteen, he started going out with an Afrikaans girl and she became pregnant. But again because he was classified Coloured and she was white they could not marry. Graham's response, in a moment of despair, was to throw himself under a train. He died instantly.'

David Harrison, *The White Tribe of Africa*

Source B: Victims of the pass laws

The Mathabane family lived in Alexandra township, Johannesburg. Mark Mathabane, who, in 1978, left South Africa to take up a tennis scholarship in the USA, remembers a police raid on his home in Alexandra township, in 1965:

[The police smashed the door down, and though Mark's mother hid successfully in a wardrobe, they soon found his father.] 'My father . . . was standing naked, his head bowed, in the middle of the bedroom . . . in front of the bed was an old, brown table, against which my father's interrogator leaned, as he flashed his light all over my father, keeping him blinking all the time . . . .

"Come, let's see your pass." My father reached for his tattered overalls at the foot of the bed and from the back pocket he removed a small, square, bulky black book and handed it over to the policeman, who hurriedly flipped through it. Stonily,

running his eyes up and down my father, he said, "The bloody thing is not in order, you know? . . . Why isn't it in order? Mine is. Anyway, look here, as an old man you ought to be back in the Bantustan. My father is back there and living in peace . . ."

The policeman confirmed my suspicion of being fresh from the reserves. The authorities preferred his kind as policemen because of their ferociousness and blind obedience to white authority. They harboured a twisted fear and hatred of urban blacks.

"I'm working, nkosi [sir]," my father said. "There are no jobs in the Bantustan . . ."

[Mark's father was arrested.] I stepped outside in time to see the two policemen, flanking my father, go up a rocky slope leading out of the yard. I saw more black policemen leading black men and women out of shacks . . . Several children, two or three years old, stood in tears outside smashed doors, imploring their mothers and fathers to come back . . . Several red-necked white men in safari suits and fatigues, guns drawn, paced briskly about the entrance gates, shouting orders and supervising the round up . . .

My father spent two months doing hard labour on a white man's potato farm for his pass crimes.'

Mark Mathabane, *Kaffir Boy*, Pan, 1986

Source C: Victims of the Group Areas Act

The Nationalists used the Group Areas Act to destroy black and coloured communities, however deeply rooted, if they stood in areas which the whites wanted. Sophiatown near Johannesburg was destroyed in 1955; District 6, a coloured settlement in Cape Town since 1838, was destroyed in the 1970s. These particular 'forced removals' hit the headlines worldwide and caused an international outcry against apartheid. The Nationalists carried on regardless. Between 1960 and 1983, they forcibly moved three and a half million blacks and in 1983 planned to move two million more.

The following account of the Tsotsobe family comes from a book called *The Surplus People* written by Laurine Platzky and Cherryl Walker for the Surplus People Project (SPP) which was published by the Ravan Press, Johannesburg. SPP was a project of South African university teachers and community workers, helped by funds from a Christian foundation in the Netherlands. It described the forced removals and their effects. Some of its workers were

District 6, above, a coloured settlement in Cape Town since 1838, destroyed by the Group Areas Act of 1950

detained by the security police, two of them for ten months.

> Jamangile Tsotsobe [not his real name, to protect him] was interviewed by SPP in 1979. He was then living with his wife and epileptic grand-daughter, in Glenmore, near the Ciskei border 200 km from Port Elizabeth. Formerly they had lived in Colchester, much closer to Port Elizabeth.
>
> They lived there for about thirty years. He found work as a gardener. Life was fairly good. They had enough food to eat and they were friends with their neighbours.
>
> But then everything changed. They were informed by the police and by Baab (the Bantu Affairs Administration Board) that they were going to be moved to a place called Glenmore. They were told that there was work for everyone...

and there were good houses which they could have for free. But they did not know this place, so they did not want to move. They were happy enough where they were, and they did not trust the police. They know that Baab would never give a black man a house for free.

But while they were still discussing these things, suddenly they were given seven days' notice to leave... That day when they were taken to Glenmore, the trucks came very early, when they were still asleep... The officials were angry men who shouted at them to get out... There was much confusion. The houses were demolished before they could get all their belongings out... Their furniture was broken. They left the place in grief and they came to Glenmore. The houses in Glenmore were bare, with draughty wooden walls they had to fix with mud.

Tsotsobe looks at us and says that now there is no hope. When he was young, he wanted to give to his children and his grandchildren a different kind of life. Now he sees that there is no hope for his children.'

1 Can you explain why the South African government continued with its strict race laws when they caused misery of the kind described in Source A?

2 How might a Nationalist politician have explained the need for the Population Registration Act? What, in your opinion, was wrong with it?

3 In Source B, what was Mr Mathabane's 'crime'? How was he punished?

4 Where did the policeman come from? What colour was he? How does Mark explain his unpleasantness? What seems to be his attitude towards apartheid?

5 Why were the pass laws so important for the day-to-day working of apartheid? Why were they so hated by the urban blacks?

6 What was Baab and what did it do to the Tsotsobes (Source C)?

7 What was Glenmore like compared to Colchester? What effect had the move had on Mr Tsotsobe?

8 Why was the Group Areas Act so vital for the 'apartheid' plan?

9 What were the aims of the SPP in publishing reports such as this? Is there any evidence that their work alarmed the South African police?

Chapter 12   South Africa and the outside world, 1960–74

The success of nationalist movements in Africa, 1956–68

In the four years from Sharpeville to the 'Rivonia Trials' (1960–64) South Africa's white government virtually destroyed the black freedom movement and drove its main political organisation, the ANC, into exile. Elsewhere in Africa, however, in more than thirty countries, black nationalist movements took control of the government of their countries from the colonial powers. The change began in 1956–57 when Morocco achieved its independence from France and the Gold Coast (renamed Ghana) gained independence from the British. The Portuguese alone among the European colonial powers clung on to its colonies. By 1968, only the four Portuguese colonies of Angola, Mozambique, Portuguese Guinea, Equatorial Guinea, plus Rhodesia (where a white settler government had rebelled against Britain rather than share power with the blacks), South Africa and South-West Africa had white governments.

Macmillan and his 'wind of change' speech, 1960

A few weeks before Sharpeville, in February 1960, the British Prime Minister, Harold Macmillan, ended a tour of Africa in Cape Town where he spoke to the white Parliament. He described his visits to other parts of Africa and explained how strong African nationalism had become. 'The wind of change,' he said, 'is blowing throughout the continent... Whether we like it or not,

An anti-apartheid demonstration in London in 1974

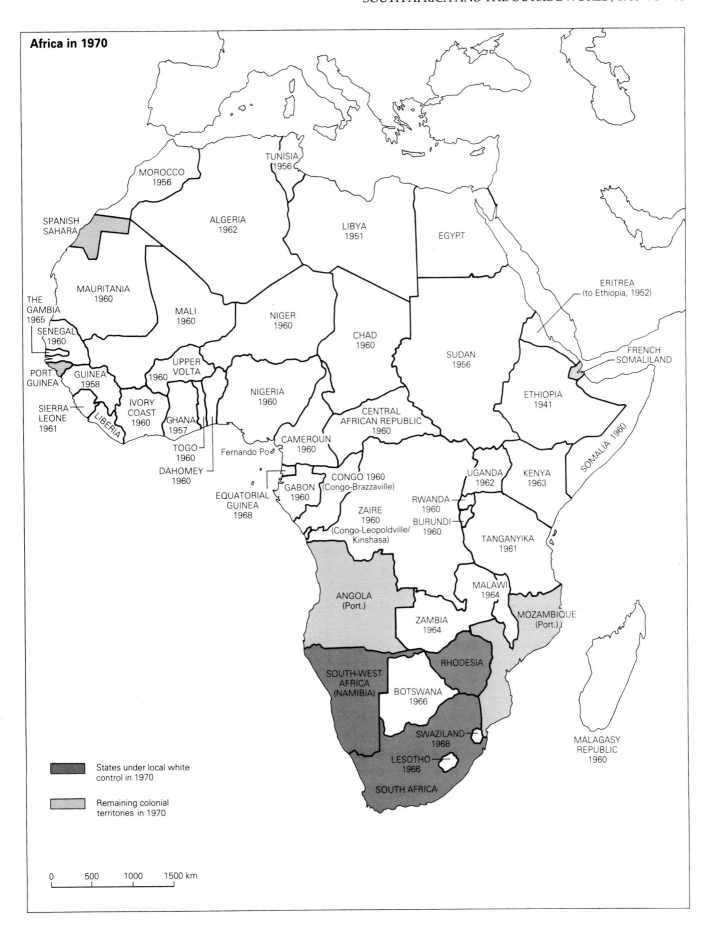

Africa in 1970

SPANISH
SAHARA

MOROCCO
1956

TUNISIA
1956

ALGERIA
1962

LIBYA
1951

EGYPT

ERITREA
(to Ethiopia, 1952)

THE
GAMBIA
1965

SENEGAL
1960

MAURITANIA
1960

MALI
1960

NIGER
1960

CHAD
1960

SUDAN
1956

FRENCH
SOMALILAND

PORT
GUINEA

GUINEA
1958

UPPER
VOLTA
1960

ETHIOPIA
1941

SIERRA
LEONE
1961

IVORY
COAST
1960

GHANA
1957

NIGERIA
1960

CENTRAL
AFRICAN REPUBLIC
1960

SOMALIA 1960

LIBERIA

TOGO
1960

DAHOMEY
1960

Fernando Po

CAMEROUN
1960

UGANDA
1962

KENYA
1963

EQUATORIAL
GUINEA
1968

GABON
1960

CONGO 1960
(Congo-Brazzaville)

ZAIRE
1960
(Congo-Leopoldville/
Kinshasa)

RWANDA
1960

BURUNDI
1960

TANGANYIKA
1961

MALAWI
1964

ANGOLA
(Port.)

ZAMBIA
1964

MOZAMBIQUE
(Port.)

SOUTH-WEST
AFRICA
(NAMIBIA)

RHODESIA

BOTSWANA
1966

SWAZILAND
1968

MALAGASY
REPUBLIC
1960

LESOTHO
1966

SOUTH AFRICA

States under local white
control in 1970

Remaining colonial
territories in 1970

0   500   1000   1500 km

this growth of national consciousness is a political fact.' As far as Britain was concerned as leader of the British Commonwealth, no citizens of a Commonwealth nation should be worse off than others because of their race or religion. Macmillan made it clear that Britain and the Commonwealth found South Africa's 'apartheid' policies unacceptable and he advised the Nationalists to be fairer to South Africa's blacks.

Verwoerd answered at once on behalf of white South Africa. 'There must not only be justice to the black man in Africa but also to the white man . . . This is our only motherland. We have nowhere else to go.' He weakened South Africa's link with Britain as a Commonwealth country by holding a referendum on the establishment of a republic in 1960. A small majority voted in favour of a republic which meant that the head of state would be an elected president rather than the British monarch. On 31 May 1961 South Africa became a republic and in the same year Verwoerd withdrew South Africa from the Commonwealth rather than waiting to be expelled.

Anti-apartheid movements, the United Nations and the Organisation for African Unity (OAU)

South Africa was increasingly isolated by the rest of the world during the sixties. All over the world, anti-apartheid groups were set up which organised demonstrations and trade and sporting boycotts.

After Sharpeville many African countries stopped trading with South Africa. Every new black African nation naturally wanted the end of apartheid so, as each joined the United Nations, that international organisation became increasingly critical of South Africa. In 1963 the black African nations formed the Organisation for African Unity (OAU) which, from its very first meeting, made the abolition of apartheid in South Africa one of its main concerns. In 1969, in Lusaka, the capital of Zambia, the leaders of fourteen Eastern and Central African nations made clear their readiness to help the blacks of South Africa in their struggle against white rule.

SOURCE WORK: The Lusaka Manifesto and Vorster's reply

Source A: The Lusaka Manifesto

Point 6: 'In Mozambique, Angola, Rhodesia and the Republic of South Africa, there is an open and continued denial of the principles of human equality and national self-determination. The societies of these territories are being deliberately organised so as to try and destroy these principles.'

Point 8: 'Our stand towards southern Africa . . . involves a rejection of racialism, not a reversal of existing racial domination. We believe that all the peoples who have made their homes in the countries of southern Africa are Africans, regardless of the colour of their skins . . .'

Point 12: 'On the objective of liberation, we can neither surrender nor compromise. We have always preferred, and still prefer, to achieve it without physical violence . . . But while peaceful progress is blocked by the actions of those at present in power in the states of southern Africa, we have no choice but to give to the peoples of those territories all the support of which we are capable in their struggle against their oppressors.'

Source B: South Africa's reply

B. J. Vorster, who became Prime Minister in 1968, after Verwoerd had been assassinated by a mentally ill parliamentary official, said:

'The outside world and especially the war-mongering leaders on the African continent must understand very thoroughly that the white man in South Africa is not expendable . . . Let them spit as much fire as they want to about the so-called immorality [evil] of apartheid . . . we in South Africa know that it is the only feasible policy . . .'

1 Give two examples of South African laws which denied the principle of human equality and two which denied that of national self-determination as understood by the black nations which signed the Lusaka Manifesto (point 6).

2 What kind of future does the manifesto suggest for white South Africans (point 8)?

3 To what extent does the Lusaka Manifesto suggest that violence should be used against South Africa (point 12)?

4 What does Vorster mean by (a) 'war-mongering', and (b) 'the white man is not expendable'? To what extent does the Lusaka Manifesto (a) warmonger (b) suggest that the white man is expendable?

South Africa defies world opinion

The South African government was particularly criticised by the United Nations and by the OAU for its policies towards Rhodesia and South-West Africa.

Rhodesia

Southern Rhodesia had become a British colony in 1890 when Cecil Rhodes' private army invaded the lands between the Limpopo and Zambezi rivers. The invaders ran up the Union Jack at a place which they called Salisbury in honour of the then British Prime Minister. Whites, mainly from Britain and South Africa, settled in the country. Most came to farm and to mine. In 1923 they were given the choice of joining the Union of South Africa or becoming a separate, self-governing colony. They chose the latter. By the early 1960s, white settlers in Southern Rhodesia numbered about 240,000, the blacks about 4,000,000.

In 1953, the British government joined Southern Rhodesia with two other British colonies, Northern Rhodesia and Nyasaland, to form the Central African Federation. However, the black nationalist movements which opposed federation persuaded Britain to end it. Both Northern Rhodesia and Nyasaland gained their independence in 1964, the former as Zambia, the latter

as Malawi. The blacks of Southern Rhodesia expected to gain their independence in the near future.

The white settlers of Southern Rhodesia, however, had other ideas. They were appalled by the move towards black rule. Not far away was what had been the Belgian Congo. In 1960, the Belgian government had suddenly given independence to an unprepared country and a dreadful civil war had followed. The Rhodesian whites believed that the same would happen if they handed power over to their blacks. When, in 1965, Britain's Labour government refused to give them independence unless they shared much more of their political power with the black majority, Ian Smith, Prime Minister and leader of the white Rhodesian Front party, declared the country independent without Britain's consent. This event became known as UDI, the Unilateral Declaration of Independence.

UDI shocked the rest of the world. Britain and the United Nations declared it to be completely illegal and recommended economic sanctions, including a ban on oil supplies. White Rhodesia survived the next few years thanks to support from South Africa. Rhodesia was South Africa's immediate neighbour to the north and most South African whites strongly supported Ian Smith and believed that, if he failed, they would be the next target of the black revolutionaries, supported by the UN, the OAU and the forces of international communism.

South Africa refused to have anything to do with economic sanctions against Rhodesia. Virtually everything that the Rhodesians needed, which they could not grow or make themselves, including oil, reached them through South Africa and the Portuguese colony of Mozambique. Vorster also sent South African police to help Ian Smith in his struggle against the guerrilla forces of the black nationalist movement.

South-West Africa (Namibia)

The Germans had colonised the area between 1884 and 1914 but during the First World War, the South African army led by Botha and Smuts easily defeated the small German defence force. In 1919, the new League of Nations gave South Africa the mandate for South-West Africa. This meant that the League would allow South Africa to run the country until its inhabitants were ready for independence. In reality, the South African government ran South-West Africa like a colony and did little to prepare the inhabitants for independence.

When the United Nations replaced the League of Nations in 1945, the South African government expected to be able to make South-West Africa more thoroughly part of South Africa, but the UN would not allow this because of South Africa's racial policies. It tried to make the South African government genuinely

S.A. Cabinet is behind Rhodesia

SUNDAY TIMES REPORTER

THE South African Government is wholeheartedly behind the Prime Minister of Rhodesia, Mr. Ian Smith, in his dramatic bid this week for sovereign independence.

This was disclosed by the Minister of Transport, Mr. B. J. Schoeman, who said at a private meeting in Pretoria this week that the Government regarded Rhodesia as South Africa's "White frontier" on the Zambesi. In this situation, he said, Rhodesia's declaration of independence called for South Africa's complete support.

The Minister said said that if Rhodesia disappeared under Black rule, South Africa's frontier would be reduced to the line of the Limpopo.

"There may be serious repercussions as a result of Rhodesia's decision," he said, "but one must keep one's head."

Mr. Schoeman was talking to a deputation of the Federal Consultative Council of the Railways Staff Association, who had come to thank him for improvements in service conditions.

It was learnt later that a number of top railway officials left South Africa this week for top level talks with the Rhodesian railway authorities.

It is understood that their talks will be connected with the enormous expansion of railway traffic between South Africa and Rhodesia if South Africa becomes the only source of supply of Rhodesian imports in the event of international sanctions and boycotts.

One of the main subjects to be discussed is the laying of the line between Beit Bridge and West Nicholson.

This is regarded to be of major importance as the present rail link between South Africa and Rhodesia runs through Bechuanaland — still under British control.

UDI in Rhodesia as reported in the South African Sunday Times, 3 October 1965

prepare the area for independence under UN supervision. Malan's Nationalist government then stated that the UN had no rights in the area and allowed the white inhabitants, who were mainly German or Afrikaners, to elect MPs to the South African Parliament. Its aim was for South-West Africa eventually to become a province of the Union.

However, the UN would not let the matter rest, nor would the OAU. In 1969 the UN declared that South African control of South-West Africa, or Namibia as the blacks preferred to call it, should end immediately. Vorster's government showed itself ready to talk to the UN but not to allow any real progress towards black rule. Within Namibia, black resistance to white rule grew stronger, especially among the Ovambo people in the north. The South-West African People's Organisation (SWAPO) was founded in 1960 and began to fight a guerrilla war in 1966. By 1969, most of the world treated SWAPO as the most representative black movement in Namibia. For its part, the South African government treated SWAPO in the same way as the ANC, declaring it illegal and banning, imprisoning or driving into exile its leaders. Up to 1974, the South African Defence Force (SADF) succeeded in keeping Namibia under it control.

South Africa ignores world criticism

The strength of the South African economy

White South Africans could defy the rest of the world because of their economic strength. They were already rich and getting richer fast. Between 1961 and 1970, their economy grew between 5 and 7 per cent each year, faster than that of any other nation apart from Japan. Business people all over the world wanted to share in this wealth so they invested their money in South African businesses. The British were the largest investors (see Sources A and B), followed by the USA, West Germany and Japan.

In addition, South Africa possessed more valuable minerals than any country other than the Soviet Union. New goldfields were discovered in the Orange Free State to add to the wealth of the Rand and more diamonds were found in South-West Africa. But this was only part of the story. South Africa was the major producer of a number of rare minerals, vital to the advanced economies of the industrial West (see Sources B and C).

Consequently, however much American and European businessmen and governments said that they disliked apartheid, they would not actively back any schemes put forward by the UN or the OAU to overthrow the white government. They themselves had too much to lose in investments and in vital mineral supplies. Many of them argued that the richer South Africa grew, the better-off the blacks would become. Slowly but surely, they said, white governments would listen more carefully to business leaders and end the more unpleasant aspects of the apartheid system.

Economic success made it possible for the government to increase the size of its army and police force and improve their equipment. It also gave South Africa an economic stranglehold on her neighbours. The mines provided desperately needed work for blacks who migrated from independent African states on South Africa's borders – Mozambique, Botswana and Lesotho. Important exports like Zambian copper, tobacco from Zimbabwe and cattle from Botswana had to be exported along South African roads or railways and through South African ports.

In 1968, the weekly magazine the *Economist*, published in London for an international readership, described South Africa as 'flourishing like a green bay tree' and likely to continue to do so. It saw no chance whatever in the near future of the blacks either inside South Africa or in the new independent nations being able to topple the white government.

South Africa and the 'Cold War'

The 'Cold War' caused the USA and Britain to treat white South Africa as a friend in their attempts to halt the spread of communism and the influence of the USSR. The term 'Cold War' is used to describe the state of fear and suspicion which the USA and the USSR had for each other in the years after the Second World War. So different was the way of life under America's capitalism from that under Soviet communism and so powerful were the two countries that the rest of the world tended to support the one or the other. Each side was sure that the other was trying to take over as much of the world as possible and each did all it could to strengthen its own position.

White South Africa was a strongly capitalist society. The South African economy had been built mainly by British, American and Western European business people who believed passionately in free enterprise. Moreover, the capitalism of America and Western Europe needed South African minerals, especially gold. South Africa also lay beside an important sea-route, the oil tanker route from the Persian Gulf to the West. Under no circumstances would America and Britain allow South Africa to fall under the control of a government which was more friendly to the USSR than to them.

Consequently 'Cold War' thinking caused America and Britain to support the white South African government, even though they disliked apartheid. Within South Africa, the Nationalists convinced themselves that a communist-inspired onslaught was directed against them and used every opportunity to tell their citizens and the outside world how dangerous the communists were and how only the Nationalists could be trusted to keep South Africa safely part of the freedom-loving capitalist West.

SOURCE WORK: Overseas business people and South Africa

Source A: Mineral production in South Africa, 1979

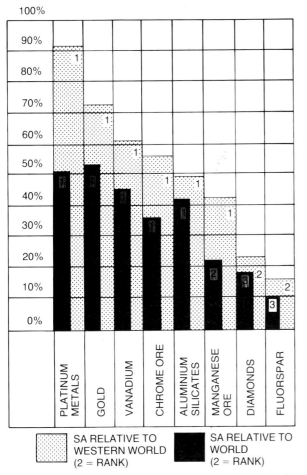

PRODUCTION 1979

SA RELATIVE TO WESTERN WORLD (2 = RANK)

SA RELATIVE TO WORLD (2 = RANK)

The figures are from a South African Ministry of Information publication, The Vital Role of South African Minerals

Source B: The 'Big Four' industrial metals

Arnt Spandau, a West German economist, explains why chromium, cobalt, manganese and platinum metals are so important to industrialised countries.

'For some strategic metals, there are no substitutes at any price. Industrialised countries must have them or write off a good part of their technological advance. The most critical of all industrial metals, known as the 'Big Four', are chromium, cobalt, manganese and the platinum group metals. As one steel executive recently (1981) put it: "Without these (Big Four) you couldn't build a jet engine or an automobile, run a train, build an oil refinery or a power plant. You couldn't process food, or run a sanitary restaurant or a hospital operating room. You could not build a computer...".'

Arnt Spandau, *Southern Africa and the Western World*, Institute of European Economic Affairs, W. Germany, 1984

1   What does Source A tell you about (a) gold (b) chrome ore (c) diamonds? What is the source? Why does it include this diagram? How reliable do you think it is?

2   What, according to Source B, are the 'Big Four' metals? Why are they so important to modern industrial nations? How important a supplier of these metals was South Africa in the 1970s?

3   Source B is a publication of an institute based on three Western European polytechnics. Would you consider it more or less reliable than Source A? Explain your answer. What information do you need to be able to check the accuracy of Sources A and B?

SOURCE WORK: The National government's fear of communism

Source A: P. W. Botha, Minister of Defence, 1977

'There is no doubt in my mind that Russia is the dominating force in international affairs today. So politically, economically and as far as relationships between people are concerned, very much depends on how successful Russia is in her expansionary total-war effort. In the first instance she is out to dominate Europe... She will only try to use force when she doesn't succeed in intimidating [frightening] enough European countries far enough, and it looks like the latter is working.

Secondly she wants to control the destiny of Africa, for its raw materials and the sea-route round the Cape – Russia is expanding her navy faster than any country in history and that can only mean that she wants to dominate the seas. If you want to dominate the seas, you must be able to control the South Atlantic and the Indian Ocean.

The moment she succeeds in either the one or the other, Russia will concentrate on isolating America from Europe.'

Source B: The 'Rivonia Trial', 1963–64

The case put by the state prosecutor against Mandela and those arrested at Rivonia was that *Umkhonto* was a communist creation which aimed to play on 'imaginary grievances' and 'to enrol the African people in an army which supposedly was to fight for African people, but in reality was fighting for a communist state'.

Mandela replied:

'Nothing could be further from the truth. In fact the suggestion is preposterous. Umkhonto was formed by Africans to further their struggle for freedom in their own land. Communists and others supported the movement, and we only wish that more sections of the community would join us... Our fight is against... poverty and lack of human dignity, and we do not need communists... to teach us about these things.'

Source C: The vital role of South Africa's minerals

(The map below is also part of Source C.)

'In view of the dependence of the West on supplies of strategic minerals from South Africa... it would surely not be an exaggeration to suggest that should a Soviet puppet regime [a black government which took orders from the Soviety Union] ever be installed in Pretoria... the Soviet Union would by this action grasp the perfect instrument for... destroying the industrial and technological supremacy of the West.'

Vital Role of South Africa's Minerals, Publications Division of the Department of Foreign Affairs and Information, South Africa, 1982.

1   For what reasons does P. W. Botha (Source A) think the USSR to be dangerous? Why do you think he specially mentions the sea-route round the Cape?

2   Why was the South African government keen to label Nelson Mandela a communist? Summarise Mandela's reply (Source B).

3   Source C comes from a pamphlet given out by the South African embassy in London. What is the message of the diagram?

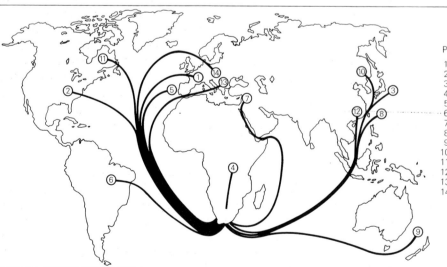

Destination of South Africa's mineral exports, 1979

Percentage of mineral exports

1	EEC	39·4
2	USA	17·7
3	Japan	13·9
4	Africa	6·2
5	Spain and other Europe	4·4
6	Latin America	3·1
7	Israel	2·2
8	Republic of China	2·0
9	Australia and New Zealand	1·7
10	Korea	1·7
11	Canada	1·7
12	Hong Kong	1·4
13	Greece	0·7
14	Comecon	0·7

Total value of mineral exports = R8 500 million

Based on a map in *The Vital Role of South Africa's Minerals*

Chapter 13   Crisis years inside and outside South Africa, 1974–80

The collapse of white power in the Portuguese Empire and Rhodesia, 1974–80

You will see from the map on page 102 that in 1970 South Africa's neighbours were the white-controlled Portuguese colonies of Angola and Mozambique, friendly white-controlled Rhodesia and black-controlled Botswana, which though politically independent had a small population and was economically at South Africa's mercy. Unfriendly black nations like Zambia were still hundreds of kilometres away across rough country.

Ten years later, Angola, Mozambique and Zimbabwe (formerly Rhodesia) were independent countries with unfriendly black governments.

Dr Antonio Salazar, the old dictator of Portugal, had refused to give independence to the Portuguese colonies in the 1960s. Instead he had sent the Portuguese army to fight the black liberation movements in costly wars which turned out to be unwinnable. His successor, Professor Marcello Caetano, followed the same policy after Salazar's death in 1970, and was overthrown in a revolt by army officers. One of the first acts of the new government was to grant independence to Angola and Mozambique.

Angola, 1974–75

In Angola, three black political groups fought to take over from the Portuguese. The Popular Movement for the Liberation of Angola (MPLA), backed by the USSR and supplied with troops from Cuba, another communist country, won control of the capital, Luanda. It was able to defeat the FNLA (National Front for the Liberation of Angola) whose support lay in northern Angola. South Africa supported a southern-based group, Unita, and sent troops deep into Angola in 1975 to help Unita against the MPLA.

It has never been clear how much fighting there was between the two groups. There were rumours but no hard evidence of a fierce battle between the South Africans and the Cubans with both sides claiming victory. What is certain is that South African troops withdrew from Angola, perhaps as a result of advice from the USA, perhaps following military defeat. Most of the world accepted the MPLA as the rightful government of Angola and the Cubans stayed to defend it. Unita, however, was very much alive in the southern part of the country, and, with the continuing semisecret backing of South Africa, was able to keep the civil war going.

Mozambique, 1974–75

In Mozambique, the Front for the Liberation of Mozambique (FRELIMO) had no serious rivals to its leadership of the blacks. Samora Machel, the FRELIMO leader, became the first President of independent Mozambique in 1975. Though Machel had Soviet backing and was as critical of white South Africa as any other black leader, it suited the South African government to accept him as Mozambique's rightful leader and it refused to send aid to a short-lived white-led revolt against him. However, before long the South African government began to support opponents to Machel.

Rhodesia, 1974–80

The collapse of white rule in Angola and Mozambique was the beginning of the end for Ian Smith's white government in Rhodesia. The USA believed that the refusal of the Rhodesian white minority to hand over power to the black majority was helping to increase rather than reduce communist influence in Africa. Henry Kissinger, the American Secretary of State, recommended that Smith should share more power with the blacks and he advised John Vorster, the South African Prime Minister, to stop supporting the white Rhodesians. Simultaneously the liberation armies of the black opposition to Smith's government redoubled their efforts. From bases in Mozambique, Botswana and Zambia they attacked deep into Rhodesia (which to them was Zimbabwe) forcing many white settlers to leave their farms for the safety of the cities.

Vorster decided that Smith could not win and that for South Africa the best solution was to gain the friendliest possible black government north of the Limpopo river. In 1974 he withdrew the South African police units which had been helping Smith and encouraged him to make an alliance with moderate black leaders like Bishop Muzorewa, and to seek a settlement with the British government, which was still, in the eyes of the world, legally responsible for Rhodesia. The liberation armies, however, proved too strong and too

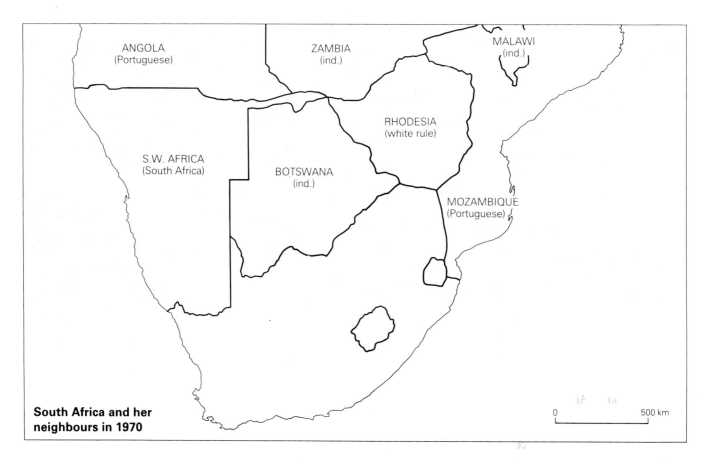

South Africa and her neighbours in 1970

ANGOLA
(Portuguese)

ZAMBIA
(ind.)

MALAWI
(ind.)

RHODESIA
(white rule)

S.W. AFRICA
(South Africa)

BOTSWANA
(ind.)

MOZAMBIQUE
(Portuguese)

0   500 km

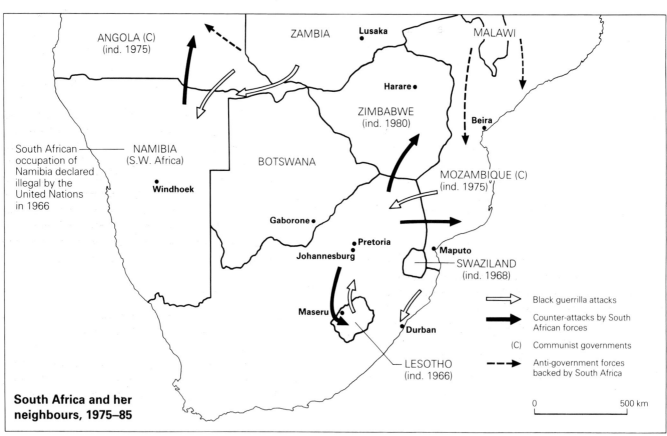

South Africa and her neighbours, 1975–85

ANGOLA (C)
(ind. 1975)

ZAMBIA

Lusaka

MALAWI

Harare

ZIMBABWE
(ind. 1980)

Beira

South African occupation of Namibia declared illegal by the United Nations in 1966

NAMIBIA
(S.W. Africa)

BOTSWANA

MOZAMBIQUE (C)
(ind. 1975)

Windhoek

Gaborone

Pretoria

Johannesburg

Maputo

SWAZILAND
(ind. 1968)

Maseru

Durban

LESOTHO
(ind. 1966)

⇨ Black guerrilla attacks

➡ Counter-attacks by South African forces

(C) Communist governments

⇢ Anti-government forces backed by South Africa

0   500 km

A convoy carrying SADF troops out of Angola crossing the Cunene river, 27 March 1976

popular. Their military success caused the British government to insist on a general election in 1980. This was won by the Zimbabwe African National Union (ZANU) with a huge majority. The ZANU leader, Robert Mugabe, who had led one of the liberation armies, became the first Prime Minister of independent Zimbabwe. Like Machel, he was a determined enemy of white South Africa.

New dangers for South Africa

These changes were very serious for white South Africa. By the 1980s the outside enemies from black Africa were no longer hundreds of kilometres away, they were at the borders. ANC guerrilla forces now had bases in Zimbabwe and Mozambique, in easy reach of Pretoria and Johannesburg, which they could and did raid. SWAPO guerrillas moved much more easily into Namibia from across the Angolan border.

The response of the South African government was twofold. In the first place, Vorster tried to appear more friendly towards his new black neighbours. Secondly, he ordered the rapid strengthening of the South African Defence Force (SADF) which patrolled the borders in larger numbers and raided across them with increasing frequency to attack guerrilla bases.

Black resistance in the 1970s

The ANC in exile

After the disaster of the Rivonia arrests (see page 88) and the crackdown by the security police on all opposition groups, black political resistance within South Africa ended for the rest of the 1960s. Oliver Tambo held together the ANC in exile. He worked to strengthen support for the ANC from foreign governments and gained most in terms of money and weapons from the USSR. Volunteer guerrilla fighters trained at camps in Tanzania and entered Rhodesia in 1967 and 1968 to fight, without much success, with the Zimbabwean guerrillas against the whites. An attempt to unite the PAC in exile with the ANC came to nothing and within the ANC itself there were arguments and personal rivalries. Tambo's main achievement was to keep the movement in existence in these difficult times.

Black Consciousness

The 1970s found South Africa's blacks in a different mood. In 1973, in Durban, determined strikers won better wages and more bargaining rights for their trade unions. A Black Consciousness movement, led by Steve Biko (see page 105), taught that blacks must stop thinking of themselves as second-class citizens who needed

Schoolchildren protesting in Soweto, 1976

white skills. They should prove to themselves that they could make their way independently. In 1968 Black Consciousness set up its own blacks-only student organisation. It followed with health and welfare services and, in 1972, the Black Peoples' Convention was established to carry its ideas into politics. Black Consciousness influenced the young. It made them more confident and less ready to be pushed around by the security police.

The Soweto riots, 1976–77

Soweto is the huge collection of townships to the south-west of Johannesburg where most of its inhabitants work. On 16 June 1976, 15,000 school pupils marched in defiance of a police ban. When the marchers were stopped by the police, they stood firm despite warning shots and tear gas. The police then fired into the crowd, killing two of the youngsters and wounding several more. News of these deaths caused first Soweto and then other townships to erupt into demonstrations, riots and destructive violence which was to last for months and, in some places, especially the schools, for years.

The most obvious cause of the riots was the government's rule that Afrikaans must be used on an equal basis with English as one of the languages for teaching in black schools. For the blacks, Afrikaans was the language of their oppressors. It was also much less useful than English since no one in the world spoke Afrikaans except Afrikaners. Black pupils believed that the white government had ordered that blacks should be taught in Afrikaans because it wanted them always to have an inferior education that would fit them only

to be servants or unskilled workers. While they had to pay for their schooling in overcrowded classes with poorly qualified teachers, white children had free education, decent buildings, smaller classes and qualified staff.

There were also other reasons for the long period of rioting. Unemployment amongst urban blacks was rising. The 'homeland' of Transkei was about to become fully 'independent' so many blacks working in the 'white' cities feared that they would soon be 'endorsed out' to the already overcrowded 'homelands'. Within townships like Soweto, houses were scarce because the government had slowed down the building programme in order to speed it up in the 'homelands' where houses were not needed because there were no jobs.

The blacks of Soweto and other townships were also angry because, in 1972–73, the government had abolished the urban local authorities and replaced them with local administration boards. By this change, the costs of running the townships, including the salaries of the white officials of the new boards, passed from white local authorities like the Johannesburg City Council, to the black residents, most of whom could ill afford the extra charges.

The main organiser of the Soweto disturbances was the Students' Representative Council. It led marches, persuaded workers to take part in one-day political strikes, attacked bottle stores and beer halls (since it believed with some reason that heavy drinking by some of the older people was weakening their will to resist white oppression), and campaigned against rent rises. It also organised an effective schools boycott which kept classrooms empty for months on end.

The riots spread

The Sowetan troubles spread swiftly to the rest of the country. The library and administration block of the University of Zululand were burnt down on 18 June 1976, the Assembly building in Bophuthatswana in August. The centre of Cape Town saw serious rioting in August and September and by November 1976 the schools were so badly disrupted that the school examinations had to be postponed.

The police met violence with violence. Other demonstrations were dealt with in the same way as that of 16 June. Nearly 6000 people were arrested between June 1976 and February 1977 and in October 1977 the main Black Consciousness organisations were banned, as was *World*, the leading black newspaper in Johannesburg.

The destruction was great, virtually all of it in black areas; 350 schools, 250 bottle stores and beer halls, 170 shops, many clinics, banks, libraries, post offices and 200 private homes. More than 700 blacks were killed, some by the police, some by other blacks who thought they were police informers. More than 100 were under seventeen and most of them under twenty-five. Two whites died, one of whom was Dr Edelstein who had devoted his life to black welfare and, in 1972, had warned of the danger if the government continued with its policies.

The effect of black resistance on the white general elections of 1977

By the summer of 1977, the arrests, bannings and strong-arm tactics of the police had brought uneasy calm to the country. In the autumn of 1977, Vorster called a general election. As far as the whites were concerned, the government's actions were a matter for praise not blame. The Nationalists won a massive victory, taking 134 seats, their greatest number ever. The white opposition parties took only thirty seats, with the Progressives (PFP) being the most successful with seventeen.

Victims of police violence

Below are details about just two of the victims of police violence during 1976–77.

Frank Chikane

In 1977, Frank Chikane was a priest at Kagiso, near Krugerdorp. Worried by the number of young people disappearing into detention, he asked lawyers to write to the police to find out what was happening to them. He was arrested and detained for six months since the police thought that because he was worried about young people being held in detention he must himself have taken part in the riots and know who the student leaders were.

While he was in detention he was tortured, being punched, beaten with a broomstick and forced to stand for hours on one spot. His torturers at one point suggested that he might as well commit suicide since he was going to die anyway.

He eventually appeared before a magistrate in January 1978 who had him released since there was no case to answer. However, the church in which he served, the Apostolic Faith Mission of Africa, suspended him from his post for being 'too involved in politics'.

Steve Biko

Steve Biko, the Black Consciousness leader, was first banned and then, in August 1977, detained by the Port Elizabeth police on suspicion of having given out revolutionary pamphlets. Biko was then thirty and in good health. In the middle of September he died of brain damage still in police custody.

According to the police evidence at his inquest, Biko was held in a cell for eighteen days, naked 'in order to prevent him hanging himself with his clothes'. He was then moved to the security police office, still naked in leg irons and handcuffs. There he was questioned by a five-man interrogation team, who, they said at the inquest, had to hold him down together because he became violent. 'In the scuffle that ensued,' said the officer in command, 'Mr Biko hit his head against a wall.'

In this assault, Biko suffered the head injuries which were to kill him but the prison doctors failed to diagnose how serious the injury was for five days. Eventually Biko was driven hundreds of kilometres naked on the floor of a police Land Rover with a blanket thrown over him for treatment in Pretoria. There he died.

BIKO AND SOLIDARITY

BLACK PEOPLE'S CONVENTION
TRIBUTE TO THE LATE
HONORARY PRESIDENT
BANTU STEPHEN BIKO
One Azania: One Nation

Steve Biko

SOURCE WORK: Children die in Soweto, 1976

Source A: To Hell with Afrikaans

Soweto, 1976, students on the march

Source B: The Children of Soweto

This is an extract from M. V. Mzame's book, *The Children of Soweto*, published in 1982. It describes the death of Muntu:

'We buried him on Sunday. There were several other funerals being held all over the township that Sunday, funerals of others who had died in the shootings earlier that week.

His death had come as a great shock to me. Life was difficult to imagine without him. In class he had always sat next to me. We lived in the same street. We had grown up playing marbles, spinning tops and flying kites together. Our street team had dominated the other street teams we played against in our football challenge matches ... He and I had formed such a deadly combination as strikers that we had been nicknamed

the "terrible twins" ... His death came as a terrible shock to me as I could not remember a time when he had not been at my side.

It was a chilly Wednesday morning in the middle of June. We were marching along the main road, some three streets away from ours, when we encountered them. They stood across the road, blocking our way. We had been marching resolutely through the townships, with children from the other schools, gathering yet more others as we proceeded. Boys and girls between 10 and 20 ... Along with them thousands of primary school children.

Addressing us first in Afrikaans and then in broken Zulu, they tried to order us to disperse. But we had grievances which could no longer wait. We surged forward, aiming to sweep them out of our path if they would not give way. By now our frenzied numbers had swelled and swelled. We shouted "Amandla" (Power), "Inkululeko ngoku" (Freedom in our lifetime) and "One Azania, One Nation" as we marched on, our clenched fists held high. The air resounded with menace. We sang... We shouted our defiance in song:

> We don't give a damn, even if imprisoned
> For freedom's our ultimate goal.

Suddenly from just ahead of us there was a great rumbling noise. Several times the thunderous explosion came, as if the very roof of heaven was collapsing over our heads. Pandemonium broke loose as we scampered for protection from the nearby houses, he and I and a handful of others hurling stones as we retreated.

He stumbled and fell, with an anguished cry... "They've hit me," he cried and collapsed to the ground like an empty sack of potatoes.

Khotso Duiker and I tore ourselves from the retreating crowd and crept on all fours to where he lay... "Hold him on the other side," I said to Khotso. We struggled on with him between us, to the safety of the nearest yard.

The shooting had lasted for seconds perhaps, but it had seemed like ages...

"Bring him over here," I said. Khotso rolled his school blazer on the ground close to the wall. We lowered him to the ground with his back to the wall.

"Where does it hurt?" I asked. Only then did I notice the streams of blood oozing through his fingers as he held his hands clasped to his tummy.'

The news reached his sister Sindiswana that he had been shot.

'Sindiswana threw herself into the small crowd of students who had gathered round her brother. One look at him, propped against a wall, his face ghastly pale and contorted with pain, and she burst into a most heart-rending wail.

"Wu! Umntana' sekhaya," she cried, "they've killed him, they've killed him!" She threw her hands into the sky and held them clasped on her head....

Sindiswana then did a most unpredictable thing. Like a woman possessed, she picked him up and carried him in her arms as if he was a baby. She staggered a little but moved resolutely towards the gate facing the main road, which was deserted except for the police and some newspaper reporters....

A few policemen detached themselves from the rest and came towards us. Many reporters, their cameras flashing, rushed forward despite efforts by the police to hold them back. I saw two policemen grab a black photographer like so much dirty washing, rip out the film from his camera and crush it under their heavy boots into near-pulp. But some of these photos, with Sindiswana carrying her dying brother in her arms, like a pilgrim bearing a sacrificial offering, found their way into the world's leading newspapers, as we were to find out later when we went into exile.

He was breathing with increasing difficulty. A faint smile played on his lips, but furrows of pain showed on his forehead and in his eyes...

We carried our friend to the back seat of the car and there laid him to rest... Khotso and I got on either side of him in the back seat. Muntu died on the way to hospital.'

Source C: Hector Pietersen, 16 June 1976

Hector Pietersen, the first child shot dead by police in Soweto, 16 June 1976

1 What do Sources A and B suggest was the main reason for the pupils' march?

2 Why did the police open fire?

3 Source C has become one of the best-known pictures from South Africa in the 1970s. Why do you think this should be so?

4 What effect did these terrible events have (a) on black opinion, (b) on white opinion and (c) on world opinion?

Chapter 14　Five minutes to midnight: how close was revolution between 1977 and 1990?

Why no revolution in South Africa in the 1970s and 1980s?

In 1977, most people outside South Africa believed revolution would soon come to South Africa. If the history of the last 200 years proved anything, they thought, it seemed to show two things: firstly, that majorities revolt against the rule of minorities, as in France in 1789 and in Russia in 1917; secondly, that coloured majorities rid themselves of white colonial governments, as in Asia after 1947 and Africa after 1957. Surely the white minority of South Africa, they argued, had no chance of holding out much longer against these world-wide trends.

R. W. Johnson, a teacher at Oxford University who had spent his childhood in South Africa, published a book in 1977 called *How Long will South Africa Survive*? It gained much attention on publication and has continued to arouse interest since then.

Johnson questioned the popular view that there must soon be a revolution in South Africa. He pointed out how the hated imperial government of Russia, for example, survived for generations and only collapsed in 1917 after the Russian army had been defeated in the First World War. In South Africa, the Afrikaners were a minority with nowhere else to go. They were determined, and controlled a strong army and police force. Johnson reminded his readers that the collapse of the white government in South Africa had frequently been predicted but had not come about. 'The opponents of the Pretoria regime [government],' he wrote, 'have continuously underestimated its formidable strength, and their wrong guesses have cost many lives.'

Certainly the Soweto riots showed that black protest was getting stronger and across the northern borders friendly white governments had disappeared to be replaced by unfriendly black ones. Certainly these new black nations provided bases for ANC guerrilla forces and white South Africans were more isolated than ever. There could be no doubt too that the South African economy was weaker. But if South Africa was close to a revolution, it was not quite there. Using the metaphor of a clock stuck at five to midnight, Johnson predicted that white South Africa would be strong enough to hold on to power until at least the 1990s.

This prediction turned out to be correct, though the country saw many changes and suffered further cruel disturbances.

South Africa and the front-line states, 1978–87

Solomon Mahlangu was one of thousands of young blacks who fled from South Africa to join the ANC in exile. In 1977 he returned to his homeland as a 'freedom-fighter' in the eyes of the ANC, as a 'terrorist' in the eyes of the South African government. He and his group killed some whites and were eventually hunted down by the security police. Mahlangu was tried, found guilty and hung. The ANC named their Tanzanian training college after him.

Solomon Mahlangu Freedom College, an ANC school in Tanzania

The term 'front-line states' describes the black states which were in the front line of the armed struggle between white South Africa and black Africa. They were Angola, Zimbabwe, Zambia, Mozambique, Botswana, Lesotho and Swaziland (see map, page 102).

The South African Defence Force (SADF) fought a

war of sorts with her neighbours throughout the 1970s and 1980s, a war of raids and counter-raids, sometimes secretly, sometimes openly, on a small scale, but a war nonetheless. At the same time South African agents fought a 'dirty war' of assassinations against the ANC leaders in exile. It has been estimated that they may have killed as many as 300 during the 1980s. One victim was Ruth First who, in 1982, was blown up by a letter bomb in her office in the Centre for African Studies at Maputo University.

Victims of an SADF raid on Matola in Mozambique, January 1981

SWAPO

SWAPO, the movement for the liberation of Namibia (see page 98), had bases for its guerrilla forces in Angola. These guerrillas struck deep into Namibia and, in retaliation, the SADF invaded Angola at least four times between 1978 and 1984. The war damaged Namibia's already weak economy. The United Nations and South Africa could not agree about the future of the country, mainly because the South African government refused to hold a general election supervised by the UN as long as Cuban troops remained in Angola.

The ANC and the front-line states

South Africa also attacked ANC bases in Mozambique. In 1983 its air force bombed a suburb of Maputo, the capital of Mozambique, in retaliation for an ANC bombing in Pretoria. If ANC guerrillas were killed, so were innocent Mozambiquan citizens. The year before, an ANC base near Maseru in Lesotho was also attacked by the SADF. Some thirty ANC guerrillas and twelve Lesotho citizens were killed.

Renamo and Unita

The South African government used another method to weaken its enemies among the front-line states by supporting rivals to the governments of these states. In Mozambique it supplied arms to the Renamo movement which opposed President Machel's government and occupied a wide area of northern and central Mozambique, while in Angola it gave active backing to the Unita forces which controlled the south-east of the country in defiance of the MPLA government.

The Southern African Development Co-ordination Conference

However much they disliked the situation, the front-line states were economically dependent upon South Africa. The major roads and railways ran to South African cities and ports. Those which did not, like the railways to Beira in Mozambique and Benguela in Angola, were closed by Renamo and Unita attacks. Between 50 and 60 per cent of the trade of Malawi, Zambia and Zimbabwe used the South African transport system and hundred of thousands of front-line citizens earned a living in South Africa.

P. W. Botha, who became Prime Minister of South Africa in 1978, tried to make use of this economic advantage to persuade the front-line states to join South Africa in a scheme of economic co-operation and development. The majority refused his offer and, instead, held a Southern African Development Co-ordination Conference (SADCC) in 1979, to seek ways of reducing their economic dependence on their hated neighbour.

The Nkomati Accord

In reality, however, South Africa was so much stronger, both militarily and economically, than the front-line states that they had to come to terms with living beside her. In 1984, the South African government agreed to withdraw its troops from southern Angola. It also signed the Nkomati Accord with Mozambique. Both countries promised not to interfere in each other's affairs. Following the Accord Mozambique gave less support to the ANC and South Africa helped Renamo less.

Despite such agreements, South Africa's relations with her neighbours remained very uneasy. Only a year later, the Angolan civil war flared up again and the SADF once more raided SWAPO bases deep inside Angola. Moreover, in 1986 and 1987, Renamo took action again against the Mozambique government, secretly aided, the Mozambique government claimed, by South Africa.

Possible solutions to South Africa's political crisis

The events of 1974–77 showed that South Africa seemed to be moving towards greater political unrest, violence and, sooner or later, a racial civil war with appalling bloodshed. How, asked South Africans, black and white, can we avoid such a catastrophe? What is the best way forward to a more peaceful future?

In the late 1970s and early 1980s, at least five clear possibilities attracted support within South Africa:

1 Continuing apartheid

The pure apartheid of Verwoerd should continue and be put into force even more ruthlessly than before. In the cities the races should continue to be strictly separated and more blacks driven from white areas. The most conservative Afrikaners supported this approach. Some of them realised that the areas allowed for the 'Bantustans' were too small to take all the blacks whom they wanted to move and they made suggestions as to how the country should be re-divided more fairly.

2 Reforming apartheid

Apartheid should be reformed but not abolished, so that it gave less offence to the blacks but the whites stayed in control. This was the approach that Botha's government tried between 1978 and 1988 and this had the support of most whites (see pages 114–15).

3 A 'grand coalition government'

Whilst agreeing that the different peoples of South Africa should generally live in separate communities and elect their own leaders, there should be a 'grand coalition government' with representatives of each of the population groups. This 'grand coalition government' should look after the needs of the minority peoples of the country with particular care and these minorities should be defended by a Bill of Rights. The term 'consociational democracy' was given to this approach which had the support of the Progressive Party, a number of church organisations and Buthelezi's *Inkatha* movement (see page 115). Between 1979 and 1983, it had some effect on the government's planning of its new constitutional proposals (see page 112).

4 Introducing a multi-racial democracy

A multi-racial democracy should be introduced with a vote for every adult. The party with the majority of votes should form the government. This was the policy of the ANC (see page 113).

5 Black government through revolution

A black government should be brought to power through a black workers' revolution. This was the policy of the Azanian People's Organisation (see page 113).

The development of business within these approaches

One important difference among these various approaches was how privately-owned (almost entirely white-owned) business would develop. In approaches 1, 2 and 3, the government would give support to private enterprise. In approach 4 the wealth of South Africa would be redistributed fairly and some private businesses would pass to public control, as suggested by the Freedom Charter (see page 77). What form that re-distribution should take and how far public ownership should replace private enterprise would be worked out, Tambo explained to a Business International Conference in London in 1987, by proper democratic discussion, once the multi-racial government was in power. In approach 5, white private enterprise would be replaced by black public ownership.

The National government tries reform

'Total onslaught, total strategy'

P. W. Botha succeeded John Vorster as Prime Minister in 1978. He came to power in unusual circumstances. Vorster was a sick man and resigned to become State President. His most likely successor as Prime Minister was Dr Connie Mulder but first he, and then Vorster too, got caught up in a financial scandal, 'Muldergate' as it became known, which forced them to resign and left the way open for Botha, who was then Minister of Defence.

By this time, the Nationalists had come to believe that white South Africa was the target of a 'total onslaught' led by the communist USSR and China who were using neighbouring countries like Mozambique and Angola and political groups in exile, particularly the ANC, to spread communist-style revolution. They also believed that the riots of 1976–77 were masterminded by the ANC as part of this 'total onslaught'. To meet this 'total onslaught', they worked out a new 'total strategy'.

Strengthening the security system and the armed forces

Part of this new strategy was to give even greater powers to the security police. Another allowed top generals and police officers a greater say in political matters through the State Security Council (SSC). General Malan, formerly the Head of the SADF, became Minister of Defence, and, after the Prime Minister, the leading member of the SSC which became the most important decision-making group in the land. A National Security Management System was set up, under the supervision of the SSC, which divided the country up into a network of security units. The main aim of these was to discover anti-government groups at an early stage and deal with them promptly.

A further part of the 'total strategy' was to increase the strength of the armed forces. After the United Nations agreed to ban the sale of weapons to South Africa, the National government expanded its own state-owned Armaments Corporation (Armscor). By 1983, Armscor produced virtually all the weapons South Africa needed to a high technical standard and was beginning to export arms to other countries. The SADF had 250 tanks, 1400 armoured cars and more than 300 fighter planes. Nor was there much doubt that South Africa had succeeded in making nuclear weapons in secret.

The regular army was about 17,000 strong of whom 5000 were black. The conscription of whites for two years' military service added another 37,000. After military service, all whites had to do another 720 days' training in the following twelve years and join the Citizen Force. In the mid-eighties, the Citizen Force numbered 130,000 and was divided into local commando units. It was trained to deal with internal rebellions as well as attacks from across the borders.

During the 1980s South Africa was the strongest military power in the whole of Africa, and by far the strongest in the southern half of the continent.

Trying to win the support of some urban blacks

Both Botha and Malan realised that if the alleged communist 'onslaught' was to be beaten back, at least some sections of the black population had to be persuaded that co-operation with the whites was worthwhile. The Soweto riots had showed that apartheid had turned most young urban blacks into bitter enemies of the whites and eager audiences for revolutionary ideas. More and more Afrikaners came to realise that Verwoerd's grand apartheid plan was not going to work and that a different approach was urgently needed. Botha and his ministers began to talk about the need for reforms. 'Apartheid as you came to know it is dead,' said Dr Piet Koornhof, Minister of Co-operation

and Development, to Americans in 1979.

The blacks whom they hoped to win over were those who had been settled in the towns for some years, who had skilled or semi-skilled jobs, whose standard of living and education was rising and who therefore had something to lose from rioting and continuous political unrest.

The Riekert, Wiehahn and De Lange Reports

The Riekert Commission (1979) reported on the situation of the urban blacks. It recommended that though the government should keep strict controls on the movement of blacks from the homelands into the cities, it should accept that the economic progress of South Africa needed a large permanent black population in 'white' areas and that this black urban population should be given better living conditions. Consequently blacks with Section 10 rights (which allowed them to live permanently in 'white' areas, see page 81) were allowed first to lease, then to buy their own homes. They could move more freely in search of employment and have first choice of jobs before the blacks from the 'homelands'.

The Wiehahn Commission (1979) reported on employment and industrial relations. It recommended greater freedom for trade unions including the formation of multi-racial ones. During the 1980s, black trade unions grew in number and became more effective in getting better wages and conditions for their members, particularly in the mines. Already the shortage of skilled labour had reduced the number of jobs reserved for whites only. This trend speeded up. Not only did a wider range of jobs open up to blacks but wages improved. In 1970, 75 per cent of all personal wealth in South Africa had been owned by whites. In 1980 this figure was down to 60 per cent.

In order to meet the employment needs of the fast-growing black population, the government calculated that the South African economy would need to grow at 5 per cent each year. It called on industry to co-operate with it in an ambitious plan of industrial development, away from the existing cities and in easy reach of the 'homelands'.

The De Lange Commission (1980–81) reported on education and recommended a massive increase in government spending on education and the end of different forms of education for the different races. While the government kept the schools racially segregated, it did raise spending on black schools considerably, both on new school buildings and on improved teachers' salaries: in 1975 the education budget for Africans stood at R 160 m; by 1983 it had risen to R 1168 m.

The traditional social segregation grew less. More theatres and cinemas allowed mixed audiences. White private schools took some black pupils. In 1985, the Mixed Marriages Act, one of the first apartheid acts to be passed after the Nationalist victory of 1948, was repealed and then, in 1986, the pass laws were repealed.

How far did these reforms really go?

Some whites thought that the reforms went too far. They saw many blacks getting better jobs and pay while their own incomes rose less fast. They also had to pay higher taxes, partly to pay for improving black conditions, such as better schools.

Most blacks did not think that they went nearly far enough. The Group Areas Act (see page 75), the cornerstone of apartheid, stayed in place. Forced removals (see page 92) continued, causing immense personal suffering. The security police were just as brutal. Most important of all, the white government seemed as determined as ever to stay in power and only carried out those reforms which did not put white control at risk.

Constitutional changes, 1983–84

The Afrikaans paper *Die Burger*, in which the picture below appeared in August 1984, reported the event as an important step towards giving other racial groups a real say in running the country and towards ending apartheid.

P. W. Botha described the constitutional changes to the country and to the world as another example of moderate reform, a cautious but genuine attempt by the whites to share power with other races.

By the new constitution of 1984, the old Senate or Upper House was abolished. The new Parliament had three sections: a House of Assembly for whites, a House of Representatives for coloureds and a House of Deputies for Indians. Representatives from these three racial groups formed the Electoral College (shown below) which chose the State President. They also attended the President's Council to advise the State President about national policy.

In fact, the new constitution did next to nothing to weaken white rule, though the more conservative Afrikaners were horrified by its apparent 'power-sharing' (see page 121). In Parliament, in the Electoral College and in the President's Council, whites could always outvote the other races.

The greatest weakness of the new constitution was that it did not include Africans. The government openly admitted that there were so many of them that they could not be included without swamping the other groups. The State President would look after African affairs. If Africans wished to take part in politics, they had, as before, the 'Bantustans' and the local urban councils.

P. W. Botha put these proposals to a white referendum in 1983 and won a two-thirds majority. He also gained the co-operation of the Coloured Labour Party and the Indian National People's Party which won general elections in 1984. However, only 30 per cent of coloureds and 24 per cent of Indians voted. The remainder thought the elections unimportant or refused to take part in what they considered a sham exercise in democracy.

Black politics in the early 1980s

The new constitution was imposed in 1984 on a country which, though more fully under the control of the security forces than in 1976–77, was still simmering.

The schools

Black school pupils remained very restless. For most of 1980 many township schools were empty since pupils refused to attend them. Although the government vastly increased its spending on black education, it

The Electoral College which elected P. W. Botha as State President. This was the first time that a multi-racial group had sat in the House of Assembly

could not convince pupils that it was providing an education equal to that of the whites.

Trade unions

Black trade unions grew in number and in confidence. They were ready to negotiate toughly with employers and to strike if need be. Where in 1974 only 14,167 working days had been lost through strikes, the equivalent figure for 1982 was 365,337. The black National Union of Mineworkers led by Cyril Ramaphosa organised major strikes in 1985 and 1987.

AZAPO

The Azanian People's Organisation (AZAPO) was a new political organisation with close links with the trade unions. It was founded in 1978. 'Azania' was the name which it would give to South Africa once it was liberated from white rule. AZAPO was the successor of Black Consciousness since it taught that blacks must free themselves from dependence on whites. It also believed that white racism and white capitalism were closely linked and looked forward to a future when South Africa (Azania) would become a black workers' revolutionary republic.

ANC

Within the townships, the ANC remained the most powerful political organisation. Led from exile by Oliver Tambo, it sent more than 4000 guerrillas back into South Africa between 1977 and 1984. Most of them were young people who had fled after the Soweto riots. Many of their targets were buildings like oil refineries and power stations which could be damaged without loss of life. However, they also attacked buildings which housed people whom they thought to be supporters of the government, like the Air Force headquarters in Pretoria (1983) and the dockyards in Durban (1984). In both these cases their bombs killed many innocent people, including blacks.

The Nkomati Accord of 1984 (see page 109) meant that the ANC had to close its guerrilla bases in Mozambique, so it then concentrated more on stirring up mass action in the townships. Nelson Mandela, the imprisoned ANC leader, was by far the most popular black leader and the ANC campaigned all over the world to persuade international leaders to put pressure on P. W. Botha to free him.

The ANC still looked forward to a future based on the Freedom Charter, a multi-racial, one-person, one-vote democracy (see pages 76 and 77), leaning towards socialism.

FIREMEN DWARFED BY A MOUNTAIN OF FLAMES AS A REFINERY BLAZES

Firemen pictured challenging a wall of flame at the Natref refinery yesterday. Late last night the fires at Natref and Sasol One were said to be under control — there was no danger of them spreading.

Picture: RAYMOND PRESTON

June 1980: ANC bombers blow up an oil refinery

SOURCE WORK: The effects of the reforms in Soweto

Source A: Life in Soweto in 1978 and 1980

In his book *The White Tribe of Africa*, David Harrison describes two interviews he had with Solly Madlala:

' "Life in Soweto is bad, even terrible (said Madlala as we filmed his candle-lit supper in 1978). There is actually no life worth living. At any moment you may be killed or murdered. You are not sure of what you are doing, or where you are when you are not white... We are unhappy with such a way that we are starving... But they live splendidly; they have got everything."

Two years later Solly Madlala was a changed man. His sons had full-time jobs, perhaps because of the uplift in the economy, perhaps *because of the Riekert proposals,* "insiders" with permanent residence were being given precedence for available work. Whatever the reason, money coming into the Madlala household had more than doubled. Madlala's own wages had gone up by ten rand a week (£5.50).

There was another respect in which Solly Madlala's life had changed: the abolition of separate queues for blacks and whites at the Post Office had transformed his working day:

"Coming to the Post Office now, and having to wait and do all that jazz because there were three whites; we had to wait hours on end, we being a hundred or so... Without any commotion everybody is being served, like a person. Even we black people are being seen as people living, human beings. Not like before." '

Source B: Black residents of Selection Park

Selection Park was a new, better quality housing scheme in Soweto paid for by the Urban Foundation. This organisation was set up by South African businesses to improve black living conditions and to create a black middle class who would support Western capitalist values. Two residents were asked whether socialism or capitalism would best serve the needs of South Africa's future. One, a personnel manager, replied:

'If there is ever going to be change in this country, the majority will not opt for capitalism, because it is seen as bringing the very suffering we are enduring now.'

Another, an insurance official, added:

'I might prefer capitalism, but I know most blacks would opt for socialism... I am part of them. I don't consider myself part of this so-called black middle class, but with the masses. That is where I have to throw in my lot.'

Source C: An advertisement in the *Weekly Mail*

Shell supports the right of all people to live where they choose.

Working to make a difference now

The international oil company Shell placed this advertisement in an anti-government newspaper in April 1989

Source D: Oliver Tambo being interviewed by a Mozambiquan reporter, July 1983

'REPORTER: What is your assessment of P. W. Botha's "reforms"...?

TAMBO: These reforms do not arise from a change of heart... They are reforms maybe in form ...but in substance there is no change. Still, the fact that Botha has to get results from the black community, and try and win over the Indians and the so-called coloureds, means that he is in desperate need of their support. The situation has changed against him . . .

REPORTER: Basically, then, apartheid cannot be reformed?

TAMBO: It is not possible. You either have apartheid or you don't. You can't amend it from the top.'

Preparing for Power: Oliver Tambo Speaks, Heinemann, 1987

1 In what ways had the life of the Madlala family improved by 1980? Explain the phrase 'because of the Riekert proposals' (Source A).

2 Why should the government and white businessmen be so concerned for the black middle class? How satisfied would they have been with the comments of the inhabitants of Selection Park (Source B)?

3 Shell is a major international oil company, one of the world's largest businesses.
(a) What particular part of apartheid is the advertisement (Source C) attacking?
(b) Why might Shell have decided to place such an advertisement in an anti-government newspaper?

4 In Source D, what opinion had the ANC of the value of Botha's 'reforms'. Why did it think Botha was trying them?

5 What did Tambo mean when he said that 'apartheid' could not be reformed?

Buthelezi and Inkatha

Another important black group was *Inkatha*, a Zulu cultural organisation, which Chief Mangosuthu Buthelezi turned into a well-organised political movement.

Buthelezi walked a tightrope, strongly criticising the government, while working within the system. In 1972 he became Chief Minister of the government-made 'homeland' of KwaZulu, but, unlike Matanzima of the Transkei, he refused to accept Pretoria's offer of full independence. Instead he had many discussions with the neighbouring white Natal provincial council and white businesses. Together they worked out a way of combining Natal and KwaZulu which included all races and was more genuinely multi-racial than the government's 1984 constitution. Not surprisingly the government refused to allow it to be used when it was first suggested in 1985.

Buthelezi agreed that Mandela was the proper leader of the blacks but he criticised the ANC for its guerrilla attacks and for its support for economic sanctions against South Africa (see page 118). Other black politicians disliked him because he was too ready to work with white business and too much the Zulu leader. 'He has left the nation and joined the tribe' was how one Sowetan leader put it. Between 1985 and 1987 the differences between *Inkatha* and other black groups exploded into violence, particularly in Natal-KwaZulu (see page 117).

UDF

The United Democratic Front (UDF) came into existence in 1983 to fight the new constitution. It was a movement which aimed to unite all the black resistance groups but not itself become a political party. The idea for it started with the World Council of Churches and churchmen like Dr Boesak and Archbishop Tutu played a leading part in it. The UDF grew at an enormous pace, reaching 2,000,000 members in 1985, coming from all the racial groups. Like the ANC it looked forward to a future based on the Freedom Charter.

Protest, violence and repression, 1984–87

The 1985–86 riots

'Sharpeville was the revolt of the parents. Soweto was the children. Now it's both,' said an experienced black news photographer in 1986.

The new 1984 constitution deeply angered the blacks. However much P. W. Botha might talk about reform and power-sharing, they now knew that he would never peacefully share power with them. At the same time, they were angry about other things; about steep rent rises, about continuing forced removals (like the one from the huge Crossroads squatter camp near Cape Town), and about the poor condition of black education. The UDF held rallies all over the country and other black political groups protested too.

As with Sharpeville and Soweto, police actions turned anger into violence. In March 1985, at Uitenhage in the Eastern Cape, police officers watching a black funeral, which was also a political demonstration, panicked and fired on the mourners, killing nineteen. Rioting spread all over the country.

Already in his New Year message for 1985, Oliver Tambo had ordered the ANC to make the urban townships ungovernable. Black tenants refused to pay their rents and ignored the orders of local councils. Black councillors and policemen who were seen as friends of apartheid were harassed. Some, fearing for their lives, fled to tents erected in white areas. Other blacks, believed to be government spies and informers, were killed by the dreadful 'necklace', a tyre filled with petrol put around their necks and set alight.

The state of emergency, 1985

By July 1985, parts of South Africa had become ungovernable and P. W. Botha declared a state emergency in thirty-six separate districts. This state of emergency, the first for twenty-five years (since Sharpeville), meant that the powers of the police were further increased and the army went into the townships.

The state of emergency had little immediate effect. Violence continued and, night after night, television viewers all over the world watched horrifying scenes of armoured cars and soldiers with guns and whips fighting against blacks armed only with knives and stones.

American banks started to withdraw their money, the value of South Africa's currency, the rand, dropped alarmingly, and in the autumn of 1985, the country faced a financial disaster which was only avoided by a deal put together in secret by international bankers.

Disorder, violence and killings (increasingly of blacks by blacks, see page 117) continued, and worldwide protests swelled to a deafening chorus. At one moment P. W. Botha would hint at further major reforms, at the next he was snarling defiance at the world. In June 1986, he extended the state of emergency to the whole country and imposed drastic controls on news reports. Many foreign journalists were expelled and the Bureau of State Information censored every report about the unrest and other aspects of political life in South Africa.

During 1985–86 the police detained at least 8500 blacks, including many young children. Thousands lost their lives in the violence and leading black politicians were banned. By the end of 1986, the security forces seemed more in control but, since most of the 'news' which came out of South Africa in 1986 and 1987 was provided by the government, it was hard to know how things really were compared with what the government wanted the world to believe.

Riot police round up protesting students, Johannesburg, 1986

SOURCE WORK: Protest and violence, 1983–87

Source A: The UDF keeps protest alive: poster, 1985

The UDF keeps protest alive: poster, 1985

Source B: The Rev Allan Boesak

He is addressing a UDF meeting in the coloured town of Mitchell's Plain near Cape Town, 20 August 1983:

'Let me remind you of three little words... The first word is "all". We want all our rights, not just a few token handouts which the government sees fit to give – we want *all* our rights. And we want all of South Africa's people to have their rights. Not just a selected few, not just "Coloureds" or "Indians", after they have been made honorary whites. We want the rights of all South Africans, including those whose citizenship has already been stripped away by this government.

The second word is the word "here". We want all our rights *here* in a united, undivided South Africa. We do not want them in impoverished homelands, we do not want them in our separate little group areas. We want them in this land which one day we shall once again call our own.

The third word is the word "now". We want all our rights, we want them here, and we want them now. We have been waiting for so long, we have been struggling for so long. We have pleaded, cried, petitioned too long now. We have been jailed, exiled, killed for too long. *Now* is the time.'

Source C: Oliver Tambo

He broadcast to South Africa on Radio Freedom, 22 July 1985

'Our own tasks are very clear. To bring about the kind of society that is visualised [looked forward to] in the Freedom Charter, we have to break down and destroy the old order. We have to make apartheid unworkable and our country ungovernable. The accomplishment of these tasks will create the situation for us to overthrow the apartheid regime and for power to pass into the hands of the people as a whole.'

Source D: 'Towards a Black Civil War in South Africa'

This extract is from *The Economist*, November 1987. It is a British journal aimed at business people:

'Around 2,600 South Africans have died as a result of political violence since September 1984. Up to the end of 1985, about half the deaths were the work of the security forces and a third resulted from fighting among rival black groups. Since then the proportions have been reversed. Last month, at least 50 people died in fighting between Inkatha and its black rival, the United Democratic Front.

The fiercest battles have been in the black townships around Pietermaritzburg in Natal. A local Christian group... calculates that 50 people were killed there between January and August. Another 80 died in September and October, after Inkatha held a youth congress...

Rather than stopping the fighting, the police are being drawn into it. The UDF complain that the police collude with [secretly support] Inkatha. Inkatha turns the accusation round... pointing to a gruesome episode... when 13 members of the Inkatha youth brigade... were killed... (and) three black policemen were later arrested for questioning about the attack...

The UDF wants simple majority rule and an immediate end to apartheid: it is generally contemptuous of Mr Buthelezi's clever gradualism [changing things slowly step by step] . . . Yet the gulf between blacks may slowly be narrowing. After three years of refusing to talk, Inkatha and the UDF announced a ceasefire for October 6th.'

1 (a) In Source A what do the initials 'UDF' stand for?
   (b) What was the UDF?

2 (a) What were the 'three little words' of which Allan Boesak reminded his audience in 1983 (Source B)?
   (b) If Boesak had had his way, what changes would then have taken place in South Africa?

3 (a) What was the Freedom Charter to which Tambo refers in Source C?
   (b) What did he wish to happen as the first step to making real the ideas of the Charter?

4 (a) Source D talks about a 'black civil war'. Who were the two sides in this 'civil war'?
   (b) In what ways did they disagree about how to end apartheid?

Economic developments

The beginnings of economic sanctions against South Africa in the 1970s

The rapid growth of the South African economy had made white South Africans rich. The growth had been fuelled by money which American, British and European businesses, supported by their governments, had invested. Now, as world opinion became even more disgusted by the actions of the National government and the way it dealt with the black protests, so Western businesses and their governments began to change their attitudes towards South Africa.

In the 1960s most Western companies had avoided criticising apartheid. They were in South Africa to make money, which meant working with, not against, the government.

The 1970s saw a slow change of attitude. In 1973 the *Guardian* newspaper published a number of articles which showed that of one hundred British companies in South Africa only three were paying their black workers wages enough to keep them out of real poverty. Famous companies like Tate and Lyle (sugar) and Rowntree Mackintosh (sweets) were paying particularly low wages. The US-based Polaroid company investigated its South African branch in 1970. It then raised black wages by 20 per cent and put one-third of its South African profits into black education. Such publicity helped to raise wages in foreign-owned companies.

The Sullivan Principles

Leon Sullivan was a black American Baptist preacher on the board of General Motors, America's, and the world's, largest car manufacturer. The company had a factory in South Africa, near Port Elizabeth. Sullivan was greatly concerned about the situation of South Africa's blacks and persuaded General Motors and other American companies to agree to the 'Sullivan Principles'. In their South African factories and offices, there would be equal pay for equal work, no segregation and no jobs reserved for whites, and better training and living conditions for blacks. However, many critics of apartheid argued that such principles were not enough. Western businesses should pull out of South Africa completely (disinvestment) and Western governments should stop trading in goods vital to South Africa's economic needs. Only if the Nationalists suffered from such economic punishments (sanctions) would they give political rights to the blacks.

Reagan, Thatcher and economic sanctions

The move towards economic sanctions gained pace in the late seventies after Soweto and the death of Steve Biko but it slowed down when Margaret Thatcher became Britain's Prime Minister in 1979 and Ronald Reagan became America's President in 1980.

Both Ronald Reagan and Margaret Thatcher said they wanted to see the end of apartheid but both argued that it would come faster and more peacefully if South Africa continued to get richer and the blacks shared more of the wealth. If British and American businesses continued trading in South Africa, they would be able to influence the whites for the better, keep the vital minerals flowing to the West and stop the communists becoming more powerful in Africa.

The growing demand for economic sanctions

The crisis of 1984–85, which the world watched on its television screens until Botha declared a state of emergency, lent new strength to the economic sanctions campaign. In the USA, anti-apartheid shareholders gave their directors increasingly rough times at shareholders' meetings. Companies' profits from their South African interests fell and South Africa's economic future looked risky. In 1985 many American companies left South Africa and sold their offices and factories to local

A MAJORITY of black South Africans oppose economic sanctions and violence as a means of ending apartheid, according to a poll conducted on behalf of the *Independent* and ITN, the television company.

Although a minority said that sanctions should be imposed on South Africa — even at the cost of their own jobs — the findings reveal that most blacks are unwilling to jeopardise job opportunities and financial well-being, and see the presence of foreign companies in the country as helping to sponsor change rather than support apartheid.

The survey, conducted by Markinor, an independent South African research company, of 550 South Africans living in all the main metropolitan areas showed that 54,7 percent were against the imposition of economic sanctions to bring about the abolition of apartheid.

Of the minority who supported sanctions, nearly three-quarters wanted them imposed even if it meant black job losses. However, a much smaller proportion of the total polled (only 8,8 percent) were in favour of sanctions if it cost them their own jobs.

According to the survey, not only do most black South Africans dismiss sanctions as a solution to the country's racial problems, they are also opposed to violence as a means of ending apartheid.

Over 61 percent said it was wrong to use violence. About one third of the more radical respondents (those who support sanctions even if it caused unemployment) believed violence was justified.

The survey shows that a majority of blacks believe South Africa's most pressing problems are economic rather than political.

Almost 58 percent said their biggest concern was either jobs, wages or unemployment. Only 13,5 percent mentioned petty apartheid regulations and a surprisingly small 1,6 percent the Group Areas Act which demarcates residential areas along racial lines.

Regardless of attitudes to sanctions, nearly a third singled out unemployment as their key concern — partly a reflection of the fact that over 60 percent of those polled were unemployed.

The greatest concern about unemployment — 33.3 percent — was registered among those who supported sanctions

FOCUS

SANCTIONS, VIOLENCE NOT RIGHT WAY — POLL

A SURVEY by the London newspaper the *Independent* and ITN television network shows surprising resistance to sanctions by black South Africans. They oppose violence as a way to end apartheid.

They fear that sanctions could jeopardise jobs and undermine living standards, and see the presence of foreign companies as a hope of bringing change.

ARCHBISHPOP Tutu . . . pro-sanctions.

MARGARET Thatcher . . . anti-sanctions.

ment by foreign companies had little popular support. The vast majority — 77,9 percent — said that foreign firms should stay in South Africa and improve the conditions of their workers.

Only just over a third of those who supported sanctions even if it produces general unemployment said that foreign firms should sell their businesses and leave South Africa.

There was also considerable support — 37,3 percent — for the notion that foreign companies have a beneficial role to play in helping to end apartheid. Under a quarter saw foreign businesses as supporting apartheid.

For and against sanctions: an article in the Sowetan, *31 March 1989*

buyers. Also in 1985, the British-based Barclays Bank sold its large South African bank network, partly because of a student boycott in Britain which had lasted many years and had damaged its home business.

Most of South Africa's black leaders – Tambo for the ANC, Boesak and Tutu for the UDF – supported international 'disinvestment' or the withdrawal of overseas companies' money from South African businesses as well as further economic sanctions by Western governments. Although black workers would suffer, they believed that short-term suffering would be worthwhile because it would lead to black liberation.

The US Congress and the Common Market back some sanctions, 1986

Within the American Congress opinion swung in favour of sanctions against South Africa. Congress pushed aside Reagan's obstinate opposition and, in 1986, banned trading in a number of goods including steel, cut airline links and forbade government investment in South Africa.

The British Commonwealth wanted to go at least as far as the USA but Thatcher, sure of the support of her Conservative Party, opposed such a move. To the great anger of the other Commonwealth leaders, Britain would only agree to minor sanctions.

Britain's coolness towards sanctions which West Germany, South Africa's most important trading partner within the Common Market, shared, meant that the Common Market countries (including Britain) would only agree in 1986 to banning the export of arms and the import of iron, steel and Krugerrands (gold coins). These bans affected only 3.5 per cent of South African exports to the Common Market. If they had included coal, which they nearly did, the proportion would have been nearer 20 per cent.

White business leaders talk to the ANC

During the crisis of 1985–86, South African business leaders became very worried. They watched the value of the rand collapse; the Johannesburg stock exchange was closed for four days during a desperate financial crisis; and their American and European friends deserted them. Some realised that the future must lie with the blacks and began talking not only to black leaders at home, like Buthelezi, but also to the ANC. In September 1985 in Zambia, at a hunting lodge in a game park not far from Lusaka, some leading South African business people, including Gavin Relly who headed up AAC, met Oliver Tambo and other ANC leaders for an apparently friendly six-hour meeting.

Not much beyond goodwill came from this and other meetings and, by 1987, white business leaders had less to worry them in the short term. The National

'Constructive and rewarding involvement': the American Fortune Magazine *supports trade with South Africa*

government had won back control of most of the townships. Although the country's financial and economic problems were serious, they had not been as disastrous as the business leaders feared. Many Western companies had left, it was true, but the local companies which had bought their businesses were prospering. Sanctions, such as they were, seemed merely a nuisance.

The economic situation

Nonetheless things were different. Before the 1984–86 crisis, white South Africans were confident that, when it came to the crunch, Western governments and banks would support them and prevent a black government coming to power. After the crisis, that confidence had gone.

In simple business terms the future did not look at all bright. The healthy expansion of the 1960s and early 1970s was only a memory. Whereas between 1964 and 1974, the South African growth rate had averaged more than 5 per cent, the 1980–84 average was only 1.5 per cent. Manufacturing production actually fell, as did the average income of the whites. Though the government seemed back in control, the long-term future of the country was so uncertain that foreign businesses were likely to continue to place their investment money elsewhere.

White politics, 1978–87

Botha's dilemma

If P. W. Botha was to win the confidence of South Africa's blacks and of the rest of the world, he had to carry out major reforms quickly. However, if he pushed ahead rapidly with whole-scale changes, he would have the greatest difficulty keeping his National Party with him. Consequently, he was extremely cautious, although he told his party that South Africa must 'adapt or die' and often talked about the end of apartheid, about freeing Nelson Mandela, and about major reforms being just around the corner. Cautious though he was, however, he could not prevent splits amongst the Afrikaners.

Splits in the National Party

The National Party had split already. In 1968, three cabinet ministers had broken with Vorster and founded the Herstigte (Restored) Nasionale Party (HNP). They thought that Vorster was betraying the pure apartheid of Verwoerd when he allowed foreign countries to be represented by black ambassadors and overseas sports teams which included black players. The followers of pure apartheid came to be known as *verkramptes* (the narrow ones) and those ready to consider reforms as *verligtes* (the enlightened ones).

In the 1981 general election, the NP won 131 seats and the PFP twenty-six. However, though the HNP won no seats, it polled 191,000 votes (13 per cent) against the PFP's 265,000 (18 per cent) and the NP's 778,000 (53 per cent). The NP could not afford to ignore its existence.

A more serious split took place in 1982. A strong group within the NP, led by Dr Treurnicht, disliked Botha's proposals for constitutional reform, especially the idea of power-sharing with the coloureds and Indians. Having tried and failed to drive Botha from the NP leadership, eighteen MPs left the NP to found the Conservative Party (CP). During the crisis of 1984–86, the CP did well in by-elections in the Transvaal. An even more extreme right-wing group appeared in 1984, the Afrikaner Resistance Movement. With its banners, uniforms, extreme racist ideas and obvious pleasure in breaking up meetings by violence, it had uncomfortable similarities to Hitler's Nazi movement.

The 1987 Election

In the whites-only general election of 1987, the NP used its control of television to try to convince the electors that it alone could defend them against the onslaught of black revolutionaries and international communism. For its part the PFP put itself forward as the one party which could bring about a real partnership between blacks and whites. In contrast, the CP criticised Botha for rushing ahead with his dangerous reforms.

At first sight, the election results suggested that Botha had won another overwhelming victory. The NP won 122 seats (52 per cent), the CP twenty-two (26 per

Year	Parties National	United	Progressive	New Republic	Progressive Federal	Conservative
1966	126	39	1	–	–	–
1970	118	47	1	–	–	–
1974	123	41	7	–	–	–
1977	137	–	–	10	17	–
1981	131	–	–	8	26	–
1987	122	–	–	1	19	22

The United Party collapsed completely in 1977 and the Progressive Federal Party replaced it as the main white opposition party.

The changing fortunes of the white political parties, 1966–87

SOURCE WORK: Sanctions against South Africa, 1985–86: for and against

Source A: Oliver Tambo

Speaking to the Royal Commonwealth Society in London, on 23 June 1986, he argued that all members of the UN should impose sanctions on South Africa:

'The argument for comprehensive and mandatory sanctions is, of course, that such a massive blow would make it almost impossible for the apartheid regime to stay in power much longer. Such comprehensive measures would naturally include financial and trade sanctions, an oil embargo [ban], the termination [ending] of all air and maritime links... The alternative... is that we will be left with nothing but... to fight it out with everything we have. The consequences of this are too ghastly to contemplate.'

Source B: Margaret Thatcher

'... was totally sceptical about [did not believe in] sanctions after the fiascos over Rhodesia; and her scepticism was reinforced by successive South African visitors to Number 10 during 1985, including Chief Buthelezi, Helen Suzman (of the PFP) and Harry Oppenheimer (chairman of AAC) who assured her that the blacks' support for the ANC was much exaggerated.... She was convinced that she had a special influence on President Botha... and believed that she could influence the Afrikaner government towards peaceful and necessary reforms if she did not threaten them .... "To me it is absolutely absurd," she said in July 1986, "that people should be prepared to put increasing power into the hands of the Soviet Union on the grounds that they disapprove of apartheid in South Africa."

Anthony Sampson, *Black and Gold*, Hodder and Stoughton, 1987

Source C

SOARING COAL PRICES WORLD WIDE PREDICTED IN FACE OF SANCTIONS

World coal prices are set to soar to more than $40 a ton if sanctions against South Africa are implemented by leading Western nations. The United States and Australia which are leading the campaign for the boycott of South African coal, uranium and steel products are high-cost suppliers.

South African steam coal is currently priced at about $26 a ton compared with the $40 a ton from the US.

South Africa is the third largest exporter of coal in the world after Australia.

In 1985 South Africa exported 44 million tons of coal mainly to the European Economic Community and Japan. More than 20 percent of Japan's coal comes from South Africa and an embargo would force the Japanese to buy the higher priced US or Australian coal which would probably escalate in price again without competition from South Africa.

Japan's Federation of Electric Power Companies says a South African coal import ban is unlikely to lead to a shortage of steam coal but it fears Australia in particular and other suppliers will take the opportunity to hike their prices.

South Africa's expulsion from the export market would have a major impact on many industries in the Western world. A one third increase in the price of coal would have a significant effect on numerous consumer pro-

ducts as well as domestic power costs in some countries.

Estimates of exploitable coal reserves in South Africa are 115.5 billion tons, of which 58.4 billion tons are considered economically recoverable.

It has been estimated that the exploitable reserves will last for at least another 400 years.

Between 1970 and 1981 the South African coal export trade grew from 1.2 million tons - one percent of the world's exports -to nearly 30 million tons, or 15 percent of world exports.

The huge Richards Bay coal terminal north of Durban has

INSIDE THIS ISSUE

WATER a new era in communication.

HOUSING and $500,000 a day on new projects.

US CORPORATIONS spend big on social projects.

SOUTH WEST AFRICA resources threatened by fishing fleets.

given South Africa the capacity to export annually up to 80 million tons of coal by the 1990's.

A survey by the South African Chamber of Mines Collieries committee, found that more than 35 000 coal workers are migrants from outside the borders of South Africa. Each black mine worker provides a living for an average of six dependants.

With a total of 95 000 blacks in the industry this represents 570 000 people dependent on continuing employment being provided in the coal industry.

Real average black wages increased by more than 300 percent in the period 1971-84 while average white real wages increased by slightly more than seven percent.

The government has also set the end of 1986 as a deadline for full participation in all job categories by blacks, thus eliminating the remnants of job discrimination in the industry.

It has given the reluctant white unions the deadline to agree on removing discrimination or have it imposed on the industry by legislation.

Sanctions will be expensive, suggests Southern Africa Business News, *October/November 1986*

1   What are economic sanctions? How far had they been imposed on South Africa by the end of 1986? To what extent were they a problem to South Africa (a) economically, (b) psychologically?

2   What post did Tambo hold in 1985 (Source A)? What sort of sanctions did he want? Although he knew that blacks would suffer from such sanctions, why did he still want them?

3   For what reasons did Mrs Thatcher oppose sanctions (Source B)? Which South Africans did she listen to rather than to Oliver Tambo? Why did she think that sanctions against South Africa would make the Soviety Union stronger?

4   What arguments does the *Southern Africa Business News* (Source C) use to put other countries off sanctions? Was coal included in the sanctions of the USA and the Common Market in 1985–86?

cent) and the PFP nineteen (14 per cent). However, the NP vote had dropped slightly from 1981 and the PFP had done badly. The Conservatives, in contrast, had done well. Worried by the fall in their standard of living and end of the colour-bar, which increased the competition from blacks for jobs, 37 per cent of Afrikaners voted CP. The large NP majority included more British votes than ever before.

During the years 1948–77, the National Party had held on to political power by keeping the Afrikaners united behind it. The success of the CP was, therefore, a serious worry to Botha and caused him to act with even greater caution.

The blacks and the white election, 1987

The blacks greeted the whites-only election day with strikes, demonstrations and school boycotts. Black newspapers like the *Sowetan* and *City Press* commented that a whites-only election had nothing to do with South Africa's real needs.

Nonetheless black leaders were shocked by the white vote which seemed to them a clear vote against reform. Buthelezi feared for the future of the country and warned that the blacks would see the vote as proving that the only way to bring the whites to their senses was by violence. 'Never in the history of the country has the white electorate been more aware of the international and external threats to the very fabric of South Africa,' he said, 'yet whites deliberately voted to support white privilege.'

At a joint press conference the day after the election, Dr Boesak and Archbishop Tutu warned that South Africa was entering into the dark ages of her history. 'The despondency in the air will deepen,' said Archbishop Tutu, 'and so will the anger of the black community, where even up until now, an amazing degree of goodwill still exists. Neither Dr Boesak nor I want sanctions but this is the only way to bring about a resolution to South Africa's problems as quickly as possible with as little violence as possible.'

The situation in 1987

After the Soweto riots of 1976–77, the revolution to bring black majority rule did not happen. Ten more years of repression, rioting, murders, bannings, detentions and war followed. Was the clock still stuck at five minutes to midnight in 1987 and had the balance of power not shifted at all from white to black?

Things had changed but in important ways they were still much the same. The whites were more divided but not divided enough to weaken their political power. The blacks, through their trade unions, the UDF and the schools, were harder to keep down, but bannings and detentions made effective political opposition impossible and rivalries like that between *Inkatha* and the UDF kept them too weak to challenge white control seriously. The ANC in exile and the front-line states could not defeat the South African army. As for the rest of the world, the Soviet Union became less and less interested in stirring up black revolution, while America, Britain and the Common Market, though ready to impose limited economic sanctions on South Africa, refused to give active support to the ANC for fear of causing a bloodbath.

Nonetheless the balance was shifting. The population was growing. Estimates showed it reaching 45 million by 2000 with the whites as a smaller minority. The ever-larger black population would be better educated, better employed and better paid. It seemed unthinkable that it should not take control of its destiny before long.

In 1987, a group of experts on South Africa met to consider how well R. W. Johnson's predictions of 1977 (see page 108) had stood up to the events of the following ten years. They decided that he had foretold the future reasonably well. They then asked themselves the same question: 'Can South Africa survive?' Their answer was much the same as Johnson's. A revolutionary overthrow of the white government was very unlikely in the near future but the country was becoming ungovernable. They concluded: 'We might not at present be much nearer the hour, but it is more conceivable [possible to see] than ever before that we shall reach the other side of midnight.'

SOURCE WORK: The 1987 general election

Source A

Dear PFP leadership,

We're three days away from the election and you still haven't grasped what it is about.

We'll try one more time. So please listen carefully to some real experts:

> **"Our aim is to gain control of the two great treasure houses on which the West depends – the energy treasure house of the Persian Gulf and the mineral treasure house of Central and Southern Africa."**
>
> Pres. Brezhnev of the Soviet Union (1973).

Even you should know that in South Africa they're working at this through the ANC – 23 out of the 30 members of the ANC national executive committee are communists on Moscow's payroll.

Yet you want to unban them?

Here's another one:

> **"The struggle in South Africa is not between Blacks and Whites. It's between the supporters of genuine freedom and stability and those who wish to force a socialist dictatorship on South Africa with the help of international terrorism."**
>
> Pres. P.W. Botha.

It must be clear even to you, that the PFP's policy of publicly, consistently and bitterly opposing laws designed to neutralise revolutionaries before they do their evil work, of condemning and criticising the Police and SADF's efforts to prevent the ANC's 'people's war', is doing a great job for the ANC.

Finally, listen to another expert on how to take over a country:

> **". . . when a country is demoralised, you can take it over without firing a shot."**
>
> Lenin.

The PFP's belief that you can talk the communists out of what they want, is naive to the point of being stupid. It's like saying the PFP can talk communists out of communism and their goal of world domination.

And by urging South Africans who truly desire peace to believe this, you're doing a great job of demoralising them. Because you simply create false hope.

Isn't it time the PFP leadership decided whose side it is on?

Because on 6 May the voters of South Africa are going to show whose side they're on.

They're going to vote for realism. They're going to vote NP.

Vote **NP** It makes sense!

Compiled and issued by J C J van Rensburg 118 Jonssen Street Braamfontein

NP electioneering, 1987: an election advertisement

Source B: Oliver Tambo

He was speaking in London, three weeks after the election:

'A terrible collision between ourselves and our opponents is inevitable [bound to happen]. Many battles will be fought and many lives lost throughout the region. In preparation for this the Pretoria regime had identified the defeat of the democratic movement as the centrepiece of state policy. Yet the outcome is not in doubt. Having reached the crossroads, the masses of our people have decided that our country must advance as rapidly as possible to the situation where they, black and white, will govern themselves together an equals. Whatever the cost, there is no doubt that we will win.'

Source C: P. W. Botha

In an interview in 1977 he said:

'Basically we [Afrikaners] are a very friendly people, a deeply Christian people and we should like to see others live in peace because we know ourselves what it is to be persecuted. I personally know what my family had to pay in the history of South Africa for our survival. But one thing you must accept from me: if they force us to hit back, we'll use everything which we have at our disposal.'

Source D: Township song sung at youth rallies in Soweto, 1986

I wonder what it will be like
When we sit with Tambo
and tell him about the fall of the Boers

1   (a)   Who could vote in the 1987 general election?
    (b)   By what arguments (Source A) did the Nationalists try to win votes?
    (c)   What was the PFP?
    (d)   Who won the election?

2   What did Tambo (Source B) think would be the main effect of the election result?

3   (a)   In Source C about whom was Botha talking when he said 'if *they* force us to hit back'?
    (b)   Comment on his statement that 'we Afrikaners are a very friendly people, a deeply Christian people . . .'

4   Will the youth of Soweto sit with Tambo and tell him about the fall of the Boers? If they do, what will it have been like?

1987–90: De Klerk succeeds Botha and the 1989 election

Almost at once the minute hand began to move nearer the hour of revolution. Under the pressure of economic sanctions the National government stayed on the path of reform. Within South Africa, it ended the pass laws and it also withdrew its troops from Namibia in return for the Cubans pulling out of Angola. Namibia gained its independence in 1989 and SWAPO, led by Sam Nujoma, won the first general election there.

Botha called another general election for September 1989 but resigned before it was held because of ill-health and arguments with his ministers. F. W. de Klerk succeeded him as State President and leader of the National Party.

The Nationalists won the election but with a sharply reduced majority. They lost seats both to the Conservatives and to the Democrats (a new reforming party in the PFP tradition). The Nationalists won ninety-three seats, the Conservatives thirty-nine and the Democrats thirty.

De Klerk fought the election as a genuine reformer who would bring changes to benefit all racial groups and give blacks a greater say in political matters. While insisting that he would not allow changes which would end his own and his party's power, soon after his election victory he allowed black political demonstrations and released important ANC leaders like Walter Sisulu who had been in prison for more than twenty-five years.

For his part, Tambo, who had suffered a stroke in 1989 and was convalescing in hospital in Sweden, offered the hand of friendship to de Klerk if he continued on the path of reform. 'He may earn a place alongside the peacemakers of our country', Tambo said, '. . . if, on the other hand, he continues to entertain the illusion that he can perpetuate [keep going] apartheid by the use of force, he condemns himself to disappear into the dim mists of history.'

De Klerk seemed determined to prove himself a peacemaker. In a major speech to the South African Parliament in February 1990 he ended the thirty-year-old ban on the ANC, the PAC, the South African Communist Party and thirty other anti-apartheid organisations. He also suspended the death penalty, eased some of the press controls of the state of emergency and declared that very soon Nelson Mandela would be released unconditionally, a promise which he soon kept. 'Walk through the open door,' he said to black political leaders, 'take your place at the negotiating table together with the government and other leaders who have important bases inside and outside parliament. Henceforth everyone's political points of view will be tested against their realism, their workability and their fairness. The time for negotiation has arrived.'

The British Broadcasting Company's television news described de Klerk's speech as 'the most radical shift since the apartheid system was introduced'. The *Independent* newspaper of London went further. It was, it declared, 'the death-knell of apartheid'.

Were they right, or was it another false dawn?

The Voortrekker spirit lives on: a family celebrating the 150th anniversary of the 'Great' Trek near Johannesburg, 1988

Sam Nujoma, the SWAPO leader, shakes hands with one of his followers to celebrate the ceasefire with South Africa, 1989

Walter Sisulu united with his wife Albertina in 1989 after twenty-five years in prison

Nelson Mandela salutes well-wishers as he leaves
Victor Verster prison, 11 February 1990

A summary of four major themes

1 Economic development: farming, mining and manufacturing

Farming, from the earliest times to about AD 1870

About AD 1100
Khoisan hunter-gatherers and nomadic cattle farmers are spread across the country. Black Bantu-speaking farmers are settling in more eastern areas.

About 1100–1650
Black farmers grow in number and settle more of the country to the east of the Great Fish river.

1652–1780
Following the setting-up of the Cape Town base by the Dutch, whites settle the area from the Cape to the Great Fish river. Their farms provide food, mainly cattle and sheep, to Cape Town and to ships passing to and fro between Europe and the Indies. The further they settle from the Cape, the more they farm simply to maintain themselves and their families.

The whites take the best grazing land from the Khoisan who, for the most part, become their labourers.

1780–1870
White farmers move further along the east coast and deeper into the interior.

1815–35
The Difaqane destroys many black farming communities in the interior and weakens black resistance to the white advance.

1835–41
The 'Great' Trek takes thousands of Dutch farmers (Boers) north-eastwards across the Orange and Vaal rivers.

Sheep rearing (wool for export to Britain) and sugar growing bring large profits to white farmers. Indians are shipped in to work the Natal sugar plantations. Whites continue to settle the best land.

Mining and farming – from 1870 to the 1930s

1867
The discovery of diamonds at Kimberley leads to mines owned by white businessmen supported by European money. Blacks provide the unskilled labour; they work as 'migrants' and live in closed bachelor compounds.

1886
The discovery of gold on the Rand again leads to white-run mines. The vast sums of money needed to get the gold-mines started comes from Europe and the USA. Whites do the skilled, well-paid jobs, the blacks the unskilled ones. As at Kimberley, the blacks are employed on a migrant basis and housed in compounds.

The success of the diamond and gold-mines causes a rapid growth of railways, ports and towns. It creates new markets for the farmers, black as well as white. Black farmers do well until the 1890s.

1913
The Land Act of the Botha government ends the right of the blacks to own any land outside the reserves. In 1913, only 7 per cent of South Africa is 'reserved' for blacks. (In 1936, this proportion is increased to 13 per cent.) The Land Act destroys independent black farming.

1920s and 1930s
White governments help white farmers and the 'poor white' unemployed. As a result of this, blacks sometimes suffer directly; for example, more jobs for whites on the railways means fewer jobs there for blacks.

Manufacturing, mining and farming – from the 1930s to the 1970s

1930s
A period of forty years of continuous economic growth begins, during which manufacturing becomes an important part of the economy alongside mining and farming.

1939–45
The Second World War speeds economic growth.

1940s
More rich goldfields are discovered in the Orange Free State.

1950s and 1960s
White farming becomes more mechanised and exports such products as citrus fruit and maize.

Manufacturing industry leads to the further growth of towns and to the need for a permanent black urban labour force. However, white governments refuse to allow more blacks to live with their families in towns. The result is more migrant labour and more crowded reserves.

The standard of living of whites rises to be amongst the highest in the world; in contrast black wages stay very low, although they are higher and rise faster in manufacturing than on the mines or farms.

From 1975 to 1990

Economic growth slows though population growth continues. The political crises of 1976–77 and 1984–86 make international business companies less ready to invest money in South Africa.

Manufacturing industry needs more skilled black labour, black trade unions become more powerful, the wages of urban blacks rise and blacks begin to set up their own businesses.

The migrant labour system continues and the rural reserves grow still more overcrowded. In the reserves, poverty and malnutrition increase.

2 The influence of the outside world

Belief in white superiority means acceptance of European actions in South Africa

AD 1487
Bartholomew Diaz, working for the Portuguese and searching for a sea-route to the Indies, is the first European to discover the Cape of Good Hope and to sail round the southernmost tip of Africa. However the Portuguese do not set up bases on the South African coast.

1652
Jan van Riebeeck sets up the Dutch base on the Cape peninsula.

1658
The Dutch East India Company (VOC) bring the first slaves into the Cape from the East Indies.

1688
French (Huguenot) settlers arrive to join Dutch and German families already farming in the Cape area.

1806
Britain takes the Cape from the Dutch during the Napoleonic Wars and keeps it when those wars end in 1815. The British government encourages emigration from Britain; for example, the 1820 settlers.

The early nineteenth century
Many missionaries from Britain and other European countries are active in the area. Some, like John Philip, persuade the British government to give the blacks a better deal.

1870–1914
The mineral revolution makes South Africa much more interesting to Europe and to the USA. Miners and businessmen flock to the Rand. Thousands of blacks from Portuguese East Africa and from other areas neighbouring South Africa also come to work in the mines.

1880–1914
The European nations 'scramble' for Africa. The Germans take possession of German South-West Africa (Namibia) in 1884, the British move into Bechuanaland in 1885, Rhodesia in 1890 and Swaziland in 1906. Meanwhile, the Portuguese extend their control of Mozambique and Angola.

1909, 1914 and 1919
Black political leaders sail to Europe to protest first (1909) against the Act of Union, then (1914) against the Land Act, and then at the end of the First World War (1919) to get political reforms as a reward for their war effort, each time without success.

The World Wars
In both World Wars, South Africa fights with the British Empire against Germany. In the First World War, the South African army conquers German South-West Africa (Namibia) and in 1919 gains the right to run the area after the war under the supervision of the League of Nations. In 1945, after the Second World War, having helped to defeat the Nazis, South Africa expects to be able to take over Namibia completely. The United Nations, the successor of the League of Nations, refuses to allow this.

As black resistance grows stronger, world opinion turns against white rule

1940s and 1950s
World opinion turns against racism. The United Nations strongly criticises apartheid. So do members of the British Commonwealth.

1960
The ANC goes into exile.

1961
South Africa leaves the Commonwealth.

Early 1960s
Many African states win independence from white colonial rule. In 1963 the Organisation of African Unity (OAU) is set up. International criticism of South Africa increases.

1966
Rhodesian whites rebel against the British who wish the blacks there to have political power. The South African government supports the white Rhodesians. Nor will it give Namibia independence and the main black resistance movement, the South-West African People's Organisation (SWAPO), begins a guerrilla war.

1968
The Olympic movement bans South African athletes from taking part in the Mexico Olympics, an early example of a sporting boycott.

1969
The UN demands that South Africa end its rule of Namibia. South Africa refuses. The Lusaka Manifesto commits the black front-line states to the overthrow of apartheid by force if necessary.

1970s
The UN leads a campaign for economic sanctions against South Africa.

1974–75

The Portuguese grant independence to Mozambique and Angola. In a civil war in Angola, while most of the world recognises the MPLA as the rightful government, South Africa gives military support to Unita. The MPLA has military help from Cuba. Black guerrilla armies operate in Rhodesia.

1978

The UN Resolution 435 demands that Namibia become independent with a government elected under UN supervision but the South African government and SWAPO cannot agree how such a plan would be carried out in practice.

1980

Blacks win power in Rhodesia (Zimbabwe). A former guerrilla leader, Robert Mugabe, becomes Prime Minister.

Early 1980s

South Africa tries to 'destabilise' the front-line states by supporting Renamo rebels in Mozambique and Unita in Angola. ANC guerrillas carry out bomb attacks inside South Africa, operating from bases in Mozambique, Swaziland and Lesotho. International campaigns for economic sanctions and for the release of Nelson Mandela grow more vigorous.

1984

The Nkomati Accord attempts to bring peace between South Africa and Mozambique.

1985

The USA and EEC impose some limited economic sanctions. Leading South African businessmen and white opposition politicians meet the ANC in exile.

1989

The South African government agrees to the UN Resolution 435, Namibia to have elections supervised by the UN and to gain independence under the government thus elected; simultaneously Cuban troops are to leave Angola.

1990

Namibia becomes independent.

3   Racist customs and laws: segregation and apartheid

The Cape under VOC Rule, 1652–1806

1658

The first slaves arrive in the Cape.

The seventeenth and eighteenth centuries

The whites are the landowners and employers, the Khoisan and the slaves are the workers. The Khoisan are sometimes hardly better off than the slaves. The whites assume their racial superiority and mixed marriages are frowned upon.

The Cape under British rule, 1806–53

1828

Influenced by missionaries like John Philip, the British governor in the Cape issues Ordinance 50 which gives blacks legal equality with the whites. Though the blacks remain the workers and the whites the employers, the former are now much freer to work as and where they wish.

1834

The British government abolishes slavery throughout the British Empire.

1835–41

The Boers of the 'Great' Trek leave Cape Colony and British rule partly because they wish to keep whites the masters and blacks the servants as they were before Ordinance 50 and the abolition of slavery.

1853

Cape Colony gains its own elected government. The right to vote is based on a property qualification, not on colour. Some blacks are able to vote in Cape elections. In contrast, the Boer republics created by the 'Great' Trek never allow blacks to have voting rights.

The coming of industry increases segregation, 1870–1914

1896

Pass laws control the movement of black miners in and out of the minefields.

1911

The Mine and Works Act makes the colour-bar legal, and also the custom of reserving certain jobs, with good wages, for whites only.

1913

The Land Act stops blacks owning land except in the reserves.

More segregation, 1923–48

1923

The Natives (Urban Areas) Act restricts the rights of blacks to enter towns. Most whites believe that towns are for whites and that blacks should, wherever possible, stay in the rural areas.

1926

The Mines and Works Amendment Act makes the colour-bar in industry stronger.

1936

The white government takes from Africans, but not yet from coloureds, their right to vote in Cape elections.

1937

The Native Laws Amendment Act further segregates the races in urban areas and tightens influx controls.

1942

Temporarily, during the Second World War, blacks suffer less from the pass laws and from the colour-bar.

Apartheid, 1948–76

1949   Prohibition of Mixed Marriages Act
1950   Group Areas Act
1952   Abolition of Passes and the Consolidation of Documents Act
1953   Separate Amenities Act and the Bantu Education Act
1954   Removal of the Cape franchise from coloured voters
1956   Industrial Conciliation Act
These laws separate the races more systematically than ever and keep the whites firmly in control.

1959
Verwoerd develops the idea of independent homelands for the blacks with the Bantu Self-Government Act.

1963
The Transkei becomes 'self-governing'.

1976
The Transkei becomes 'independent'.

The beginnings of reform, 1976–86

1979
Following the Wiehahn Commission, the colour-bar grows less firm and the blacks can form trade unions.

1984
By the new constitutional arrangements, Indians and coloureds can vote for representatives in their own Parliaments and a coloured and an Indian join the Cabinet. Africans, however, have no such rights.

1985
Mixed marriages are made legal.

During the 1980s, many 'whites only' signs disappear and many places hitherto for whites only, like concert halls, beaches and picnic spots, become free for everyone. Pass laws abolished.

4   Racial conflict

The white wars of conquest, 1659–1881

1659
The Dutch defeat the Khoisan in a fight over grazing lands.

1673–77
The Dutch again defeat the Khoisan in a more serious war over land.

The eighteenth century
Trekboer commandos attack the San. Those they do not kill they drive away from their grazing lands.

1790–1878
Nine frontier wars (the Kaffir Wars) take place along the eastern coast between the whites (mainly British) and the blacks (mainly Xhosa).

1835–41
The Boers of the 'Great' Trek defeat Mzilikasi, the Ndebele chief, on the inland plateau, and Dingane of the Zulus in the eastern coastlands.

1850s and 1860s
The Boers of the Orange Free State fight Moshoeshoe, the Sotho leader. They take some of his best farmland in the Caledon valley and force him to seek the protection of the British.

1879–81
The British army attacks and defeats first the Zulus and then the Pedi. These victories bring to an end the independence of most blacks in South Africa.

Violent resistance, 1906–90

1906
Chief Bambatha leads a rebellion against the Natal government. Twenty-four whites die, and more than 3000 blacks.

1920
Black miners strike on the Rand and some are killed when the police end the strike by force.

1946
Another major black miners' strike again ends with loss of life.

1952
During the demonstrations of the Defiance campaign, twenty-five die; twenty-one black, four white.

1960
Police shoot and kill sixty-nine blacks at Sharpeville during an anti-pass-law demonstration. One hundred and eighty others are wounded and 18,000 later arrested. The ANC and PAC decide to turn to violence, sabotage in particular.

1976–77
The disturbances in Soweto lead to the deaths of between 500 and 700 blacks, many of them schoolchildren. Thousands more are arrested and detained without trial.

Early 1980s
ANC guerrillas carry out bomb attacks in major cities. The South African army raids their bases in the front-line states.

1984–87
During these years of frequent serious political disturbances which cause the government to declare a state of emergency, thousands die, almost all of them black.

1989–90
The dawn of a new age? President de Klerk releases ANC leaders like Nelson Mandela and Walter Sisulu and calls for negotiations with the leaders of all races to bring about peaceful change.

Index

Acknowledgements

We are grateful to Longman Group UK Limited for permission to reproduce an extract from *Children of Soweto* by Mbulelo Mzamane © M Mzamane 1981.

We are grateful to the following for permission to reproduce photographs and other copyright material: Africana Museum, Johannesburg, pages 4 *above*, 5, 12, 14, 19, 22, 30, 44, 58; The Associated Newspapers Group Ltd, page 91; Associated Press, page 127 *above*; Abe Berry, page 75; Marita Bailey, page 26 (photo: Africana Museum, Johannesburg); G. Boonzaier (photos: Africana Museum, Johannesburg), pages 63, 66, 70; Cape Archives Depot, pages 16, 17, 21, 23, 42; *Daily Graphic*, June 1902, page 56; De Beers Consolidated Mines Ltd, pages 33, 34; *Die Burger*, page 112; *Die Gelofte*, The Covenant, Le Serment, Das Gelubde, 16.12.1949, page 65; Drum Archives, page 79 *left*; *The Eastern Province Herald*, Port Elizabeth, Cape of Good Hope, 31.5.1910, page 55; Reprinted by permission from a paid Advertising Section which appeared in the October 1, 1984 issue of FORTUNE Magazine, page 120; Free State Archives Depot (11176); page 48; Robert Harding Picture Library, page 6 *above*; Hulton-Deutsch Collection, pages 4 *below*, 40, 52, 83, 94; IDAF, pages vii *above*, 35 *above*, 36, 57, 59, 60, 68, 71, 76, 78, 80 *below*, 86, 87, 88, 89, 103, 104, 106, 107, 108, 109, 113, 117, 126 *below*; Illustrated London News Picture Library, pages 39, 61; Helen Joseph, *Side by Side*, Zed Books Ltd, 1986, page 82; Library of Parliament, Cape Town, page 29 *above*; Link Picture Library, pages vii *below* (photo: Greg English), 6 *below* (photo: Orde Eliason), 116 (photo: Trevor Samson), 126 *above* (photo: Photo Group); Mansell Collection, page 49; Mrs Marais, page 74; *The Natal Mercury*, 28.5.1948, page 73; National Monuments Council, page 29 *below*; Popperfoto, page 127 *below*; Shell South Africa (PTY) Ltd, page 114; *South African Sunday Times*, 3.10.1965, page 97; *Southern Africa Business News*, Oct/Nov 1986, page 122; *Sowetan*, 31.3.89, page 119; Tempo, page 80 *above*; United Press International, page 81; Voortrekker Monument, Pretoria, pages 28, 64. We are unable to trace the copyright holders of the following and would be grateful for any information that would enable us to do so, pages 8, 47, 50, 67, 79 *right*, 93, 105.

Cover
Painting of the Battle of Isandhlwana; National Army Museum, London.
Students demo in Beacon Hill Valley, Capetown: Frank Spooner Pictures (photo: Eric Bouvet).
Zulu Shield: Africana Museum, Johannesburg.

Source information

Publication details for primary source material are given after the extracts. If several extracts are taken from the same source, full details appear after the first extract. Details for extracts from secondary source material are given below:
V. Alhadeff, *A Newspaper History of South Africa*, Don Nelson, Cape Town, 1976, page 50 (Source B); M. Benson, *Nelson Mandela*, Penguin, 1986, pages 90 (Sources A and B) and 100 (Source B); J. Bird, *Annals of Natal, 1498–1845*, vol. 1, P. Davis and Sons, Pietermaritzburg, 1888, pages 24 (Source B) and 26; L. Callinicos, *Gold and Workers*, Ravan, Johannesburg, 1981, page 56 (Source B); T. Cameron and S. B. Spies (eds), *An Illustrated History of South Africa*, Jonathan Ball, Johannesburg, 1986, pages 10 (Source A) and 96 (Source A); P. Delius, *The Land Belongs to Us*, Heinemann, 1984, page 41 (Sources C and E); J. Frederickse, *South Africa – A Different Kind of War*, Ravan, Johannesburg, pages 114 (Source B) and 117 (Source B); W. Hancock, *Smuts* (vols 1 and 2), CUP, 1962, page 66 (Sources C, E and F) and page 72 (Source C); A. Hepple, *Verwoerd: Political Leaders of the 20th Century*, Pelican Books, 1967, pages 85 (Source A) and 96 (Source B); W. C. Langsam, *Historic Documents of World War II*, Van Nostrand, 1958, page 72 (Source A); P. Maylam, *A History of the African People of South Africa*, St. Martin's Press, New York, 1986, page 41 (Source D); Desmond Morris, *The Washing of the Spears*, Sphere Books, 1966, page 41 (Source B); A. Sampson, *Black and Gold*, Hodder & Stoughton, 1987, page 125 (Source D); D. M. Schreuder, *The Scramble for Africa*, CUP, 1964, page 41 (Source A); A. Starke, *Survival*, Tefelberg, Cape Town, 1978, pages 100 (Source A) and 125 (Source C); M. Wilson and L. Thompson (eds), *The Oxford History of South Africa*, vol. 2, OUP, 1975, page 66 (Source B).